THE MACK

CHARLES RENNIE MACKINTOSH
AND THE GLASGOW SCHOOL OF ART

THE MACK

CHARLES RENNIE MACKINTOSH
AND THE GLASGOW SCHOOL OF ART

ROBYNE CALVERT

YALE UNIVERSITY PRESS
NEW HAVEN AND LONDON

For my mother, Robin, who taught me to read;
for my grandparents, Jack and Margaret, who gave me the world;
and for John, who saw me through.

CONTENTS

HOPE IN HONEST ERROR

Late in the evening on Friday 15 June 2018, a major fire took hold of the Mackintosh building at the Glasgow School of Art (GSA) (fig. 0.1). It burned fierce and hot throughout the night, destroying the building.

That day, many of the staff and students had been enjoying graduation celebrations, and early reports of the fire on social media around 11.30 pm were met with disbelief. A colleague texted me a photo of flames crowning the east wing, which I assumed was fake. But concern sent me to Twitter, where within moments the veracity of the image was confirmed by, of all people, the actor Sam Heughan of *Outlander* fame: 'Huge fire in Glasgow! Hope everyone is safe. Looks like Glasgow School of Art? So sad.' The photo was no hoax. Somehow the unthinkable was happening: the Mack, as the building has been affectionately known in recent memory, was on fire *again*.

My colleague rang me: 'What can we do, who can we call?' Shocked, I replied vacantly: 'Nothing. No one. Everyone who needs to know will already be on their way. We can't disturb them. They will be busy. There is nothing we can do.'

It was the second fire to beset the building, and from the raging flames moving furiously westward it was clear that this fire was going to be much worse than the one that damaged it on 23 May 2014. At the time of the first fire, I was a lecturer in architecture and design history at GSA. I remember standing downhill from the

Mack on the corner of Sauchiehall Street, among many staff, students and passers-by, watching heartbroken as flames consumed the Mackintosh library, destroying my favourite room in the world. I then joined many from the GSA community at the nearby State Bar, where we could collectively drown our sorrows. The atmosphere that night shifted from profound distress to fond reminiscing, and even some merriment with so many friends gathered, rather like a wake.

In 2018 the fire that raged all night allowed for no such congregation. This time I did not rush down to the campus, as I feared I would be in the way of those required in an emergency. Many colleagues had gone down in the middle of the night though, including the architects from Page\Park who were leading the rebuilding of our masterpiece. They stood on the nearby roof of GSA's Blythswood House residence halls, watching the Mack become engulfed in flames.

The prognosis looked very bleak indeed. Although my history with the Mack is not nearly as long as many others', I have nevertheless loved the building since my first visit in 2006 as a budding Mackintosh scholar and was privileged to teach in it since 2008. In 2015 I was appointed Mackintosh Research Fellow at GSA as part of the wider project to restore the building after the 2014 fire, and was tasked with research and teaching on the activities and discoveries of the building's conservation and reconstruction. Being so closely connected to this project, it was not just heartbreak but despair that took hold of me at the second fire, thinking of the loss of both the building and the admirable conservation work. I spent much of that terrible night under my duvet, communicating with friends and

PREVIOUS PAGE (FIG. 0.1) The Glasgow School of Art Mackintosh building in the early hours of 16 June 2018.

FIG. 0.2 The Mack, 11 July 2018, with finial still in situ.

colleagues and finally, desperate for comfort, a tearful phone call with my mother.

And yet in the morning, after little sleep, hope subtly glimmered. It was first raised by an early morning chat with my colleague Bruce Peter, an expert on industrial material culture. His practical discussion of the century-old steel making up the structure reminded me that the Mack was made of sturdy stuff. I then went to Blythswood Hill, where I found many of my Mack restoration project colleagues and friends trying to make sense of what had happened. As I wandered the outskirts of the police cordon some three streets away, alongside the swarm of journalists, I finally got clear sight of the building. It was devastating, yet somehow still beautiful in its new state of ruin, its Scots baronial profile more evident than ever. Surveying the roofline, I noticed that, perched proudly atop the parapets, the ironwork finials appeared unscathed (fig. 0.2). Like symbols of its mighty ramparts, Mackintosh's clever interpretation of the Glasgow coat of arms still crowned the building, as if to signify to us that the Mack had not been beaten.

After nearly four years of restoration work, I knew the best possible team was already on site working tirelessly to save the building. The restoration team members who had become the world experts on the Mack – and whose work informs much of this book – were already there devising salvage and recovery plans. This fact kept me in decent humour that morning while listening to a local architect opining to a news crew that we would have to tear the whole building down, insisting we should build something new in its place. He must not have been aware of the incredible body of knowledge generated about this building through its restoration, including the 3D scans and superbly detailed plans created for its reconstruction, and the knowledge of the craftspeople employing traditional skills to expert effect in its remaking.

For me and many others, working on what is now the first restoration project was a labour of love. This book strives to tell that story through an updated history of this beloved, ruined building. At times the disaster has felt too raw to write about. But previous texts, wonderful as they are, are now out of date given what

was learned through rebuilding the Mack, and what has befallen it since. I am grateful to the many people, particularly my former colleagues at the Glasgow School of Art, who have said that writing this story now is more important than ever, that it is significant for the history of design and the built environment and for the heritage of Glasgow. The biography of the Mack now has another tragic chapter, but it is not the final one.

* * *

This book only scratches the surface of the Mack's history. It was originally intended to accompany an edited volume of essays telling the story of the Mack restoration, with contributions from many of those directly involved. The 2018 fire disrupted that ambition, but this book does highlight the restoration project where possible. I have consciously chosen not to focus on some of the more contentious or dissenting opinions about the Glasgow School of Art as an institution or its governance. These debates have been well rehearsed elsewhere in the press and in the Scottish parliamentary proceedings referenced in this book. Such political and institutional dimensions certainly have an impact on the management and rebuilding of the Mack, but the purpose of this book is not to weigh in on the wide-ranging opinions about institutional fault or dereliction of duty. Where I have taken liberties or made generalisations about the feelings of the GSA community, it is based on countless conversations with my peers; but I offer apologies to anyone who might feel their views have not been represented.

I wish to acknowledge at the outset that the Mack was not the only casualty on 15 June 2018, and perhaps in some ways it was the least important one. We can be very thankful that no lives were lost, particularly while the horrific fire at London's Grenfell Tower, in which at least seventy-four people tragically perished, was still fresh in everyone's minds. Livelihoods were significantly affected, however. Not only was the GSA community of staff and students largely displaced, but out of necessity a large police cordon was put in place that

FIG. 0.3 Interior of the gutted Mackintosh building, February 2020.

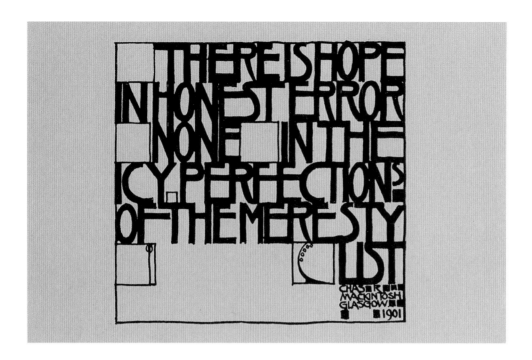

had an extremely detrimental impact on neighbours in Garnethill. Businesses remained shut, jobs were lost and, perhaps most critically, a small group of residents remained without access to their homes for over ten weeks. It must always be remembered that this was a very difficult time for the local community. I hope this book might not only capture the amazing work that was done in the 2014–18 Mack restoration project but also honour the community in Garnethill that has lived so long with this beautiful but unruly neighbour.

The first draft of this prologue, written in September 2018 shortly after the second fire, claimed 'This book is not a memorial.' However, as time and the state of the world have offered perspective, I have changed my mind and acknowledged an undeniable fact: in June 2018 the Mackintosh building was destroyed. I have been inside since and walked through the ruins left behind (fig. 0.3). Its damaged finials have been brought down, along with any other fragments that could possibly be salvaged, and stored for safe-keeping. But whatever is erected in its place will be a new entity, even if it is to the old design. Will it be the Mack again? That remains to be seen, but the graceful liminal carving over the front entrance endures undamaged, a sentinel during this uncertain time (*see* fig. 0.6). The design also exists, both in its

FIG. 0.4 Charles Rennie Mackintosh, original design for lettering sample, 1901.

archived plans and through the incredible body of work of the 2014–18 Mack restoration project, only a fraction of which could be shared here. That design is still an excellent one in terms of the needs of an art school.

Mackintosh is known to have loved a particular declaration by the nineteenth-century architect John Dando Sedding (fig. 0.4). Since the night of the second fire, part of that phrase has echoed in my mind every time I see the Mack: 'There is Hope in Honest Error.' I know I am not alone in feeling it.

Robyne Erica Calvert
February 2024

INTRODUCTION

A PLACE OF DREAMS

INTRODUCTION
A PLACE OF DREAMS

The Mackintosh building at the Glasgow School of Art was a masterpiece of dichotomies: light and shadowy; commodious and cosy; practical and complex; direct and symbolic (fig. 0.8). Designed at the turn of the twentieth century by Charles Rennie Mackintosh, it both invoked the past in its Scots baronial parapets and looked to the future through minimalist spaces and embrace of new technologies. The Scottish painter and GSA alumna Alison Watt called the Mack 'a place of dreams', commenting that, 'It has always had a particular hold over those who studied there, not only through its remarkable physical presence but also as an idea'.[1] For over one hundred years it was a point of pride for Glasgow and a physical and emblematic representation of the city's creative spirit.

As Mackintosh's last major commission for a complete building, the Mack represents the pinnacle of his architectural achievement; it was his 'masterwork', in part because he never had the chance to outdo it. In 2009 it was awarded the Royal Institute of British Architects-sponsored 'Stirling of Stirlings' prize as Britain's favourite building of the last 175 years. It was thus a devastating blow when late in the evening on 15 June 2018 the Mack was shockingly overwhelmed by fire for a second time, severely injuring its walls and gutting its magical interior. The school was nearing completion of an estimated £35 million restoration project after a fire had badly damaged the west end of

FIG. 0.7 The opening of the Reid building (School of Design) at the Glasgow School of Art, April 2014.

the building on 23 May 2014.[2] All the hope invested in its reconstruction turned to desolation as the beloved Mack became utterly engulfed in a nightmare inferno.

The Mack has been transformed not just by recent fires but by a century of folk who have passed under its enigmatic carved threshold, which, rather metaphorically, still stands strong (fig. 0.6). It has been a living building, even in its more recent period of supposed dormancy, and it yet shows resilience even in its most dramatic chapter.

Although the Mack's interior was destroyed, much of its physical aspect survived, buttressed by nearly seven hundred tons of scaffolding at the time of writing in 2023. It still imposes its presence on the GSA campus and Garnethill community, perhaps most forcefully when viewed from the sleek glass windows of the Steven Holl-designed Reid building (2014) across Renfrew Street (fig. 0.7). It does not let us forget its dignity, and seems to demand a response from us: what shall we do now?

As Watt suggested, this building is more than the sum of its parts: it represents an idea that is not so easily

PREVIOUS PAGE (FIG. 0.5) Charles Rennie Mackintosh, 'The Tree of Influence' (1895), published in *The Magazine* (Spring 1896). Pencil and watercolour on grey paper, 32 × 25 cm.

FIG. 0.6 OPPOSITE Relief sculpture over the main entrance.

FIG. 0.8 The Glasgow School of Art building by Honeyman,
Keppie & Mackintosh, 1897–9 and 1907–9.

dismantled. Numerous people who have worked in it have reflected on the ways it affected them, particularly in the wake of the recent disasters. Christopher Platt, former Chair of Architecture at GSA, spoke about how his time in the building, both as student and teacher, influenced his practice:

> *Every physical place has an impact on us ... Time seems to slow down in such places. In the case of the Mackintosh building, I think it influences me as an architect in its simple plan and section configuration ... its sequence of dark and light, its uses of timber in direct and memorable ways ... [and] Mackintosh's ability to transform utility, making the everyday special (a newel post, the end of a steel beam, a library which had no aspirational brief except an area to work in). I am still influenced by how the building belongs to a particular architectural and constructional culture and yet is breaking away from it. These experiences, which I later understood as ideas, have remained with me in approaching the design of new buildings or adapting existing buildings. It felt like 'our place', domestic, homey, but mysterious and willing to be explored and discovered. It did not reveal itself in one single atrium and a few repetitive floors.*[3]

The Mack was seductive, slowly offering intriguing revelations through repetitive engagement with its spaces. In its clever subtlety it has been a source of creative stimulus for generations of people and was often called the 'beating heart' of the institution. But in the most practical sense, the Mack was a working building, a highly adaptable masterpiece of architectural design. That design still exists, and we arguably know more about this building than we ever have, from previous scholarship and the vast amount of research generated from the 2014–18 restoration project, and even through current post-fire stabilisation efforts. The Mack *can* be rebuilt just as it was. But should it be?

In 2014, after the first fire, the decision was made to restore the building because it was deemed the best possible solution given that the relative extent of the damage was not insurmountable. Much of the building remained; statistically just ten percent was damaged, although what was lost – notably the beloved library – was significant. To allow any contemporary intervention to the damaged spaces seemed anathema to the holistic, albeit phased, design of the building. As such, GSA quickly decided that the best course of action was to rebuild it, but admittedly wasn't sure how to tackle the project at first, or even if it could be accomplished at all. Despite having possibly the most extensive institutional archive of any art school in the UK, there were still many unknowns about the building 'as built'. But GSA set forth to reconstruct, embarking on a programme of forensic research, expert consultation and an embrace of traditional skills, including apprenticeship and collaboration with Historic Environment Scotland (HES), the lead public body looking after Scotland's heritage, to create a faithful reinstatement of what was damaged.

However, some critics felt that rebuilding would not just be a mistake but against the very spirit of Mackintosh – that if he were alive today, he would of course build something new (an argument reiterated after the 2018 fire). Aside from any complications presented by second-guessing the desires of the dead, such arguments contradict good conservation practice, particularly when so much of the integrity of a building lies in the unification of its design. Perhaps the reticence to rebuild is due to a tendency to perceive buildings as immovable monuments of architecture rather than fluid iterations of design. If we can replicate a tea-room chair, why do we baulk at copying a building's interior, its ornamentation, or indeed its structure?

We tend to see buildings as fixed expressions of the time and place in which they were built. We mentally imbue their fabric with powerful notions of permanence and immutability, finding comfort in such places as physical and symbolic manifestations of our cultural immortality. But the truth is, buildings are in a constant state of flux. They are transformed through the wear of their users, wrought over time. Rooms are made over. Doorways are inserted or sealed up. Grand interiors become subdivided, their tall windows awkwardly

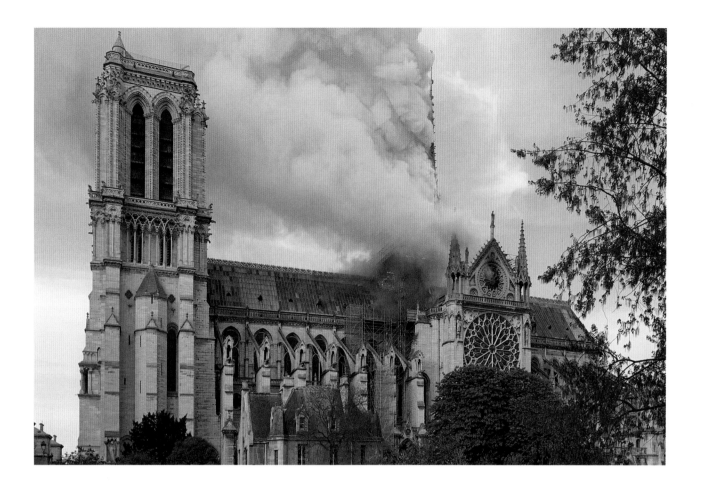

spanning multiple floors. Schools become flats, churches become bars and nightclubs, and even the grandest of icons are subject to health and safety interventions, many of which we simply take for granted. Watching monuments slowly crumble may even reinforce feelings of their resilience, but when faced with their unexpected demise we are shocked by their tangible fragility.

In the wake of the destruction of the roof and spire of Paris's Notre-Dame Cathedral in 2019 (fig. 0.9), French Prime Minister Édouard Philippe called for a competition to design a new spire even while the building was still smoking, without consultation from the wider expert community.[4] President Emmanuel Macron supported the idea, with plans to fast-track reconstruction within five years in time for Paris to host the 2024 Summer Olympics. This was not well received, and soon after the French Senate stopped Macron's proposals with a bill legislating that conservation efforts must restore Notre-Dame 'in the same way visually as

before' and 'If the [conservation team] uses materials different from those in place prior to the disaster, it [should] publish a study giving the reasons for these changes'.[5] The famous spire at the centre of this debate was part of the 1845–64 'restoration' programme directed by Eugène Viollet-le-Duc, using a research-based but rather liberal approach. For example, he replaced the crumbling medieval gargoyle waterspouts with his imaginative *chimères*, guardian-demons that had no function beyond the decorative. These objects have gained popular appeal (notably the iconic figure of Le Stryge, fig. 0.10) and consequently their own cultural significance, which today we would seek to protect, even though the conditions of their making would not be viewed as acceptable conservation practice now. If Le Stryge had been lost, what are the odds he would

FIG. 0.10 'Henri Le Secq near "Le Stryge" at Notre-Dame Cathedral', photograph by Charles Nègre (detail), 1853.

for the honesty of the original fabric, even to the extent of preferring a ruin to any kind of restorative intervention, which he deemed 'a lie' in his *Seven Lamps of Architecture* (1849).

These views still hold weight with the Society for the Protection of Ancient Buildings (SPAB), founded in 1877 by designer William Morris and architect Philip Webb, along with others who were profoundly influenced by Ruskin's views. SPAB's manifesto, written the same year, sought to highlight the great damage done to buildings under the banner of 'restoration', declaring:

> *those who make the changes wrought in our day under the name of Restoration, while professing to bring back a building to the best time of its history ... destroy something and to supply the gap by imagining what the earlier builders should or might have done ... in short, a feeble and lifeless forgery is the final result of all the wasted labour.*[7]

Today SPAB remains a positive force in the conservation of the built environment. Its current methodology, 'the SPAB Approach', is considered the standard among many conservation professionals, but still puts primacy on a materialist philosophy as laid out by Morris and Webb:

> *Building fabric is precious. A concern for its protection helps ensure that the essence of an old building survives for future generations to appreciate. The SPAB Approach therefore stands against Restorationist arguments that it is possible and worthwhile to return a building to its original – or imagined original – form ... [it] generally rejects arguments that original design or cultural associations are more important than surviving fabric.*[8]

be replaced? Is this sculpture's agency somehow more potent than the spire (which replaced a bell tower that was dismantled in the French Revolution)? Why would these fanciful additions not be consigned to memory, given they are not original to the building? In September 2021 it was announced that Notre-Dame had been 'shored up' and was ready for restoration, and that Viollet-le-Duc's spire would in fact be rebuilt.[6]

Projects like these provide us with an opportunity to scrutinise ideas and policies regarding the preservation of our built heritage. For example, some experts might argue that when substantial original fabric of a building is lost, creating any kind of replica would be dishonest, unethical even. Such arguments are partially rooted in nineteenth-century attitudes that sought to circumvent deplorable 'conservation' practices that would often rely on aesthetic (sometimes damaging) 'improvements' in the name of restoration. In opposition to these practices were conservationists such as John Ruskin, who argued

SPAB places emphasis on fabric in order to preserve the history, craftsmanship and labour of place. Yet, although SPAB 'values' state that 'buildings should be valued for their entire history, recognising, understanding and respecting change', this is in reference to the physical, material aspects of place. Contemporary conservation theorists are increasingly attempting to broaden their methodology in this regard. The most widely accepted

FIG. 0.11 Utagawa Kuniyoshi, *Depiction of the Relocation of the Grand Shrine of Ise, c.* 1849. Woodblock print, 25.1 × 37.2 cm.

'best practice' guide is the Burra Charter, conceived by the International Council on Monuments and Sites (ICOMOS) in 1979 and regularly updated. It aims to set a standard of practice for decisions about places of cultural significance. The core of its philosophy goes beyond the materiality of place, speaking of more intangible ideas about 'who we are and the past that has formed us'.[9] This is in line with contemporary thinking in the heritage field, for example UNESCO moving beyond guarding just physical places (World Heritage Sites) towards protecting 'Intangible Cultural Heritage'.[10] Nonetheless, the Burra Charter 'advocates a cautious approach to change: do as much as necessary to care for the place and to make it useable, but otherwise change it as little as possible so that its cultural significance is retained'.[11] But what if the significant material has been destroyed, through accident, or nature, or an act of violence or conflict? And what if it can be replicated in a transparent – or honest – way?

The word 'restoration' still sits uncomfortably within debates around good conservation practice. Some excellent recent scholarship on the value of replicas and

on the more intangible aspects of heritage – notably the emotional and social value of the built environment – has come out of the field of archaeology and is a welcome contribution to conservation discussions.[12] Many heritage professionals now invite a broader, more global viewpoint that considers other values alongside material authenticity. An often-referenced example is the interest in Japanese Shinto shrines, like the Grand Shrine at Ise (fig. 0.11), which are rebuilt every 20 years to symbolise the death, renewal and impermanence of all life and as a means of passing on traditional building skills and techniques to each generation. In such practices the honesty or authenticity of place is not rooted in the material of an original building but in the design and the process of making and remaking and in the integrity of intention. It may be argued that it would be inappropriate to apply this philosophy to Western architecture, with its aspirations of permanence. Indeed, some recent scholarship has noted that Japanese

FIG. 0.12 Reconstructed roof structure in Studio 58, 2018.

conservation approaches also follow ICOMOS best practices. However, there is much to be learned from Eastern viewpoints that honour the built environment as being not just about monolithic structures but also about the people and ideas that see them to fruition. Such approaches have successfully informed recent and ongoing conservation of two other notable Mackintosh properties, the Willow Tea Rooms on Sauchiehall Street in Glasgow and The Hill House in Helensburgh (*see* pp. 179–80).

Like Notre-Dame – like any building really – the Mack was not the static monument that is fixed in so many minds. It was transformed over many years – and, incidentally, it was not the work of one man, one creator-genius. Although Mackintosh was at the helm throughout its two construction phases (1896–9 and 1907–9), he shared the role with his boss, then partner, John Keppie, steering the many craftsmen (for they were surely all men) that contributed to its making: the joiners, stonemasons, electricians, decorators and many others whose individual skill and creativity is too easily overlooked when admiring the harmony of the building's completion. A century of steady alteration followed, modified by its community of users to suit their needs, casually at first, then more carefully as the building was listed in 1966 and Category A-listed in 1983. The Mack was made over again and again, from

partitions and balconies that expanded studio space to updated technical services, including the more recent needs of the digital age. After the fire of May 2014 the building was repaired, remade and rediscovered. Its conservation and reconstruction were mammoth tasks accomplished by the teamwork of many women and men performing assiduous research and traditional building skills with care and passion. The beauty of handcrafting in their nearly completed plasterwork and joinery was being revealed and is now sadly lost (fig. 0.12).

This book relies on the painstaking work of the 2014–18 Mack restoration team: architects, engineers, project managers, traditional craftspeople and researchers who together have revealed a new and wealthy body of knowledge about the Mack that we did not previously possess. Their story underpins this new history as much as Mackintosh's did the old one. After the second fire, work to stabilise and consolidate the Mack was necessarily slow due to the precariousness of the building's condition, and then was impeded further by the effects of the Covid-19 global pandemic that took hold in the UK in March 2020. Indeed, events since the second fire have added quite another dimension to this project. How can we place such importance on a single building amid an international health emergency, the climate crisis and the widespread social and political unrest we are presently experiencing? Can such events provide opportunity for reflection and reconsideration of how we treat heritage and conservation both in theory and in practice?

In terms of how we write about our heritage, long overdue discussions of diversity, inclusion and the decolonising of our histories have been a welcome development in recent scholarship. Through these lenses, we must acknowledge the uncomfortable truth of how the history of the Mack is dominated by privileged narratives: from the makers of the building – as far as we know – to most of the scholars and architects who have written about it. As a starting point to address this and re-evaluate the 'genius-creator' narrative that Mackintosh has been subject to, this book highlights the women who were part of the early contextual history of the Mack; non-white people were also likely among those who originally built the building, but individual workers are undocumented. In the extant archival material, the systemic nature of this problem was glaring in researching images for this book, with a few notable exceptions such as Tsoo Hong Lee, the first Chinese student to earn a Fine Art degree in the UK (fig. 0.13). Only in recent photographs, from the late twentieth century on, do we begin to see increasing diversity in the school, in the student population more than the staff.

There is also deeper research needed in terms of decolonising the history of the Glasgow School of Art. Further investigation could be made into its funding history, for example, much like other projects are doing in Glasgow and across the UK. In fact, a recently published report revealed that 'the Bellahouston bequests [given to the University of Glasgow] were provided by the Steven siblings who accumulated a fortune of £500,000 in 1875 (worth as much as £243 million in 2016, depending on the comparator used), much of which came from their father, Moses Steven, a partner in a West India firm in Glasgow during the 1820s'.[13] This is significant as it was a £10,000 donation

FIG. 0.13 Tsoo Hong Lee (standing, second row from top, second from right) attended GSA from 1907 to 1912. He studied painting with GSA Director Francis Newbery (seated, centre, holding book) and tutor Maurice Greiffenhagen (seated next to Newbery). Lee went on to study sciences at the University of Glasgow before returning to China and becoming a professor of art and engineering in Beijing.

from the Bellahouston Trust that purchased the site on Garnethill and launched the initial fundraising for the building. Thus the very foundation of the Mackintosh building itself was funded through monies derived from the trade and labour of enslaved peoples. Given Glasgow's economic history, a similar legacy project at GSA would likely reveal further evidence of funding linked to enslavement and colonial oppression. GSA library staff have done some work in this area through the 'Emancipating our Collections' project, but that was a departmental initiative and not institutionally driven. While a focused investigation to decolonise GSA's institutional history is outside the scope of this book, it is imperative that these facts are recognised, and it is hoped that GSA will follow the University of Glasgow's lead in researching these legacies and creating a programme of reparative justice at the school.

Much like the Mackintosh building itself, this book is based on the work of many hands and minds, past and present. Telling this story requires recounting the Mack's history with consideration of those new to the subject, but with fresh ideas and information to offer a revised and updated understanding of this much-loved building. What we know about Mackintosh's life story and his ideas around architecture and design has been well rehearsed since his first biography was written by Thomas Howarth in 1952.[14] In reframing this narrative, this book owes a debt to recent projects that have aggregated key primary sources, along with valuable critical commentary, especially the University of Glasgow's indispensable digital archive *Mackintosh Architecture: Context, Making and Meaning* (2014).

This book is not a traditional architectural history, but rather embraces a variety of approaches from art and design history, material culture studies, heritage studies, archaeology and social history to tell the story of this masterwork. As evidenced in the prologue, I am not an unbiased author. Consider me part of a growing community of academics who acknowledge emotion in historical scholarship, especially in relation to intangible heritage. As a Mackintosh researcher at GSA, I was welcomed on the restoration project design team that undertook the key work of the project. As such the tone of this book is not what I originally planned. It

was to be a document of the resurgence of the building, but instead it is the story of what has befallen it, told through my own experiences and research as well as those who have worked on the project, and at times it drifts into the realm of memoir. I hope that instead of diminishing the book, the inclusion of my own and others' memories adds interest, because the destruction of the Mack feels personal to all who have loved it.

The history of the Mack and the uncertainty of its future is reflected in the language of this book. The building as a whole is referred to in the past tense because, as an entity, it has been destroyed. But the plans and designs and some of its fittings still exist, so these are referred to in the present tense. This is also true for extant components of the building, for example exterior walls. The names of rooms and spaces have changed over the years and I have tried to be clear about this within the text. In his drawings Mackintosh labelled the studios by function, but eventually they just became numbered rooms for ease. For example, his Composition Room at the top of the building became Studio 58. Some spaces have been named, either formally or through colloquial use. The original board room was the Design Room in 1908 plans but was named the Mackintosh Room in 1947 when it was used as a museum for the furniture collection. Most famously, Mackintosh's elegant glass pavilion at the top of the building has almost always been called the Hen Run (*see* p. 72). Even calling the building the Mack is a recent development – for some the 'Mac' is still the Mackintosh School of Architecture, specifically. It can be confusing, even for locals.

It is useful to remember that when the Mack was built, Mackintosh was just an architect, working to a brief. Although history has laid all the 'genius' of this building at his door, this book strives to contribute to a fuller understanding of how his vision came to be. This includes a contextual discussion that gives due credit for the Mack's existence – and indeed for the environment in which Mackintosh's style came to fruition – to Francis Henry Newbery, the director of the school from 1885 to 1917. While this book raises some questions around accounts that Newbery 'hand-picked' Mackintosh to design the building, it also seeks to show the ways

in which his vision – subtly performed through the educational and social camaraderie he cultivated at GSA – shaped the building both formally and conceptually.

Some readers may be surprised to see that there is very little mention of 'The Four' in this book. Margaret Macdonald Mackintosh, Frances Macdonald MacNair and Herbert MacNair (fig. 0.14) are included only as relevant to discussion of the Mack, but leaving them to the side entirely would feel awkward. As Mackintosh expert Roger Billcliffe states in his book *Charles Rennie Mackintosh and the Art of the Four*: 'From 1890 to 1910 the work of The Four can be seen, overall, as interrelated ... They shared a common aim, frequently a common palette and iconography, and a still secret and personal language.'[15] However, he goes on to state that his text excludes architecture 'because it was an art form specific to Mackintosh alone and where he worked outside the orbit of The Four'.[16] This book does not fully share that view. While it is certainly true that Mackintosh's architectural work was largely manifest through his day job at John Honeyman & Keppie (from 1901 Honeyman, Keppie & Mackintosh), can these design ideas be so easily segregated from the

FIG. 0.14 'The Immortals' at the 'Roaring Camp', Dunure, Ayrshire, *c.* 1893. Left to right: Charles Rennie Mackintosh, Jessie Keppie, Agnes Raeburn, Janet Aitken, Katherine Cameron, Frances Macdonald, John Keppie (bottom), Herbert MacNair, Margaret Macdonald.

rest of his artistic work? Mackintosh's ability to move fluidly between art, architecture and design was key to what made his work so potent. He met his circle of friends around 1893, around the time that he began taking the lead on architectural projects. His personal and creative relationship with Margaret Macdonald bloomed while he was working on the first phase of the Mack, and they married in 1900 just after it opened. It is worth noting that Mackintosh seems to have acknowledged her influence in this sphere specifically. In 1927 he wrote to her from France: 'You must remember that in all my architectural efforts you have been half if not threequarters [*sic*] in them.'[17] The context for this oft-quoted remark is usually omitted: Mackintosh was writing to Macdonald to ask if she would give a short interview to Christian Barman of the *Architects' Journal* before a pending trip to Glasgow and was assuring his wife that she was fully capable of discussing his architectural designs. This is perhaps debatable evidence that Macdonald was a collaborator in these efforts, but it would seem to indicate, at least in Mackintosh's eyes, that she was quite a significant source of inspiration, if not an outright artistic partner. While this book does not suggest that Macdonald should be attributed authorship of the Mack, it does take the position that the building is part of a larger body of Mackintosh's work that was conceived within the creative camaraderie, aesthetic sympathies and imaginative pleasure that flowed naturally from the artistic education, stylistic development and close personal relationships he enjoyed.

The Mack's wider significance as a masterpiece of early modern architecture – as recognised in 1936 by Nikolaus Pevsner[18] – is partially due to its eclectic relationship with the art, architecture and design movements of its era: Arts and Crafts, Aestheticism, Art Nouveau and Symbolism. This latter category is under-appreciated in the canon of architectural history; in fact Symbolist architecture does not exist as an established genre. In 1985 the architect Charles Jencks theorised a historically based 'Symbolic architecture' within postmodernism, suggesting that architects work with their clients to create symbolic programmes for domestic buildings, even using Mackintosh as an example of this approach.[19] However, fin de siècle Symbolism in literature and art was not concerned with overt representation in an iconographic manner, but rather the evocation of experiences, states of mind and universal truths. If works could render a synaesthetic sensation, so much the better.

While the Symbolist movement had roots largely in Belgium and France, it was not neatly fixed to a particular time, place or group. It spans across several genres, including Pre-Raphaelitism, Aestheticism and even Post-Impressionism, and overlaps with Art Nouveau, Jugendstil and Secessionism. So to say Mackintosh was a Symbolist is not a refutation of his other stylistic connections. Recent scholarship has established that Mackintosh was engaging with the artistic ideals of Symbolism, particularly in his art and design of the 1890s and early 1900s (fig. 0.5).[20] In fact, one might argue that the Glasgow Style, often

referred to as Scottish Art Nouveau, could equally be called Scottish Symbolism. Such a category might include some of the paintings of the Glasgow Boys and could be national, including the work of Phoebe Anna Traquair, for example. This book does not seek to establish a new canon of Symbolist architecture, but it is worth considering how past architectural scholarship has perhaps overlooked the engagement with Symbolist art and design interests in the built environment – another casualty perhaps of the modernist marginalisation of anything seen to be too feminine or decadent (queer). Mackintosh's Symbolist ideas appear in his architecture as much as the rest of his oeuvre, especially in the collaborative decorative schemes he crafted with Macdonald, some of which were directly inspired by Symbolist literature like the plays of Maurice Maeterlinck.[21] It is worth remembering Herbert MacNair's reflections on the work of The Four, as reported by Howarth: 'not a single line was drawn without purpose, and rarely was a single motif employed that had not some allegorical meaning.'[22]

As this book illustrates, the Mack's Symbolist design programme was not obvious and offered the pleasure of sensory engagement and discovery. This idea is perhaps best expressed by the Symbolist poet Stéphane Mallarmé:

To name an object is to remove three-quarters of a poem's pleasure ... suggestion, that is the dream.[23]

Throughout this book, possible interpretations of space are offered as suggestions. But through a Symbolist lens there is no one 'correct' meaning, and by relation nor is there an incorrect reading of this building. We may search for the ideas Mackintosh wished to impart, but we will never have a certain answer, even if we feel we have absolutely puzzled it out. Ultimately, the space of meaning exists between the building and its users and can represent whatever it is they may imagine. The story the Mack tells is not just one of bricks and mortar, but of its overall effect on the people who have been part of its life, its death and, hopefully, its resurrection.

BEFORE THE MACK

CHAPTER 1
BEFORE THE MACK

Oh! Mackintosh – he built a School
And Newbery – he filled it full
With Painters and Sculptors and Arkerytects
Of various ages and every sex ...

**DUMBLE-DUM-DEARIE, OR HOW FRA NEWBERY GOT HIS
CLOAK AND HAT: THE GLASGOW SCHOOL OF ART SONG**[1]

Perched near the top of Garnethill at 167 Renfrew
Street, the Glasgow School of Art's first purpose-built
building is often referred to synonymously with the
school itself; even locals aren't always aware that it is
now part of a larger campus of premises. For them, the
Mack *is* 'the art school'.

Mackintosh's building was built in two phases, in
1896–9 and 1907–9, in a city brimming with industrial
and architectural ingenuity. Glasgow is situated in the
west-central lowlands of Scotland, stretching over a
hilly landscape flanking the River Clyde that even today,
with its many parks, is true to its Brythonic Celtic name
meaning 'dear green place'. It has ancient roots, budding
from a medieval village to become one of the key British
seaports in the eighteenth century. Consequently, in the
nineteenth century Glasgow underwent a significant
population boom, growing from an estimated 77,000
in 1801 to 762,000 in 1901.[2] Its rapid expansion ran
parallel to that of other British industrial hubs like
Manchester and Birmingham, as well as emerging

North American cities like New York, Chicago and
Toronto, largely built on the 'new money' made from
robust international commerce. It was not for nothing
that the nouveaux riches in Glasgow called themselves
the 'tobacco lords' and the 'sugar aristocracy'; like
industrial counterparts such as Liverpool and Bristol,
much of Glasgow's wealth was made on the brutal
transatlantic trade in and labour of enslaved people.[3]
Colonialism built the mercantile industries that by the
mid-nineteenth century shifted focus to manufacturing,
particularly ship- and locomotive-building, among
other heavy industrial products like coal and chemical
engineering. The strength of shipping trade on the
Clyde, and the expansion of the Caledonian Railway in
particular, became a vital network for the infrastructure
of Scotland and for collaboration in industry, engineering
and design across the British Empire.

Children have been educated in Scotland from
the fifteenth century, and by Mackintosh's time many
schools were free, and government funded. Manual and
professional trades would be pursued via apprenticeship
or higher education, with Glasgow home to one of the
oldest universities in the world. Within this system,
technical and creative education also grew to feed
the Victorian industrial machine. This confluence
of industry, economy, wealth and education powered
the social and physical growth of Glasgow, creating
conditions in which creative artisans were in demand to
furnish villas, townhouses, tenements, office buildings,
railway stations and even ocean liners with an
abundance of joinery, stained glass, metalwork, textiles
and furnishings. To help meet that need, Glasgow
required an art school.

PREVIOUS PAGE (FIG. 1.1) Francis Newbery and
Ann Macbeth discussing a student's work, *c.* 1905.

FIG. 1.2 Portrait of Charles Rennie Mackintosh, 1893.
Modern bromide print, photograph by James Craig Annan.

ART SCHOOLS, BRITISH DESIGN REFORM AND GLASGOW

The Glasgow School of Art was established in 1845 as the Glasgow Government School of Design, part of a national programme of design reform that sought to improve British product standards in the service of economic improvement.[4] The Industrial Revolution created a rapid increase in manufactured goods but with diminishing quality and, to some critics, poor aesthetic value. By creating highly skilled local artisans, the government schools supported efforts to ameliorate design standards and educate consumers on taste across the nation. The first of these schools was established in 1837 in South Kensington, London, and similar schools opened in key industrial cities across Britain, notably Manchester in 1838, Birmingham and Sheffield in 1843 and Leeds in 1846.[5] By 1853 they all came under the direction of the newly created Science and Art Department that was established with funds and ideas generated by the 1851 Great Exhibition. The department's first superintendent was Henry Cole, who had been the exhibition's director. Cole enlisted the help of Owen Jones, a design theory expert who decorated the exhibition's famous Crystal Palace, to assist in rethinking approaches to art education across Britain.[6] Jones was tasked with collecting examples of 'good' and 'bad' design at the Great Exhibition for the teaching collections at South Kensington, and according to many critics there was an abundance of the latter.[7] Jones gave his appraisal in an 1852 lecture:

> *There was no unity, the architect, the upholsterer, the paper stainer, the weaver, the calico printer, and the potter run each their independent course; each struggles fruitlessly, each produces in art novelty without beauty, or beauty without intelligence.*[8]

Jones's words echoed the sentiments of his fellow design reformers, who aimed for a more integrated approach to creative production. This was a clarion call for the Arts and Crafts movement to come, and it underpinned the National Course of Instruction (also known as the South Kensington system) that Cole devised with Jones's

support. Their new 23-stage curriculum became the foundation for teaching art across Britain, setting itself apart from traditional methods of the Royal Academy by prioritising the production of skilled workers in applied (industrial) art, design and architecture.

While this new education system was key to design reform efforts, equally influential were the architects, designers and craftspeople who argued for a more thoughtful and cohesive balance between beauty and utility through their own creative work and through teaching and writing about their theories. Figures like John Ruskin, William Morris and Walter Crane (fig. 1.3) celebrated the past to make a new future. Each saw improved artisanship as a means to advance social conditions for workers, rejecting the industrial approaches to manufacture and labour conditions that earlier design reform strategies set out to boost. The socialist principles of these and other Arts and Crafts leaders took root in Victorian art schools, especially in Scotland and the north of England. This was the system that shaped Francis Newbery.

Born in Devon, Newbery studied at the National Art Training School in London and taught there before being appointed Headmaster at the Glasgow School of Art in 1885.[9] In 1911, a year after the Mack opened, the *Glasgow Herald* reported on a lecture given by Newbery, which outlined his views on the function of art schools in society:

> *The ideal he had always held before himself was that the school should be a centre of art culture, art education and technical education which should make for the good of the commonwealth as a whole by furnishing it with workers in every medium, means or material, whereby beauty could reveal itself through art. These ends were accomplished by educating any member of the community who came there – future producer or future consumer, lay or professional.*[10]

We can see the influence of the South Kensington system and Arts and Crafts ideology in Newbery's desire not only to encourage creative producers but also to educate the 'consumer' in matters of taste. He

FIG. 1.3 Walter Crane, design for the cover of *The Scottish Art Review*, c. 1898. Pen and watercolour on paper, 36 × 24.5 cm.

advocated for the ways in which Glasgow benefited from being part of this system, and enjoyed support for this approach from the chairman of the board of governors, James Fleming, according to a report on the annual meeting of February 1897:

> *The South Kensington Department was not very popular in some quarters, but there was no question that it had done more to promote the teaching of science in this country than any other institution whatever. Some people wished to separate Scotland and England, but [Fleming] considered it was an enormous advantage to them that they should have their work exhibited alongside work done in the great schools of Manchester, Birmingham, and Liverpool, and that it should be examined by such men as Mr Walter Crane and the late William Morris.[11]*

Newbery brought these connections to Glasgow, arranging for Crane and Morris to speak to Glasgow School of Art students in 1888 and 1889 respectively. It is not known whether Mackintosh attended these talks, but given that they were offered in the evening, when he was a part-time student at the school, it is hard to imagine he would have missed them. Certainly the Arts and Crafts ethos found its way into Mackintosh's 1893 lecture on 'Architecture':

> *To get true architecture the architect must be one of a body of artists possessing an intimate knowledge of the crafts, and no less on the other hand the painter & sculptor & other craftsmen must be in direct touch & sympathy with architecture. There must be a real communion, a common understanding & a working together towards the highest & best aim.[12]*

Among the artistic movements of the era permeating art school curricula was Aestheticism, also associated with the design work of Morris and Crane. Aestheticism arose in parallel with the Arts and Crafts movement and was a notable influence on Mackintosh and other late nineteenth-century designers. It considered beauty to be the singular purpose of art, taking its cue from the French literary philosophy *l'art pour l'art*, or art for art's sake. In architecture, to create spaces that were holistically designed as artistic symphonies and even to dress in a manner that was complementary to the space one occupied was not just to show oneself as a person of refined taste but to present a beautiful mind and soul.[13] These ideas inspired the subsequent development of Art Nouveau and Symbolism in the fin de siècle, of which Mackintosh and his circle were the nexus in Scotland.

All these artistic movements were heavily influenced by non-Western cultures, particularly those of India, China and Japan. Wide-reaching British colonial enterprises brought goods and ideas from across the globe that provided rich source material for objects such as textiles, ceramics and prints. While we may now appreciate the problematics of the appropriation that ensued, for the Victorians such items were merely exotic feasts for the senses, consumed with admiration more for their aesthetic than cultural value.

Glasgow and Japan enjoyed direct exchange, with exports of trams and steam locomotives, and according to architectural historian Neil Jackson:

While Japan benefited from Glasgow's industries, Glasgow soon benefited from Japan's culture. In 1878, in exchange for a wide range of Scottish industrial products, the city of Glasgow received over a thousand items of Japanese artware which were exhibited at both the Corporation (or McLellan) Galleries in Sauchiehall Street and the City Industrial Museum in Kelvingrove Park. In December 1881, the Oriental Art Loan Exhibition opened at the Corporation Galleries, displaying pieces gathered from private collections as well as from the South Kensington Museum and Messrs Liberty's & Co. of London.[14]

FIG. 1.4 120 Mains Street, drawing room fireplace, photograph by T. & R. Annan, 1900–1.

Japonisme flourished in Glasgow and Japanese art and design are a well-documented influence on Mackintosh's work.[15] Its impact can be seen in the first home he designed for himself and Margaret Macdonald at 120 Mains Street (1900–1), where Japanese prints – gifts from their close friends Hermann and Anna Muthesius – were displayed over a pagoda-inspired hearth (fig. 1.4). A chair in the lounge is decorated with roundels similar to those atop the Mack's fence-posts. Jackson has compared these to Japanese *mon*, heraldic symbols usually inscribed within a circle, which influenced many other artists in this period, for example the 'butterfly' signature of James McNeill Whistler or the initials used similarly by Walter Crane.[16] An early library book in the GSA collection is an 1881 edition of Kikuo Tanaka's *Iroha biki monchō*, an illustrated

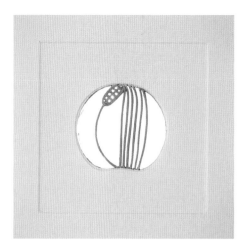

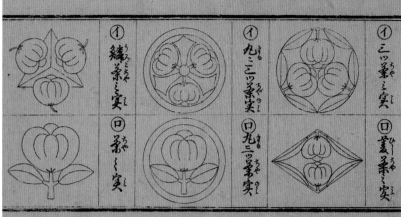

FIG. 1.5 Detail of the window in the Director's office door.

FIG. 1.6 Kikuo Tanaka, *Iroha biki monchō* (Illustrated index of Japanese coats of arms), 1881.

index of Japanese *mon*.[17] It was in the collection when Mackintosh was a student, and looking at some of the illustrations it is easy to see where it may have given him design ideas (fig. 1.6). In the Mack, this Japanese sensibility was found in the rounded stained glass in some of the internal doors (fig. 1.5), and perhaps most prominently in the immense yet elegant post-and-lintel roof supports of Studio 58 (*see* fig. 0.12).

Aestheticism and the Arts and Crafts movement had flourished in Glasgow for some time before the presence of Newbery and Mackintosh. Its earliest manifestation was perhaps found in the architecture and interiors of Alexander Thomson, a direct contemporary of Ruskin and Jones who might in some ways be seen as their Scottish counterpart. The interior of his St Vincent Street Church (1859), built just a few streets from the Glasgow School of Art, features boldly coloured decoration and beautifully polychromed cast iron columns and was a collaboration with the famed designer Daniel Cottier (fig. 1.7). Several of Scotland's prolific designers trained with Cottier, including the prominent stained-glass artist Stephen Adam, who acquired commissions across Scotland, largely for churches but also for homes, pubs, Glasgow City Chambers and even for Mackintosh at Miss Cranston's Ingram Street Tea Rooms in 1900.[18] Adam represented Glasgow's abundant artistic society in a set of stained-glass windows made for Maryhill Burgh Halls in 1873.[19]

FIG. 1.7 Alexander Thomson and Daniel Cottier, St Vincent Street Church, Glasgow, detail of interior, 1859.

FIG. 1.8 Charles Rennie Mackintosh, *Glasgow Cathedral at Sunset*.
Watercolour, 39.3 × 28.4 cm.

They depict all the varied trades that drove Glasgow's industrial machine, from joiners, glassblowers and calico printers to teachers, engineers and chemical workers. This creative economy was observed by Sir Thomas Armstrong, Director of Art for the Science and Art Department, who visited the Glasgow School of Art in January 1899 to oversee the annual prize-giving:

> *In Glasgow ... I became aware that many trades were being carried on in which decoration – the element of beauty or tastefulness, added to the element of utility – was a most powerful factor in effecting saleability or success. I found also that there was preserved here, more than in England, a good tradition in some of the minor arts, among others in carving in stone and wood, and in plaster work, and, more important than all, I found a great power of work, a willingness among the young to sacrifice their pleasure and comfort to achieve skill in those branches of Art Education which might lead to advancement in their walks of life.[20]*

Mackintosh's building at the Glasgow School of Art was emblematic of the environment described, and Armstrong surely saw the building as it was moving rapidly towards the completion of its first phase during his visit. It may even have been on the building site where he witnessed that 'great power of work' and the 'good tradition of the minor arts'. As Armstrong testifies, Glasgow was a city brimming with architectural promise and Mackintosh grew up watching it flourish, quite literally, in the streets and neighbourhoods of his youth.

MACKINTOSH'S EARLY LIFE AND ARCHITECTURAL TRAINING

Charles McIntosh was born on 7 June 1868 and grew up in a large family, the fourth of eleven children. His father, William McIntosh, was a police administrator who, according to Alan Crawford, had 'a passion for gardening, and the McIntoshes' flat was always full of flowers'.[21] Charles's mother, Margaret Rennie, whose surname he adopted for his artistic moniker, married William in 1862. Little is known about her apart from

reports of being much loved by all who knew her. The atmosphere of Charles's childhood must have been colourful and busy, but his youth was certainly not without its hardships. It has been thought that he may have had some form of dyslexia, based on patterns of error in his writing; if so, school may have been difficult.[22] He also had a contracted sinew in his left foot, which caused a characteristic limp as he grew older. Perhaps most profoundly, four of his siblings died in infancy, followed by his beloved mother when he was just 17.

Mackintosh's childhood environment surely shaped his artistic imagination. He spent his first six years in a three-room tenement at 70 Parson Street, Townhead, not far from Glasgow Cathedral (fig. 1.8) and the city's Necropolis in the most ancient heart of the city. The east end neighbourhood included the fifteenth-century manor house Provand's Lordship (fig. 1.9), which Mackintosh sketched in 1889.[23] Originally part of a hospital complex, its stalwart, slightly irregular façade and asymmetrical composition of windows and doors is typical of medieval Scottish architecture and a consequence of centuries of additions and renovations. This typology inspired the nineteenth-century Scots baronial revival style and was one of the early sources of inspiration for Mackintosh's architectural approach, alongside the countryside castles he would sketch later in the 1890s (fig. 1.10).

FIG. 1.9 Provand's Lordship, the oldest extant house in Glasgow, built 1471, extended 1670. A conservation project to reinstate the harling was completed by John Gilbert Architects in 2023.

By 1874 the McIntosh family had moved to a larger five-room flat a short distance away in Dennistoun, just behind the hill of Glasgow's Necropolis, at 2 Firpark Terrace. Mackintosh lived there with his family until 1892, when he was 24. Though he grew up in tenements, and no doubt watched many of them being built in his youth, they are seldom mentioned when considering his possible architectural influences. Like many such urban dwellings that were being built in Europe and North America at the time, Glasgow tenements adjoin terrace-like, rhythmically stretching along suburban streets (fig. 1.11). Their interiors have high, airy ceilings, often feature large bay windows and are reached by a central stairwell called a 'wally close', referring to

FIG. 1.11 Tenements stretched along Waverley Gardens in Glasgow's southside, built *c.* 1898.

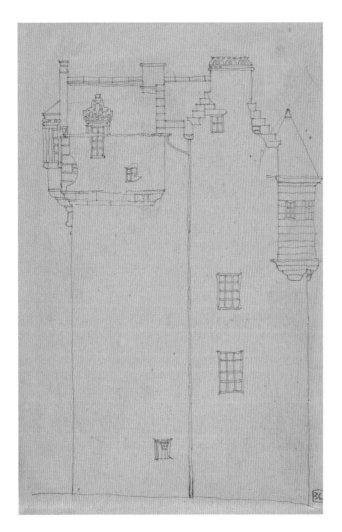

FIG. 1.10 Charles Rennie Mackintosh, east elevation, Maybole Castle, Ayrshire. Pencil on paper, from *Sketchbook of travels in Scotland and a tour to Kent* (1895), 34.

FIG. 1.12 Tiles at the apex of the Mack's east stairwell.

the decorative ceramic tiles lining the walls. These colourful, locally made tiles also perform a hygienic duty for the communal close. They undoubtedly stuck with Mackintosh, who incorporated a range of richly coloured tiles in the School of Art stairwells within his more austere scheme (figs 1.12, 3.37).

Mackintosh started at Reid's Public School at the age of seven, and at nine was enrolled at Allan Glen's Institution, a school established in 1853 for 'the sons of tradesmen or persons in the industrial classes of society'.[24] In 1876, two years before Mackintosh's attendance, the school had shifted its focus from trade and business towards science and technical education, and so it may have offered him the foundations needed to establish an architectural career. By the time of Mackintosh's first architectural apprenticeship in 1884, Glasgow was just out of a relatively brief financial depression after bank failures in 1878, and within ten years it had largely recovered due to the strength of Clydeside industry. Mackintosh's route to school and work throughout the 1880s and 1890s would have taken him from the east end, through what is now called the Merchant City, and past the construction site of the Glasgow City Chambers (1882–8; fig. 1.13). He will have passed the many banking and business premises of recent design, such as the Ruskinian Gothic Stock Exchange (1874; fig. 1.14) by John Burnet Snr,[25] whose son John James Burnet was Mackintosh's contemporary and at times competitor, notably for the Glasgow School of Art project.

An important local building from the period is the Venetian Gothic Templeton's Carpet Factory, designed by William Leiper in 1888 (fig. 1.15). Made for the manufacture of James Templeton and Son's Axminster carpets, it was erected just a few minutes' walk from Mackintosh's home. Modelled after the Doge's Palace in Venice, the richly patterned façade seems to mimic the textiles made inside. It experienced disaster when on 1 November 1889 its insecure façade was blown down in high winds, tragically killing 29 women weavers in an adjacent shed. A fire then beset the building in 1900, just eight years after its completion, resulting in more deaths. This incident prompted changes to fire regulations that impacted the second building

FIG. 1.13 George Square, built *c.* 1890, with Glasgow City Chambers designed by William Young. *c.* 1883.

FIG. 1.14 John Burnet Snr, The Stock Exchange, Buchanan Street, Glasgow (*c.* 1875–7). Photomechanical print, *c.* 1895.

FIG. 1.15 William Leiper, Templeton's Carpet Factory, Glasgow, *c.* 1892.

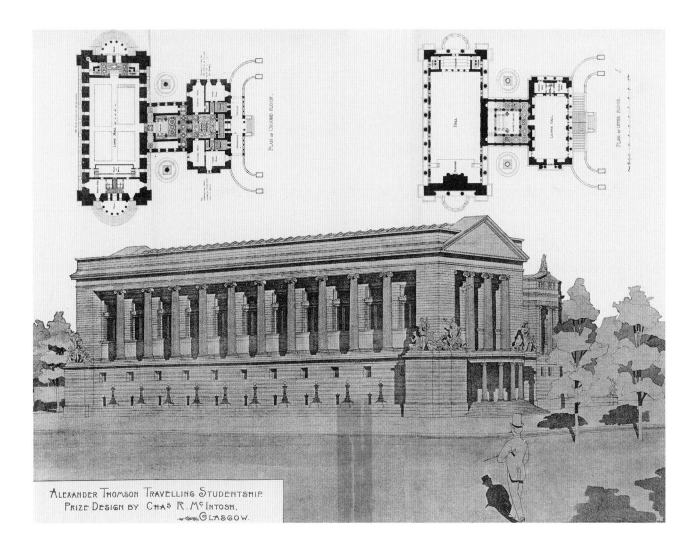

FIG. 1.16 Charles Rennie Mackintosh, plans, elevation and sections of a student design for a public hall, reproduced in *British Architect* (November 1890), 34.

phase of the Mack, creating a more robust material structure that has enabled it to endure as much as it has.[26]

We can trace the progression of Mackintosh's early career from the Glasgow School of Art registers. He enrolled in drawing courses in 1883 at 15 years old, and the first entry lists his father's occupation ('Clerk') rather than his own. But from 1884 until 1889 he is listed as 'Apprentice Architect', reflecting his first professional pupillage in these years with the architect John Hutchison. In 1889 he joined the firm of John Honeyman & Keppie, and from the second term of 1889 until 1891 the GSA registers list him as 'Architect & Draftsman', and finally from 1892 until 1894, his last enrolment, he is simply 'Architect'.

Mackintosh was apprenticed to Hutchison for nearly five years, but we know little of his work in this period.[27]

Of the few known buildings Mackintosh may have worked on, the only scant evidence is for R. Wylie Hill's department store on Buchanan Street, for which it was reported that he made drawings of unique Ionic capitals for the interior.[28] The connection may have been helpful as Robert Wylie Hill was related by marriage to Francis Newbery's wife, Jessie, and Mackintosh would later execute a private commission for the mantelpiece of Wylie Hill's home.[29]

In 1890, during his second year as a draughtsman at John Honeyman & Keppie, Mackintosh won the Alexander Thomson Travelling Studentship from the

Glasgow Institute of Architects for his design for a public hall (fig. 1.16). The plan demonstrated that from the combination of his art school education and his standard architectural apprenticeships he was able to design the most conventional of neoclassical buildings. Mackintosh's submission met the brief of a public hall to accommodate 100 seated people and committee rooms, in the 'early classic style'. It is a functional, Graeco-Roman revival composition that exhibited his skill in drawing an appropriate architectural plan and section, even including a replica Parthenon frieze, ubiquitous in the nineteenth century. It is lacking in details that we might label 'Mackintosh'; however, the cross-section does show some originality in the asymmetrical composition of space, perhaps in homage to Thomson. The plan also won a silver medal in the Department of Science and Art National Competition and is a great example of a talented applied architect-in-training.

Between March and June 1891 Mackintosh used his scholarship to travel across Italy, making studies of 'ancient' architectural sites and pausing in Paris, Brussels, Antwerp and London on his return journey. His diary of this journey – a requirement of the scholarship – offers hints that he was already familiar with many of the masterpieces he was to see, for his gallery visits were like meeting 'old and well-known friends'.[30] He makes amusing and insightful commentary on his travels, sometimes effusive, sometimes bitingly critical, but little that is terribly personal. A sketchbook of the northern leg of this journey is still in the Glasgow School of Art's collection,[31] and several beautiful watercolours are extant from his travels. He was particularly taken with Venice, having made an exquisite watercolour sketch of the Lido that is reminiscent of etchings made there by Whistler.[32] It has been generally accepted in Mackintosh scholarship that his trip to Italy had no lasting influence on his work in any obvious way,[33] but it surely shaped his imagination in some perhaps intangible manners. He was extremely impressed with the cityscape; of San Marco he wrote, 'A more noble assemblage was never exhibited by Architecture'. And perhaps like many architects, he is rather rapturous

about the fall of light wherever he sees it. In one passage he describes how he found himself in the Doge's Palace at dusk, 'not without respect leaning against the beautiful balustrade', when his reverie was interrupted by a custodian telling him they were about to close. On his exit, he recalled:

The various portals, the strange projections in the short striking irregularities of those stately piles delighted me beyond idea; and I was sorry to be forced to abandon them so soon especially as the twilight, which bats and owls love not better than I do, enlarged every portico, lengthened every colonnade, added a certain misticism [sic], *and increased the dimensions of the whole just as the imagination desired.*[34]

Anyone familiar with a Mackintosh interior might consider this passage as foreshadowing one of his greatest artistic abilities – the way he used light in his interiors, perhaps most masterfully in the Mack. Light and dark play on each other, bringing his spaces alive, a situation he deliberately crafted in the arrangement of space, fenestration, lighting and scale. Just as he observed in Venice, his interiors create an intentional psychological effect for the stimulation of the imagination and environmental experience that might be termed 'mystical' for some, or at least mysterious. We know very little as to what literature Mackintosh was studying, but he certainly read *Architecture, Mysticism and Myth*, published in 1891, the same year as his Italy trip. Its author, W.R. Lethaby, was an English Arts and Crafts architect and theorist who was a close friend and colleague of Morris and Webb. The book promoted the symbolic programmes of buildings as vehicles for meaning, rather than just ornamentation. In examining their sculptural and decorative schemes, Lethaby also considered geometric forms as signifiers, particularly the most basic ones such as the circle and square, which also marked the title page of his text.[35] Mackintosh had obviously read this by 1893 when he gave his lecture on 'Architecture', and lifted a passage from it (without credit) almost verbatim:

FIG. 1.17 Charles Rennie Mackintosh and John Keppie for John Honeyman & Keppie, Glasgow Art Club, gallery, 1891–2.

FIG. 1.18 Charles Rennie Mackintosh for John Honeyman & Keppie, Glasgow Art Club, chimney-piece, 1891–2.

Old architecture lived because it had a purpose. Modern architecture, to be real, must not be a mere envelope without contents. As [French architect and critic] *Cesar Daly says, if we would have architecture excite an interest, real & general, we must have a symbolism immediately comprehensible by the great majority of spectators.*[36]

Here we find the young Mackintosh using Lethaby's words to express his own developing design ideas. The notion that he advocates, via Lethaby, a 'symbolism immediately comprehensible' may seem at odds with the Symbolist ideal of 'suggestion', as well as the more enigmatic aspects of some of his spaces. However, these things are not necessarily mutually exclusive. Symbolism is full of narratives, as are Mackintosh interiors, for example the exciting narrative spaces he created for Catherine Cranston at her tea rooms (*see* fig. 5.4),[37] but

also the quiet, contemplative places in the Mack, like the library, that are remembered most fondly for the ways in which they subtly inspired the creative process. But we see the first signs of what we recognise as the 'Mackintosh style' the year before this talk, in his designs for the extension of the Glasgow Art Club (1891–2).

The commission was acquired by John Keppie, a member of the Art Club who, alongside his architectural work, was a keen watercolourist and moved in Glaswegian artistic circles. The overarching design for the space is a straightforward top-lit gallery, with an abundance of floor space for exhibition and social activities (fig. 1.17). A basic and functional rectangular plan, it is possibly Keppie's overall design. However, the large chimney-pieces at either end, as well as the door-frames, are a combination of neoclassical scroll-work and details like undulating carved garlands that hint at Mackintosh's developing style as a junior draughtsman (fig. 1.18). Sketches for the overall scheme were made by Mackintosh and published in Glasgow magazine *The Bailie* in June 1893, captioned in the curious hand lettering he experimented with in this period (fig. 1.19). They included a decorative frieze under the cornicing – an abstract motif of ribbon-like plants adjoining spiky Scottish thistles – and there is some evidence it was executed, but it has long been painted over. A recent refurbishment of the gallery offered an opportunity to recreate the stencilling based on the sketch, and its presence serves to unify the decorative scheme throughout the room. The sinuous garlands echo those found over the doorways, and stylised flora have the same kind of Mackintosh 'otherness' as details on the chimney-pieces and door fingerplates (fig. 1.20). While the overall effect is one that at a glance seems rather historicist, in its details we find the young Mackintosh searching for a language of his own.

The fourth son of a successful tobacco trader, Keppie studied at the Glasgow School of Art and continued his involvement there until, having been named one of its governors, he resigned his official post when the School of Art competition was won in 1897. Just a few years older than Mackintosh, Keppie was an especially ambitious young architect who had left Glasgow to study for a year at the École des Beaux-Arts in Paris. He had already won prizes as a student and nationally from the Royal Institute of British Architects. In 1888, the year before Mackintosh joined the firm, Keppie entered partnership with the respected older architect John Honeyman, and his dynamism and determination reinvigorated Honeyman's practice. Taking on the young Mackintosh was surely a sign of this.

The University of Glasgow's *Mackintosh Architecture* project highlights the challenge of attribution in some

FIG. 1.19 Charles Rennie Mackintosh for John Honeyman & Keppie, sketches for the Glasgow Art Club, published in *The Bailie*, 1893.

FIG. 1.20 Charles Rennie Mackintosh for John Honeyman & Keppie, Glasgow Art Club, door fingerplates in the gallery, 1891–2.

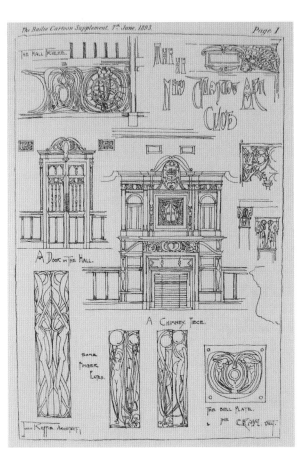

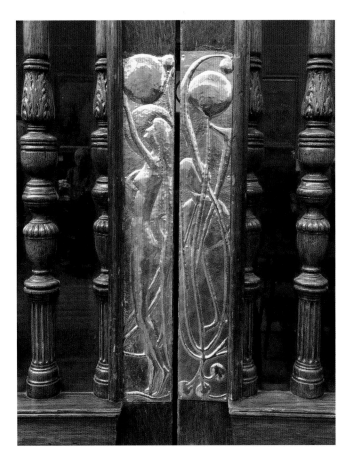

FIG. 1.21 Charles Rennie Mackintosh for John Honeyman & Keppie, perspectival drawing of the Glasgow Herald building, 1893.

FIG. 1.22 The Glasgow Herald building, 1893–9.

of the early projects Mackintosh was involved with, but also the ways in which his work can be clearly identified as his confidence and responsibility grows. Architectural historian Joseph Sharples notes, 'In the beginning, not surprisingly, Mackintosh seems to have assisted the partners while enjoying little scope for personal creativity'.[38] By the early 1890s we begin to see evidence of Mackintosh's developing style emerging from Keppie's Beaux-Arts preferences.[39] Sharples observes: 'The dividing line between Keppie and Mackintosh is particularly difficult to establish in the key work of this period, the Glasgow Herald building' (fig. 1.21).[40] When writing Keppie's obituary for the *RIBA Journal* in 1945, Andrew Graham Henderson, who joined the firm around 1904 and would later become a partner, recalled:

Mackintosh was an assistant with the firm for some time prior to being named a partner, and it is natural, therefore, that traces of his original and questing genius should be seen in Keppie's work, notably in the tower of the Glasgow Herald *buildings in Mitchell Street … [Later] Keppie and Mackintosh worked almost entirely, in an architectural sense, as individuals – Mackintosh blazing the trail for the 'modernist' and Keppie upholding the traditional outlook.*[41]

The Herald building was designed in 1893–4 after a fire damaged its extant property and destroyed the adjacent building on the corner of Mitchell Street and Mitchell Lane. The corner site was acquired and Mackintosh had a key role in a new extension design, under the

direction of Keppie. The most noticeable feature of his is the 44.5-metre (146-foot) water tower marking the corner of the building, which held a tank for the 'roof-drencher' fire suppression system (fig. 1.22).[42] The decorative stonework, with its scroll-work emerging from its surface, shows a further progression from the classically inspired Art Club-era designs towards the more organic forms of the Mack (fig. 1.23). Mackintosh saw himself as author of this building, as he lamented to the respected German architectural critic Hermann Muthesius, who would become a close lifelong friend:

> *You must understand that for the time being*
> *I am under a cloud – as it were – although the*
> *building in Mitchell Street here was designed by*
> *me the Architects are or were Messrs Honeyman*
> *& Keppie – who employ me as assistant. So if you*
> *reproduce any photographs of the building you*
> *must give the architects' name – not mine. You will*
> *see that this is very unfortunate for me, but I hope*
> *when brighter days come I shall be able to work for*
> *myself entirely and claim my work as mine.*[43]

This was written on the cusp of Mackintosh's 30th birthday, and although referencing the Herald building, his complaint may also derive from him having leadership on several notable projects of the period but without professional recognition for his authorship. He would not be made partner until Honeyman's retirement in 1901. It is even possible the project foremost in his mind when writing this was the Glasgow School of Art, as the note was sent to Muthesius on 11 May 1898, shortly before the foundation stone was laid for the new School of Art building on 25 May. He was also in the midst of finishing the new Queen's Cross Church (1896–9; fig. 1.24), a significant building in terms of establishing Mackintosh's visual language and one which we shall see has several stylistic connections to the Mack. He had a hand in numerous commissions during this period,[44] including Martyrs' Public School (1895–7; fig. 1.25), a new school building on the very street he was born. The commission came to the firm apparently without competition and followed the basic plan prescribed by the Glasgow Education Board.[45] It was being built during the time of the competition for the art school, and Mackintosh's hand can be seen emerging in some of the stonework. The experience of planning a 'school' building type must have helped Mackintosh think through ideas for his GSA project, though the two share little in common design-wise. More valuable, though, would have been his own experiences of a decade working in the crowded studios at the McLellan Galleries, home to the Glasgow School of Art when he was a student there from 1883 to 1894.

ART SCHOOL STYLE: MACKINTOSH, NEWBERY AND THE IMMORTALS

Mackintosh complemented his professional architectural training by honing his technical skills at the Glasgow School of Art, furthering his artistic

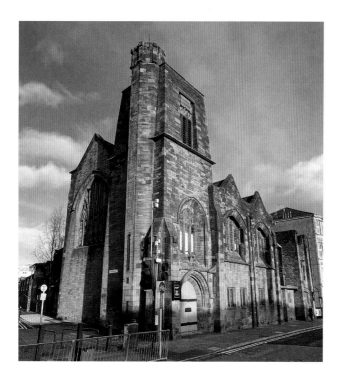

FIG. 1.24 LEFT Queen's Cross Church, 1896–9.

FIG. 1.25 ABOVE Martyrs' Public School (north-east corner), 1895–7.

impulses. Art school study allowed for creative development in a manner that the demands of the architectural office may not have. GSA did not yet offer a formal course in architecture; rather, relevant skills were offered through the National Course of Instruction – architecture came under the very last of the 23 stages. The courses were traditional and practical in their content, including, for example, visual analysis through studies made from the extensive plaster cast collection. He also designed classical and Beaux-Arts-style buildings, for which he passed local exams and won national prizes and awards for architectural plans and drawings in 1891 and 1892. His study is reflected in some early graphic work, notably an 1892 invitation to the Glasgow School of Art Club meeting (fig. 1.26). Made after his tour of Italy, here we find figures drawn directly from Michelangelo's Sistine ceiling amid a rather busy tableau of garlands, vines, putti and, at the centre, an ornate frame for the text that would be equally at home housing a Baroque painting. The hand lettering is anything but historicised, however, and marks the beginning of Mackintosh experimenting with letterforms, also seen in the *Bailie* sketch, that are elaborate outlined

flourishes: bold, if a bit awkward. This lettering also finds its way into similar invitations made by the Macdonald sisters the following year (*see* figs 1.37, 1.38).

Classes were held near the current campus in the McLellan Galleries on Sauchiehall Street, then the home of the city art collection. Mackintosh would have passed through an array of displays – perhaps a mix of Egyptian artefacts, Italian icons, medieval tapestries, Chinese figurines and Japanese ceramics and prints – on his way to cramped classes on the upper floors. The need for a larger permanent school was already pressing and Mackintosh would have experienced first-hand the practical requirements of the teaching studios, which were restricted in such close and limited quarters. As the Glasgow School of Art Song quips (*see* p. 29), Mackintosh may have 'built the school' – or rather the permanent home it needed – but it was Francis Newbery who helped to realise the school's community by recruiting gifted staff from across Europe to tutor students of varied age, class and gender to foster an atmosphere of artistic camaraderie. Newbery's charisma and connections built the esteemed reputation of the Glasgow School of Art – and by association Mackintosh – beyond Glasgow, eventually to continental Europe. He was appointed the fifth Headmaster of GSA in 1885, the title later changing to Director, and served until 1917. He expressed his educational philosophy in a lecture and demonstration he gave to the governors, staff and students on taking up his post, as the *Herald* reported:

> *He particularly insisted that students should be individualised as well as classified, and pointed out that no two students need ... be treated alike ... the personality of the student should be not lost sight of, for the teaching power in school was there to guide and direct, not to put itself in the place of the powers of the student, but by means of an intelligent and, above all, interesting course of teaching draw out the latent powers of the student, and direct them to the right channel.*[46]

This individualistic approach to students was coupled with a preference for an atelier-like method of teaching, a workshop-based approach where students were taught by practitioners in the field, professional artists,

designers and architects.[47] Newbery was himself a gifted painter and taught regularly in the studios, particularly championing his women students. In 1889 he married Jessie Rowat, who was a student at the school from 1884 (fig. 1.27). At a time when it was expected that married women give up their profession, Newbery instead enlisted her to establish the Department of Embroidery in 1894, a highly subscribed course that became part of the teaching certification for women. Though best known for her needlework, Jessie Newbery also taught other subjects, including mosaic and book illustration. She mentored some of the leading Scottish designers of the early twentieth century, including Jessie M. King and Ann Macbeth (fig. 1.28), both of whom would also go on to work in the school, King teaching book design from 1899 to 1907 and Macbeth, a prominent educator in needlework, becoming assistant mistress of the department in 1902. Highly respected at the school,

FIG. 1.26 Charles Rennie Mackintosh, invitation to the Glasgow School of Art Club meeting, 19 November 1892. Lithograph on paper, 12.6 × 21.6 cm.

FIG. 1.27 Jessie and Francis Newbery in 'fancy' dress, *c.* 1900. Pageants and masques were a favourite form of creative expression at the Glasgow School of Art in its early years.

FIG. 1.28 Ann Macbeth, Glasgow School of Art banner, *c.* 1900–5. Linen, wool and appliqué, 65 × 23.5 cm.

both were called on to craft ceremonial documents celebrating the new building.

The broader activities of the school, such as exhibitions, arts societies and clubs, also served the creative economy of Glasgow. These activities brought together night school students like Mackintosh and his friend and colleague Herbert MacNair with many of the day students. These were predominantly women and included two who would be vitally important to Mackintosh, the sisters Margaret and Frances Macdonald. Howarth credited Newbery with introducing the Macdonald sisters to Mackintosh and MacNair in the early 1890s because he saw something kindred in the work they were producing.[48] It is equally likely that they met each other through the activities of the Glasgow School of Art Club, the student group Newbery fostered. On Mackintosh's death in 1933, Jessie Newbery reflected that her husband 'remembers little of Mackintosh' until he won the Thomson travelling scholarship, but from then he was never 'out of sight, out of mind'.[49] She goes on to discuss the 'four epoch-making events of his life', stating that the first:

> *was contact, through the medium of 'The Studio', with work of the following artists: Aubrey Beardsley (his illustration to the play 'Salome' by Oscar Wilde); illustrations to Zola's 'Le Rêve' by Carlos Schwabe; reproductions of some pictures of [Jan] Toorup ...; the work, Architectural and Decorative of CFA Voysey. These artists gave an impetus and a direction to the work of 'the Four'.*[50]

FIG. 1.29 'The Immortals' at 'the Roaring Camp', Dunure, Ayrshire, *c.* 1893. Left to right: Frances Macdonald, Agnes Raeburn, Janet Aitken, Charles Rennie Mackintosh, Katherine Cameron, Jessie Keppie, Margaret Macdonald.

This is the first place Mackintosh, MacNair and the Macdonald sisters are called 'The Four', and she informs us that they exhibited together in a student show the following autumn, likely to have been in 1894.[51] Newbery tells us they 'isolated their contribution' and it was met with mixed reviews, but it gained an invitation to be featured in *The Studio* in articles by the Newberys' friend Gleeson White. This series, 'Some Glasgow Designers and Their Work', appeared in four parts in 1897–8 and helped to foster international attention for The Four and the Glasgow Style more generally.[52] While it is certain that these four worked closely together, usually in pairs rather than a quartet, this perhaps undermines the fact that when they met they were part of a larger group of students and friends who were exploring new modes of creative expression at the art school. Their wider interests in nature, faerie tales and European Symbolism in painting and design were shared among their cohort. This was particularly true for the group of women artists, writers and designers who called themselves 'The Immortals'.

We know of this group's nickname from an album of photographs donated to the GSA archives by Jessie

Keppie, younger sister of John. The album documents a sketching trip (or trips) to the nearby Ayrshire countryside by these women and a few of their male companions, notably John Keppie, MacNair and Mackintosh. They stayed at the Keppie family house in Dunure, known as the 'Roaring Camp', which certainly suggests a place for free-spirited and boisterous fun. Looking at the carefree images, one might think that their being 'Immortals' could just be down to a youthful feeling of possibility and invincibility, but Jude Burkhauser suggests the name may have been inspired by Celtic mysticism.[53] She also posited that it might represent an ironic reference to the kind of posterity usually reserved for male academic artists, which very few females got to enjoy. In one photo (fig. 1.29) the women stand three and three with Mackintosh perched between them: Frances Macdonald, Agnes Raeburn, Janet Aitken to the left and Katherine Cameron, Jessie Keppie and Margaret Macdonald to the right. Aitken and Cameron have bridged their hands to frame the young Mackintosh, and the image overall is one of bucolic merriment.[54] It is rather a dreamy group portrait of young artists who collectively found inspiration from nature, folklore and, notably, each other.

These women became friends at the art school, possibly in drawing and painting classes taught by Newbery himself: they all appear in a class portrait with Newbery, taken in a painting studio at the school around 1894–5 (fig. 1.30). Around the same time, Agnes's sister Lucy Raeburn created an 'artistic and literary magazine', simply titled *The Magazine*. It was a unique compilation of handwritten stories, illustrations and photographs by The Immortals and their friends, clearly inspired by *The Studio*, and compiled into four handmade albums created in November 1893, April 1894, November 1894 and Spring 1896.[55] The November 1894 issue contains one of Frances Macdonald's most renowned works, 'A Pond', as a frontispiece (fig. 1.31). It depicts symbolic embodiments of pond life through two elongated winged females mirroring each other as stylised tadpoles hovering about them. A few pages thereafter we find Margaret Macdonald's 'The Fifth of November' (fig. 1.32), a

mysterious vision which, given the date, may represent the fireworks in the night sky (although it is also the date of Macdonald's birth, and the figure at the bottom might represent the artist herself). These early works show the young artists already interested in Symbolist modes of expression, offering inscrutable, dream-like visions that are suggestive of narrative but leave all interpretation up to the viewer.

Mackintosh's contributions to the last three volumes of *The Magazine* in 1894–6 seem to evolve from mythological study, such as the 'tree of life' watercolours of 1895, inscribed 'The Tree of Influence, The Tree of Importance, The Sun of Cowardice' (*see* fig. 0.5) and 'The Tree of Personal Effort, The Sun of Indifference' (fig. 1.34). Loosely painted and abstract, each contain the *mon*-like circular shapes at their centre, with only

FIG. 1.31 Frances Macdonald, 'A Pond', published in *The Magazine* (November 1894). Pencil and watercolour on grey paper, 32 × 24 cm.

the suggestion of trees evident in the barren twig-like forms that frame and overlap. The poetic titles of each hint at frustrations of the artist, perhaps professional, if we recall his lament to Muthesius in 1898 that he was 'under a cloud'. The titles also serve as interpretive guides to these incredibly metaphysical Symbolist compositions.

Mackintosh was already experimenting with Symbolist abstraction in the rendering of both subject and idea, exemplified by the decorative details at the Glasgow Art Club of 1892. A watercolour from that same year, *The Harvest Moon*, is a subject purely from

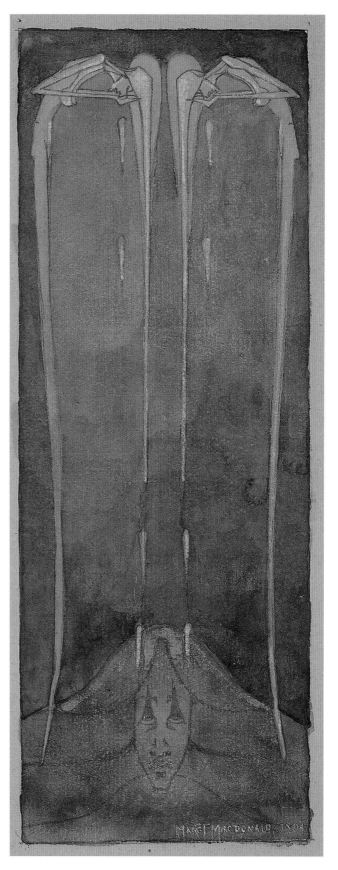

FIG. 1.32 Margaret Macdonald, 'The Fifth of November', published in *The Magazine* (November 1894). Pencil and watercolour on light grey paper, 31.5 × 19 cm.

FIG. 1.34 Charles Rennie Mackintosh, 'The Tree of Personal Effort' (1895), published in *The Magazine* (Spring 1896). Pencil and watercolour on grey paper, 32 × 25 cm.

Mackintosh's imagination, a divine feminine figure presiding over the ripened fruits at her feet, perhaps offering a blessing on a frosty night (fig. 1.33). At the centre, the angelic being floats above a bare and spiky thicket. Her wings encircle and frame the full moon at her back, and an ambiguous cloud-like form projects from the left below her feet, providing a suggestion of a horizon line. The bottom half of the composition is full of brambles and berries, while the upper half is largely watery blue sky. Timothy Neat, among others, has suggested the central figure is modelled after Alexandre Cabanel's *Birth of Venus* (1863), in which Venus reclines sinuously in her shell.[56] But there is another possible source for the composition of the central figure: the penannular shape of brooch pins used to fasten clothing, particularly in early medieval cultures across Britain

FIG. 1.33 OPPOSITE Charles Rennie Mackintosh, *The Harvest Moon*, 1892. Watercolour, 35.2 × 27.6 cm. Inscribed on back: 'The Harvest Moon, Chas. R. Mackintosh, 1893, To John Keppie, October 1894'.

(fig. 1.35). These objects are descended from both the Iron Age and Roman periods, and numerous examples have been found in Viking cultures. They most often take the form of an open decorative ring with a sliding pin-clasp that effectively bisects the circle. During the eleventh century in Scotland and Ireland, these pins often took the form of thistles. We find similar penannular motifs throughout the visual culture of post-Roman Britain and Ireland. This complex mix of Pictish, Germanic and even Mediterranean styles is known as Insular art, but for Mackintosh and his contemporaries it was 'Celtic'. Much of his oeuvre might be viewed as part of the Celtic Revival, which in late Victorian design culture was on trend and lucrative, championed commercially through decorative objects including jewellery commissioned and sold by firms such as Liberty with its Cymric range of silver (fig. 1.36). For The Immortals and Mackintosh, such themes would have aligned to their interests in a romanticised notion

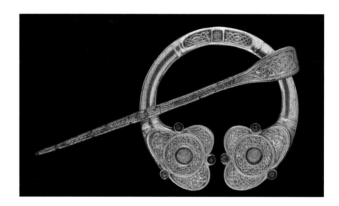

FIG. 1.35 Silver pennanular brooch with interlaced ornamentation, from Rogart, Sutherland, 8th century.

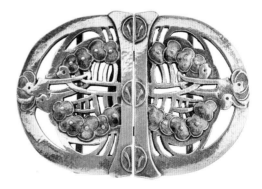

FIG. 1.36 Jessie M. King, buckle designed for Liberty & Co., 1906. Silver and enamel, 5.8 cm wide.

FIG. 1.37 Margaret Macdonald, invitation for a Glasgow School of Art Club 'at home', 1893. Lineblock print, 13.1 × 15.6 cm.

FIG. 1.38 Frances Macdonald, programme of music for the Glasgow School of Art Club 'at home', 1893. Lineblock print, 13.2 × 11.8 cm.

of Scotland's past, evidenced in their artistic work. Like Mackintosh's architectural responses to Scots baronial styles, we might view works like *The Harvest Moon*

FIG. 1.39 Maquette for the relief sculpture over the main entrance.

as having a relationship in theme and form to local folkloric traditions. The Celtic penannular brooch form would be found again in the Macdonald sisters' graphical work for the School of Art Club (figs 1.37, 1.38) and, most significantly, chosen by Mackintosh to grace the threshold of his School of Art (fig. 1.39), where it stands sentinel, through two fires, even today (*see* fig. 0.6).[57]

The Magazine and The Immortals offer unique evidence of the kinds of collaborative communities cultivated by Newbery during the 1890s – the proof of his successful experiment to gather art students 'of various ages and every sex', as the song put it. The young Mackintosh thrived in this atmosphere; it supplemented his architectural training to create a fully rounded artistic vision. The collaborative work, social events, camaraderie and shared philosophical and artistic styles are evidence that rather than being a 'lone genius', Mackintosh was energised by the collective nature of working in practice with others. Thus Newbery was setting up a diverse artistic community even before the Mack existed – and a new building was quickly becoming a dire necessity.

DESIGNING THE MACK

DESIGN BY

FOR THE GLASGOW School of ART: DESCRIPTION AND SCHEDULE OF CONTENTS.

CHAPTER 2

DESIGNING THE MACK

What is required, is a building with class rooms conveniently arranged and well lighted.

CONDITIONS OF COMPETITION, 1896[1]

Almost since its establishment in 1845, the Glasgow School of Art struggled with sufficient accommodation for its ever-growing student population. In Newbery's time, while initial enrolment numbers were declining, his ability to retain students year after year meant that overall attendance was increasing.[2] Evening classes, designed for working people like Mackintosh, were particularly crowded.[3] For nearly forty years, the school managed with rented accommodation at 12 Ingram Street in the city centre, then moved to the McLellan Galleries on Sauchiehall Street in 1869. Newbery's leadership expanded the curriculum and increased funding for the school by establishing a reputation for excellence in national exams and competitions. This funding, much of it from Scottish municipal tax schemes, meant that Newbery could begin to increase the school's facilities.[4] This initially focused on expanding the technical studios to serve the growing requirements of local industry, but it was clear that purpose-built accommodation would be critical to the future success of the school.

The benefits of sharing accommodation with Glasgow Corporation Galleries at the McLellan inspired the initial idea for new school premises within the city museum in Kelvingrove Park that was being planned with surplus monies from the 1888 Glasgow International Exhibition. The scheme was vetted by several municipal committees over the next few years.[5] However, in 1891 the city decided not to include an art school in the new gallery, even though most, including the Lord Provost James King, agreed that GSA's accommodation situation was untenable.[6]

Yet the desire to have arts education closely connected with Glasgow's museum collections remained strong, inspired by the relationship enjoyed by the South Kensington Museum and the National Art Training School. In service of this idea, a deputation was sent to visit South Kensington in 1893, as well as the schools of art in Birmingham and Manchester. The group included Newbery, the three architects on the GSA board of governors – James Salmon, William Leiper and J.J. Burnet – and the board chairman James Fleming. Their main agenda was to study the technical studios, and the relationship each had with municipal museums.[7] This trip provided essential encouragement for the planning of a new school building, but it would be another three years before a formal building committee was convened as funds needed to be secured for the project.

Substantial support initially came from the Bellahouston Trust, which purchased the Renfrew Street site on the steep rise of Garnethill for £6,000. This was done with the stipulation that the school raise matching funds from the public (which they did), at which time the Trust would offer a further £4,000,[8] giving them an initial total of £10,000 to launch their building fund after site purchase. The governors

PREVIOUS PAGE (FIG. 2.1) The main entrance of the Mackintosh building, photograph by Thomas Annan, *c.* 1910.

FIG. 2.2 Charles Rennie Mackintosh for John Honeyman & Keppie, 'Merrythoughts' illustration on cover of competition entry, 1896.

ultimately decided that a funding target of £21,000 would be desirable and, on condition of reaching their public fundraising goal, Glasgow Corporation (the city government) agreed to contribute £5,000 for 'a plain building affording accommodation equal to that at present in use'. This note, from a September 1895 meeting of the board of governors, may be the genesis of the notion that the building should be 'plain', that is, not lavish but practical and economical in function as well as execution. It was not to be a grand statement but a useful composition.

THE BUILDING COMMITTEE

An extraordinary meeting of the board of governors was convened on 16 March 1896, at which many critical decisions were made, notably the formation of the building committee. The board chairman James Fleming was named convenor.[9] Fleming, who attended the art school in his youth, was the director of Cochran & Fleming Potteries (later Britannia Pottery) and sat on several important committees for arts and education in the city.[10] In many ways he was as vital to the building of the new school as Newbery, particularly for his financial connections. The importance of his role was such that a plaque in his honour was commissioned from the sculptor George Frampton in 1903 and placed in the Mack's central stairwell, where it remained until it was sadly destroyed in the 2018 fire.

Two independent assessors for the competition were also selected: Sir James King, 1st Baronet, who had served as Lord Provost of Glasgow from 1886 to 1889 and championed the need for better premises to the council, and Sir Renny Watson, a mechanical engineer, city council member and chair of the Bellahouston Trust. Alongside the authorities in South Kensington, their recommendations would appoint the winning architects.

At this initial meeting the board directed Newbery to prepare a block plan for the competition, showing how the site might be used and with a complete list of building specifications, including room dimensions and lighting requirements.[11] By May 1896 Newbery and committee member Robert Leadbetter prepared the final version of all the building requirements in the 'Conditions of Competition',[12] which were approved by

Thomas Armstrong of the Science and Art Department, South Kensington. They were also reviewed by the property surveyor of the School Board of Glasgow, for although they were not the governing authority for the art school, the practicalities of the building were not unlike those of public schools being built. Everything was in order, and with a final decision to increase the number of invited architects from eight to twelve, the competition was set to begin.

THE COMPETITION

In June 1896 the shortlisted architects were invited to compete (fig. 2.3). The three architect governors – Burnet, Salmon and Leiper – were included in the initial list. Only Leiper refused the invitation, stating:

I don't think any Architect holding office as Governor or otherwise should enter the competition but that it should be left to some of the younger men whose names I have already mentioned to make designs.[13]

There was, however, an issue that the committee had to tackle at the outset: the inadequacy of their £14,000 building budget. The £21,000 the committee raised was inclusive of the £6,000 that purchased the site, and the remaining £1,000 was for building the retaining wall, assessors' expenses and other contingencies. The £14,000 sum was to 'be the full limit given as the total cost of the building inclusive of lighting and heating and ventilating apparatus, draining, paving, and altering Streets, ready for occupation; also of architects, measurers and clerk of works fees'.[14] For comparison, both Martyrs' School and Queen's Cross Church had been completed for under £10,000, but both were much smaller buildings on easier sites than the steep slope of Garnethill.[15] Scotland Street School (1903–7), a building of more comparable size, cost £20,541.[16]

After the competition launched on 24 July 1896, a provocative letter was received from the competing architects regarding the insufficiency of the budget:

We the undersigned ... are of the opinion that this accommodation cannot be provided in an

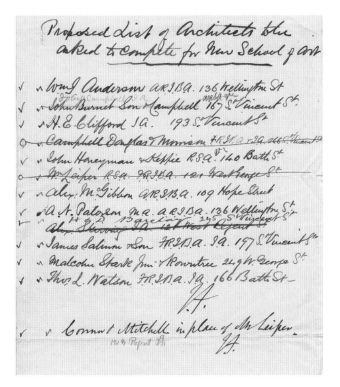

FIG. 2.3 The proposed list of architects.

Core to their concern was the difficulty of the site itself, as Watson explained in his letter of 20 August 1896:

> It is quite understood that the building must be one of great simplicity and plainness, and the Competitors have no wish to induce the Governors to incur any expense that can possibly be avoided … the accommodation required by the conditions cannot be provided on the site within or near the limit of cost that has been laid down even in the plainest building that would be tolerated by the Governors. I may point out that the accommodation scheduled is that of a large School of a complete and thoroughly equipped kind. The site that has been acquired is an excellent one for the purpose but on account of its long frontage and steep gradients it is a costly one to build upon and necessarily involved a large amount of underbuilding.[19]

Because of this more reasoned complaint, the governors acquiesced and amended the 'Conditions':

> Should it be found that the accommodation required as above cannot be adequately provided in their plan for this sum of £14,000 then Architects are asked – 1) To mark on their plans by shading or other means such portion of their design as can be carried out for the Sum, and 2) To State the cost of the completed plan covering the whole ground.[20]

This is the reason the Mack was built in two phases. The difficult slope was made even more complicated by the encroachment of the buttresses from the Glasgow Real Ice Skating Palace (previously the Panorama) on the south-west property line. Mackintosh's solution, as seen from his earliest drawings like the perfunctory block plan of September 1897, was not to give the Panorama building clearance but simply to design recesses into the very wall of the building (fig. 2.4). The structure thus filled the rectangular foundation to maximum capacity, a clever solution but one that had catastrophic consequences for the neighbouring building in the 2018 fire.

> adequate manner within the limit of cost laid down. We suggest that the competing architects should be asked to State what portion of their design could be carried out within the limit of £14,000 and to give also their estimate of the completed scheme.[17]

After some deliberation, the governors declined the request, emphasising that 'although not mentioned in these conditions, it is but a plain building that is required'.[18] This implies that the assumed expense would come from unnecessary addition or embellishment of what was asked for in clause 20 of the 'Conditions', simply: 'What is required, is a building with class rooms conveniently arranged and well lighted.'

A further letter from the architects of 17 August 1896 emphasised the impossibility of the budget, followed by a 'deputation' of the group, led by the architect T.L. Watson, apparently doorstepping Fleming to debate the matter. Fleming seems to have understood their misgivings and requested that Watson lay them out more clearly in a further letter to the governors.

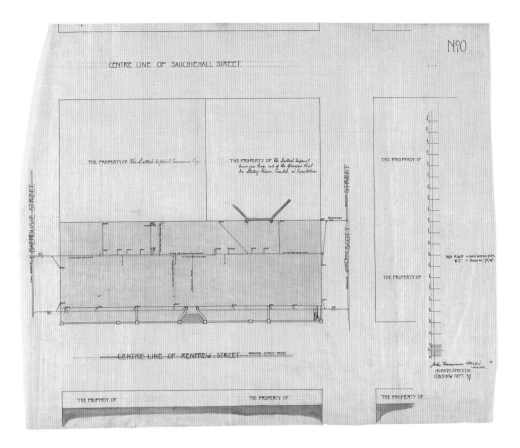

FIG. 2.4 Charles Rennie Mackintosh for John Honeyman & Keppie, block plan, September 1897.

With the budget issue settled, the competition moved forward. It was standard to judge such competitions anonymously, and in this case architects were to submit their drawings 'marked with a seal, sign or motto, and be accompanied with a sealed envelope, enclosing a replica of this same seal, sign or motto, together with the architect's name and address'.[21] John Honeyman & Keppie's submission was marked with Mackintosh's choice of motto, a small ink drawing with the motif of three interlocked 'merrythoughts' or wishbones, composed in another *mon*-like roundel (fig. 2.2). Surely intended as a good-luck charm, the resilient arched wishbone is poetically architectural. Although submitted anonymously, the 'merrythoughts' motif, alongside the distinctive lettering of the cover, must have been recognisable to Newbery as the work of Mackintosh. Howarth was adamant that 'it was well known that Newbery had done all in his power – short of flatly refusing to accept any design but Mackintosh's – to secure the only building he thought worthy to house his School of Art'.[22] Although he was writing near

Mackintosh's lifetime, Howarth often did not include sources for his conclusions, so some reports cannot be substantiated. This statement seems particularly speculative when considering Newbery's personal and professional connections to several of the other contestants, especially those on the board of governors and through his own membership of the Glasgow Art Club. In fact James Salmon II, grandson of the firm's progenitor and son of the governor, studied at GSA at the same time as Mackintosh, from 1888 to 1895, before joining the family firm. He also undertook his apprenticeship with Leiper, indicating what an insular architectural world Glasgow was at the time. Therefore Mackintosh was not the only one of Newbery's students to have strong connections to the committee, nor to compete.

Even if Newbery did favour Mackintosh's design and the adjudicators had a degree of familiarity with local architects, the competition was assuredly fair for the South Kensington authorities were judging blind. The London judges – Armstrong and Major-General Edward Robert Festing, the first director of the Science Museum – identified Mackintosh's building as the superior design. The local judges, King and Watson, were pleased that their decision was unanimous: 'Accordingly we beg now to recommend to your most favourable consideration the design which bears as a distinguishing mark Three "Merrythought" OR CROSSED BONES.'[23] They also added a suggestion as to how the scheme might go forward, which was carried out:

> ... in our opinion it would be advantageous, as well as economical, if (in carrying out the design) instead of erecting at present the dark shaded Central Block, which we assume can be built within the specified cost and leaving the two ends unbuilt, the design should be modified as to begin the present building at Dalhousie Street and carrying it westwards as far as the able funds will allow thus leaving only one end to be built at a later date.

The winners were notified in early January 1897, and by March a set of plans was submitted to the Science and Art Department. This is the earliest extant set, and we can assume these plans were very close to the original scheme as laid out by Mackintosh.

MACKINTOSH AND KEPPIE'S ORIGINAL DESIGNS FOR THE SCHOOL

Except for the winners, the unopened envelopes with mottos were returned to the unsuccessful architects;[24] however, all contestants agreed to have their submissions exhibited with their names in Corporation Galleries alongside the annual exhibition of student works on 1–6 February 1897. It is regrettable that none of the competition drawings is extant for comparison, especially given the competitors' contemporaneous buildings, for example Salmon & Son's elegant and astonishing St Vincent Street Chambers, known locally now as the Hatrack (1899–1902; fig. 2.5).

FIG. 2.5 James Salmon & Son, the 'Hatrack', St Vincent Street, 1902.

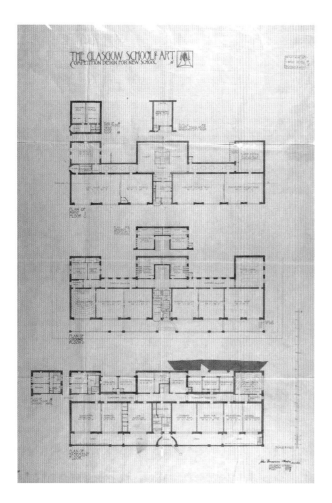

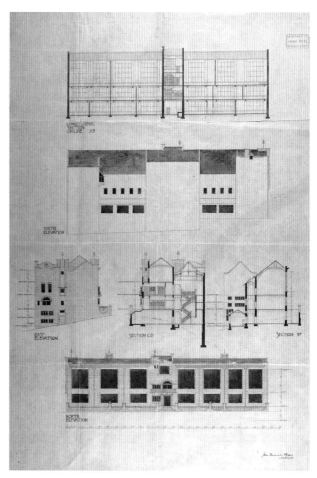

FIG. 2.6 Charles Rennie Mackintosh for John Honeyman & Keppie, GSA competition plans – all levels, February 1897. Photo-mechanical reproduction and wash, with ink inscription, 91.3 × 61.7 cm.

FIG. 2.7 Charles Rennie Mackintosh for John Honeyman & Keppie, GSA competition plans – all elevations, February 1897. Photo-mechanical reproduction and wash, with ink inscription, 86.7 × 61.8 cm.

We also do not have the original competition drawings for the Mack, just the written description of the building, in Keppie's hand, with a detailed schedule of the rooms as delineated in the 'Conditions' in Mackintosh's recognisable script.[25] The description itself begins: 'The authors of this design …', which serves as another reminder that even though Mackintosh has now been attributed singular authorship, Keppie was heavily involved in conceiving the building. With similar experience to Mackintosh, having studied at the school, he surely had valuable input, if not authority, over the revisions in the building. It was Keppie who attended building committee meetings as needed during the first building phase; Mackintosh would attend throughout the second phase. Honeyman, who

was nearing his retirement, was notably not present in any documentation.

From the room schedule and the earliest drawings for the building, Mackintosh and Keppie addressed every single requirement of the 'Conditions' (figs 2.6, 2.7). Newbery's original room schedule included details such as dimensions and other key instructions like room position and lighting requirements. For example:

C. *One Design Room, say 49' × 35' – 1715 sq. ft. This room need not necessarily be lighted from the north.*

D. *One School Library and Reading Room with a floor space of from 1000 to 1200 sq. ft. This room should adjoin and communicate with room C.*

The architects were exacting in seeing that these features were realised. Just a few small adjustments were made on square footage where necessary, and usually to provide space for other accommodations suggested in the brief, such as a lecturer's room in the lecture theatre or dressing rooms for models inside the studios. Yet the architects were also thoughtful in the way they composed the rooms, taking the freedom to stray where they thought the school would be better served. For example, instead of placing the library in the basement, they used the area for the architectural studios there (rather than the suggested ground floor) to make space for the library more centrally, as Keppie explains: 'This has been done … as it makes the library more available for all departments of the school than had it been placed on the basement floor.'[26]

Mackintosh's drawings improved on the client's requirements where they could, offering new ideas that exceeded the brief. He and Keppie offered a handful of new spaces that Newbery hadn't thought of or hadn't fully included in his list. For example, the 'Conditions' emphasised corridor spaces be provided for the plaster cast collection, a critical teaching tool for any art school. It was also suggested that this space should be flexible for periodic exhibits of student work and clarified that 'The School Museum need not be a special room, but might be a feature in connection with the staircase.' Mackintosh obliged by designing the central stair to open on to an impressive first-floor gallery, with great timber trusses soaring some ten metres above the floor (fig. 2.8). An anatomy studio was also added, 'an essential of a wholly equipped school of art',[27] and a common room for the students as, like Newbery, both Keppie and Mackintosh understood the value of fostering a creative community:

This room would provide a place of meeting for the students between the hours of study, it could also be the headquarters of the School of Art Club and be available for meetings lectures etc. under the auspices of that society.[28]

The original configuration of the building was three levels on a rectangular foundation (*see* cats 15–21). The

FIG. 2.8 The museum, photograph by Harry Bedford Lemere, *c.* 1909.

FIG. 2.9 The main staircase, photograph by T. & R. Annan, *c.* 1910.

upper two floors were recessed on the south, between the eastern, central and western blocks, to allow more light to filter into the rear of the building. As per Newbery's instruction, most of the messier and louder studios – clay, metal and woodworking – were arranged on the basement level (*see* cat. 5). Also on this level, in the south-east corner, was a janitor's house, a clever little flat arranged over two levels within the nine-metre height of the basement floor. The ground floor (*see* cat. 6) contained the entrance hall with janitor's office leading on to the main staircase (fig. 2.9). Airy studios were arranged along the north side of the central east–west corridor, culminating in each tower end. The east end was to be a lecturer's room, attached to a planned lecture theatre in the north-east corner, but this was abandoned in favour of more studio space. South of the corridor at the east end were the male and female teachers' rooms – flexible office-type shared spaces – but not their studios, which were planned for the floor above. At the opposite west end, a library and reading room comprised the whole of the south-west corner. Like the janitor's house, this was designed over two storeys within the height of the volume. This drawing is a rather plain affair compared to Mackintosh's final iconic library; however, it shows a charming spiral stair, which originally adjoined the two floors with each other and the basement below.

Flanking the central stair were female and male lavatories, and on the half-landing (entresol) above them staff dining rooms, again making the most of space that does not need to utilise the full height of each floor. It is worth highlighting here that providing space for women was a feature of this building, as directed by Newbery. The Glasgow School of Art was not singular in this; Newbery would have seen male and female studio spaces at the other schools he visited. But unlike at Manchester and Birmingham, Newbery's plan did not divide studios along gender lines, except for the life rooms initially, but even these became mixed in phase II revisions. Rather, rooms were planned on subject/use requirements. Rawson states:

> *Newbery had no need to waste space in providing for elementary classrooms or in dividing the sexes unduly. Manchester seems to have been the most encumbered in this regard in not only providing separate male and female elementary classes, taking up as many as four rooms, but in also accommodating a 'ladies' and gentlemen's painting class' in a fifth.*[29]

Newbery's plan was more focused on providing sufficient accommodation for women in terms of offices and toilets, a point that does not seem so radical now but which shows the value he placed not just on the education of women, but also on them as staff members in the school. It is an intriguing notion that such concerns have always been part of the building's plan, especially considering decisions in the 2014–18 restoration project to provide gender-neutral facilities when the building reopened, in keeping with present-day positions on diversity and equality.

The first floor (*see* cat. 7), which was the top level until the phase II expansion, had just four large studios across the front. The board room was planned for the south-east tower with a dropped ceiling to provide space for male and female teachers' studios above it. The south-west tower comprised the flower painting room with a cantilevered conservatory attached. The central block contained the headmaster's office and, again bisecting vertical space, his studio above. Outside this to the south and filling the whole of the southern central area surrounding the main stair was the spacious museum.

Much of this plan is recognisable in the final building, in form if not in function. Although the phase I drawings render the building as a whole, everyone knew that only half would be built when laying out the studios. The architects seem to have allocated most of the core South Kensington system classes (ornament, life, modelling) to the east and central wing, along with key spaces for staff (offices, studios, dining rooms). In reality, these studios would need to be much more flexible in use since the entirety of Newbery's programme needed to be served. Part of the solution for this was that technical studios were housed in a purpose-built shed nestled in the unbuilt western portion of the site (fig. 2.10). These were not in any case the final configurations for these studios, as Mackintosh's phase II revisions saw him boldly add

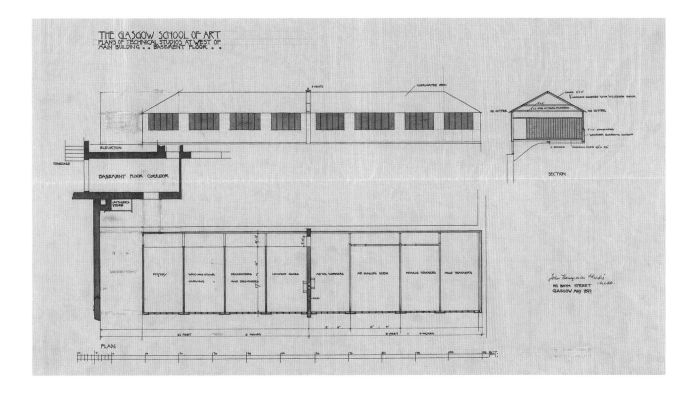

FIG. 2.10 Charles Rennie Mackintosh/John Honeyman & Keppie, plan, north elevation and section of temporary technical studios, May 1899, 37 × 69.8 cm.

a whole new floor to the school, enabling the upward movement of the library to the first-floor level and the expansion of studio space above, as well as below in a new sub-basement.

PHASE I: 1896–9

At an extraordinary meeting of the board of governors on 11 October 1897, it was noted that the first phase of construction would comprise 'that portion of the building ... which commences from the eastern boundary and runs west to the western wall of the main entrance and includes the western walls of the museum and stair case.'[30] By that time much preliminary work was accomplished: drawings had been revised and contractors had been solicited. At the same meeting the following tenders were accepted:

1. *Excavator Mason + Brick Work*
   John Kirkwood

2. *Cast Iron Work*
   Kesson & Campbell
3. *Steel Work*
   P. & R. Fleming
4. *Carpenter & Joiner Work*
   James Morrison
5. *Glazier Work*
   McCulloch & Co
6. *Slater Work*
   John Anderson
7. *Plumber Work* [and Gasfitter]
   Moses Spiers & Son
8. *Plaster Work*
   R.A. McGilvray
9. *Marble & Tile Work*
   Galbraith & Winton[31]

Further works were not yet contracted, and the committee also asked for power to approve further work 'without having to return for authority' each time. All was unanimously agreed, and later contracts include electric lighting (over gas, decided at the same meeting) by Osborne & Hunter and 'speaking tubes', an early intercom system, by James Hutcheson.[32]

Minutes of 5 November 1897 report that 'ground had now been broken for the building of the new School of Art'.[33] Work progressed throughout the early winter and by April 1898 it was agreed that a ceremony to lay a 'memorial stone' (foundation stone) should take place on the afternoon of 28 May 1898, 'to which Representatives from various public bodies associated with Art should be invited'.[34] The Lord Provost of Glasgow presided and included in the formal ceremony were Watson, Fleming, the Bishop of Glasgow, the school secretary E.R. Catterns, Newbery and Keppie.[35] Speeches lauded Newbery's recent successes, noting that 'For the second year in succession the School has taken first place in National Competition, having been awarded the greatest number of medals given to any school of art in the Kingdom.'[36] Craftspeople were invited on the dais to offer ceremonial tools to city officials, but no mention of Mackintosh was made in local reports.[37]

It was also decided that a time capsule would be placed inside the stone itself. A glass jar containing items such as annual reports and other school ephemera (fig. 2.11) was placed inside the cavity alongside one unique document, a short history of the school illuminated on vellum by student Jessie M. King.[38] It was signed by the representatives at the event and sealed with the seal of the school. Similar documents were made for the first and second opening ceremonies by other celebrated women students, both now in the GSA archives. In 1899 Ann Macbeth made an exquisitely detailed black ink drawing on vellum,[39] and in 1909 a spectacularly intricate illumination was designed in green and gold leaf by the lesser-known illustrator Edith Lovell Andrews (fig. 2.12), complete with a clever detail of Mackintosh's grand door to the school. Judging by these, one can only dream what King's must have looked like, but there may now be a chance to discover it. There is little to celebrate about the current condition of the building; however, it may have made investigating the location of the foundation stone a possibility, using current archaeological technology. The extent of dismantling needed for reconstruction might even allow access, documentation, conservation and another ceremonial placement of this time capsule. There may still survive an original

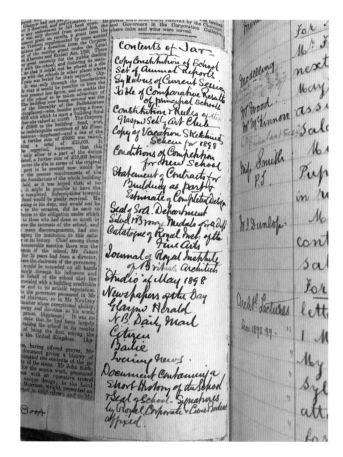

FIG. 2.11 Handwritten list of time capsule contents for foundation stone. Pasted in 'Report of the Governors of the Glasgow School of Art', Session 1897–8, 4.

illuminated document by the celebrated artist Jessie M. King inside the remaining walls of the Mack.[40] What a discovery that would be!

Not a lot is known about the actual construction process of the building, but the *Mackintosh Architecture* project includes a brief chronology derived from the building committee minutes, public records and site inspections.[41] The bulk of the heavy work took place in 1898. The year began with laying the foundations and a steam crane was on site by 3 May, in time for the laying of the memorial stone on 25 May. The walls of the eastern portion were complete and the roof was under construction by July, with plasterwork and finishing already taking place in the autumn. Interior construction carried on and the technical studios were planned and built adjacent to the main building by late October 1899.

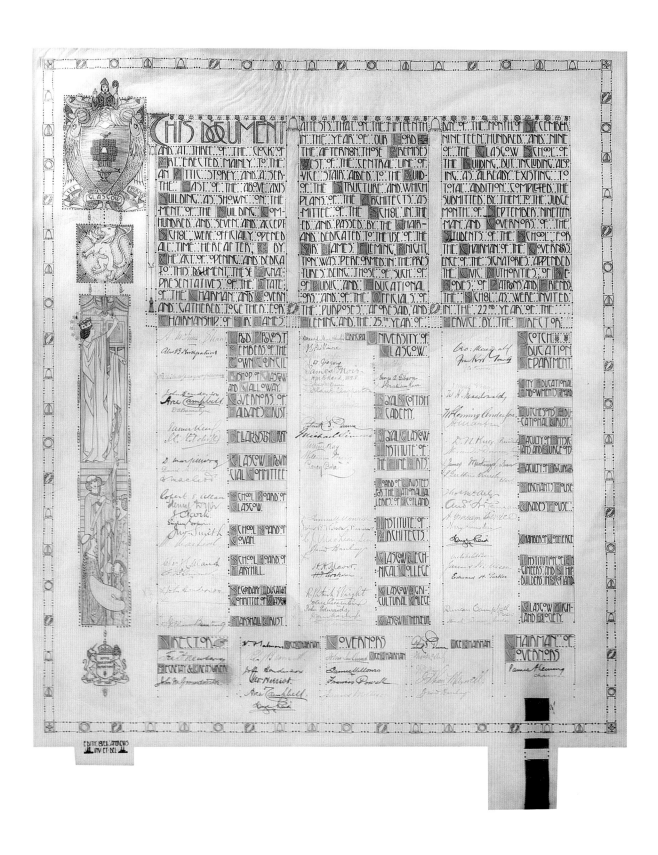

FIG. 2.12 Edith Lovell Andrews, illumination for the second phase opening of the Mackintosh building, 1909.

FIG. 2.13 Charles Rennie Mackintosh, 'Design for a Library in a Glasgow House', *c.* 1894–6. Watercolour and graphite on paper, 17.1 × 87.3 cm. The Metropolitan Museum of Art, New York.

In terms of the execution of the first phase of the building, Mackintosh's earliest interior drawings – one of the few extant sections of his Mack – offer a much more decorative vision than was realised, particularly for the museum. A small sketch for the frieze depicts a processional (*see* cat. 18), including a composition of figures that is like those he would design with Margaret Macdonald for the gesso panels at the Ingram Street Tea Rooms in 1900. This design is also reminiscent of an unrealised 1894 'Design for a Library in a Glasgow House' (fig. 2.13). We also find an elaborately designed front door to the school and many ornamental suggestions throughout the sage panelled interior, which were never realised. As completed, the first phase of the building was more austere than Mackintosh planned, but not without some decorative surprises. The interior building was not the 'white walls' of living memory but an 'artistic green', according to the *Evening Times*.[42]

The first phase of the building was delivered on time, but not under budget. There was a £4,500 overspend that took two years to pay off, with help from Fleming and a further grant from the Bellahouston Trust. Just as Mackintosh was seemingly absent from the memorial stone proceedings, nor was he mentioned as present at the formal opening for phase I on 20 December 1899. But again, as he was not a partner in the firm at that point, it would of course be Keppie who was mentioned in the press and who represented the firm for these ceremonies (whereas Mackintosh *was* included, as a partner, in the phase II opening in December 1909). Mackintosh was not slighted and he was surely present, and probably not just lost in the crowd. A ceremonial key of his design (fig. 2.14) was presented to Sir James King, carried by Newbery's daughter Mary on a white satin cushion that she later stated was embroidered by her mother, Jessie, and Jessie's friend Margaret Macdonald.[43] Another report in a ladies' society magazine noted both of these women beautifully dressed for the dance held later that evening:

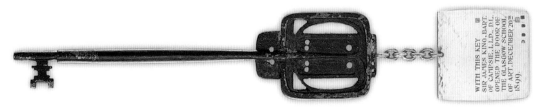

FIG. 2.14 Charles Rennie Mackintosh (designer), George Adam & Sons (ironwork), possibly James Reid & Co. (silver), ceremonial key, 1899. Presented to Sir James King.

'Mrs. Newbery was artistically gowned in green satin, the green bodice and sleeves being slashed with white ... Miss Macdonald's auburn hair was well set off with her fawn frock.[44] Mackintosh was certainly there too; it was just not remarked on.

INTERIM PHASE: 1899–1906

When the building opened at the end of 1899, hopes were high that remaining funds would be secured quickly:

The portion of the new building to be opened, though equal to the present needs of the School, makes little provision for growth and development, and the Governors feel that they should not relax their efforts until the whole building is completed.[45]

But it would take nearly seven years for building to recommence (fig. 2.15). In the interim, Mackintosh married Margaret Macdonald in November 1900 and became a partner in the firm in 1901. He also finally received recognition as the architect of the new school that year, in a review of the Glasgow International Exhibition by Lewis F. Day. In critiquing an exhibition stand Mackintosh designed for the school, Day commented: 'A similar severity is to be observed in

FIG. 2.15 Alexander McGibbon, sketch of the Glasgow School of Art (phase I completion) from the north-west, 1907. The temporary technical studios also appear here.

Mr Mackintosh's permanent building for the Glasgow School of Art – planned apparently on lines nakedly utilitarian, yet everywhere revealing the marked individuality of the artist.[46]

These years were Mackintosh's most prolific in terms of architecture, when he completed some of his most famous commissions, including Kate Cranston's tea rooms, The Hill House in Helensburgh and Scotland Street School. He undertook numerous smaller domestic commissions, including his own homes in 1900 and 1906, alongside entering competitions for notable buildings such as Liverpool Cathedral (lost to Giles Gilbert Scott). Exhibitions also occupied much of his time in these years, for example a display featuring his collaborative work with Margaret Macdonald at the Eighth Vienna Secession Exhibition (1900), featuring their monumental gessoes before they were installed in Miss Cranston's Ingram Street Tea Rooms. He also co-curated the Scottish section with Newbery at the International Exhibition of Modern Decorative Art in Turin (1901–2).[47] This exhibition is notable for bringing further international attention to the Glasgow School of Art, since the exhibition basically comprised the work of current and former students and staff. Mackintosh also continued to work on the art school. He designed the metal surround for the James Fleming memorial relief panel in 1903, and in 1904 he was asked to design a suite of furniture for the headmaster's office. All the while he must have been thinking about his revised vision for completing the building.

In 1901, when the school came under the responsibility of the Scotch Education Department, Newbery established four distinct departments: Drawing and Painting, Modelling and Sculpture, Design and Decorative Art, and Architecture.[48] Despite providing such excellent studios, or perhaps even because of this success, conditions at the school were again cramped in just a couple of years, as the fundraising pamphlet for the school reports:

> *Not only has the scope of study been enlarged, but the conditions attached to the production of work have entirely altered, and the School ... has become a Central Institution fulfilling National requirements ... The Life Classes are overcrowded and about double the present space is required ... Since the organisation of the Glasgow School of Architecture, the Classes in this subject have grown in number and importance, and more and better accommodation is urgently needed ... The accommodation for the Sculpture and Modelling Department is meagre and in many respects unsuitable, while the Technical Studios are housed in a temporary shed ... There is no Lecture Theatre in the School and the Library is situated in a part of the School Museum, the remaining portion of which is used as a class room.[49]*

The appeal also clarifies the finances needed for completion, and reveals how significantly the first phase went over its £14,000 budget:

Cost of the present Building:

For Site	*£6000*
Tradesmen's Accounts	*£21219*
Fees, etc.	*£1626*
Sundry Charges	*£286*
TOTAL	*£29131*

Subscriptions	*£28397*
Bank Interest	*£734*

[Breaks even]

Estimated cost of completion Western Extension, including furniture, fittings, etc. say	*£22000*
New Service Stair in East Portion of School	*£680*
Cloak Rooms and Lavatories	*£500*
Architects' and Measurer's Fees and Sundry Charges	*£1820*
Total	*£25000*

The appeal does not at this point state that a whole new top floor and sub-basement were part of Mackintosh's vision for phase II, but it must have been under discussion to determine the required sum. The east stair was necessary due to increased concern about fire safety in the building, given its current capacity. A western stair would also be an integral part of the new extension.

In September 1906 a new building committee was formed, with Fleming, Burnet, Salmon and Dunn returning and the addition of several others including the highly respected shipping merchant and arts patron and collector William Burrell.[50] Honeyman, Keppie & Mackintosh were appointed on 1 February 1907; however, the new contract had some very specific conditions that hint at fiscal difficulties in phase I:

> It was agreed to appoint Messrs Honeyman, Keppie and Mackintosh as Architects ... on the understanding, that they are not at liberty to instruct any extra work or any alterations on the plans of specifications as endorsed by the Committee, involving any additions to or modification of the work, without the written authority of the Building Committee.[51]

It appears that Mackintosh was developing a reputation for extravagance, having incurred overspend and undertaken alterations without approval at Scotland Street School.[52] As such, while Mackintosh was the architect in charge of the design, Keppie was left in charge of the financial side of things.[53] Plans were revised in discussion with Newbery and the building committee approved them in May, the governors approved in June and, finally, the Glasgow Dean of Guild Court gave approval for the second phase to commence in November 1907.

PHASE II: 1906–9

Over the course of the project, hundreds of revised drawings would have been made; we know of approximately seventy-five existing.[54] Because we are missing revisions or as-built drawings for the 'half building' from the first phase, it is difficult to know exactly how individual spaces were used in its first ten years. However, looking at the drawings for the completion of the school gives us some insight into changes of curriculum and even approaches to pedagogy and artistic practice that took place in the interim.

FIG. 2.16 Design Room, photograph by Harry Bedford Lemere, *c.* 1909.

FIG. 2.17 Junior Architecture Room, partitions open, photograph by Harry Bedford Lemere, *c.* 1909.

The basement levels still contained the messier studios, including a new sculpture suite in the sub-basement (*see* cat. 16), with its own (pretty steep) access from Scott Street, and a bespoke ceiling-mounted hoist for moving large blocks about the stone-carving studio. The basement (*see* cat. 17) contained the various noisy technical studios on the east: glass-staining, wood-carving and metalworking as in the original plans, but needlework – now called embroidery – was raised up to beautiful airy studios on the north-east top of the building (fig. 2.16). Weaving was added, along with silversmithing and ceramics. The anatomy room was also in the eastern basement across from the technical studios and, just inside the entrance, across from the janitor's house, was the living animal room, into which live animals were brought as models. In a letter to a colleague, Newbery once wrote:

As regards the relating between Art and the Animal World, yes! We make excursions into Zoology and borrow very largely from the neighbouring Zoo as well as from other quarters. We have not yet essayed the Lion, but the Camel has humped its way into the School, as have also Yaks, Reeky Mountain Sheep and other strange creations. We find the study very useful and enjoyable.[55]

In addition to periodic animal traffic, the western basement was reserved for muddy clay activities, with four studios designated for antique modelling, ornament modelling and two life-modelling rooms, one for day and one for evening students (presumably because full-figure clay models could not be easily set aside between day and evening class changes). The basement also housed the lecture theatre, with its notoriously uncomfortable benches that humorous GSA lore quips Mackintosh designed to ensure no student would ever fall asleep in class!

On the western ground floor (*see* cat. 18), an additional ornament studio was added, with the rest of the other studios designated to the new Glasgow School of Architecture established by Newbery in 1904.[56] The senior architecture studio occupied the south-west corner and adjoined the junior architecture studio to the north. The junior studio was a clever space, taking up most of the north-west ground floor, with full-length partitions that could be removed as needed to divide the space (fig. 2.17). But in living memory these screens merely formed the walls of each of the painting studios. According to architectural historian Ranald MacInnes, 'there is anecdotal evidence that the movable partition elements were so heavy that the janitors were reluctant to move them – each one had to be lifted out and fitted into place.'[57] At the time of the 2014 fire and restoration project many were surprised to find this system was flexible, when the spaces were heavily smoke-damaged but largely survived intact.

On the first floor (*see* cat. 19), life rooms were more numerous, increasing from just two (male and female) to five studios, no longer designated by gender and each with changing rooms for the models. Four adjoined the whole of the west wing and one was placed in the south-east corner in the small space previously assigned to staff studios. These sat above the former board room, now a design room like the north-east corner studio. The small narrow cupboard space at the east end of the corridor was simply labelled 'Professor' and was presumably an office (as it was in later years) rather than a studio. The museum had been used as

FIG. 2.18 Library, photograph by Harry Bedford Lemere, *c.* 1909.

both library and studio space during the first-phase occupation of the building but was freed from this function with the completion of the west wing, and notably the famous library (fig. 2.18).

The second floor (*see* cat. 20) at the top of the building was an entirely new composition. The north-eastern wing was made up of studios, notably the large, airy embroidery room (*see* fig. 2.16). At the west, four new professors' studios adjoined each other via a sub-corridor. The west end comprised composition rooms in a similar configuration to the architecture studios on the ground floor. The south-western room, known more recently as Studio 58 (fig. 2.19), was notable for its substantial posts and roof structure and its cantilevered conservatory (fig. 2.20).

Mackintosh was faced with a challenge on the top floor: how to connect the east and west wings when he had built the soaring A-frame museum roof on the southern central block below. Only a narrow passage between these would work, and his solution became one of the most breathtaking moments in the building: a brick loggia of three bays (fig. 2.21) connecting to a pavilion (labelled 'Glass Pavilion' in an earlier 1908 drawing). This elegant name would not stick though. No one is quite sure when it came to be called the Hen Run, but the story handed down from generations of students relates to the Scots use of the word 'hen' for 'dear' or 'woman', still a term of endearment in Glasgow today. Legend has it that the name arose because it was the main thoroughfare between the embroidery studios at one end and Studio 58, where design courses were held, both largely populated by women students. This provided not only extra circulation space but also extended studio capacity and allowed for the gathering places Mackintosh so desired, as the students' common room did not make the final plan. Such spaces are found throughout the building and are looked at more closely in the next chapter.

The final important feature of the top floor is a technical one: fire regulations had changed between phases I and II, so not only did the whole of the west wing need to be built under these conditions but for fire protection the flooring needed to be concrete slab (*see* cat. 21). This of course meant interventions into

FIG. 2.19 Studio 58, photograph by Harry Bedford Lemere, *c.* 1909.

FIG. 2.20 Cantilevered conservatory after the 2014 fire. The burnt-out windows of the loggia can be seen to the right.

the existing fabric on the east too and 'Plan Shewing Alteration of Second Floor from Wood Construction to that of Steel and Concrete' from April 1908 shows how this was accomplished. What is truly critical about this concrete-and-steel slab though is that it worked: after the 2018 fire it was instrumental in holding the building together, keeping it from collapsing and tumbling down Garnethill into Sauchiehall Street.

In terms of finishes there was still colour in the building, but the 1909 palette was more subdued it seems. Joseph Sharples notes: 'Dissatisfaction with the original colouring is suggested by a request from the

Building Committee during construction of the W. wing in 1909, that "all the stained wood in the new building should be kept light in tone".[58] There was the 'artistic green' reported in 1899 (fig. 2.22), but recent paint sampling in the restoration project revealed blue and red paint in the museum and some of the studio spaces as well: 'distemper was used extensively across all of the different surfaces and substrates either as colour paint or colour stains on timber.'[59] This was applied as a 'thin wash' that allowed the grain of wood to remain visible through the stain. Wood grain was still visible in the library and board room as the only places in the school that were never painted over. It also underscored the variety of texture in the finishes throughout the building when it was new, from the rich red exposed brick of the loggia to the suede-like plasterwork that Mackintosh instructed be 'finished off the float', leaving a soft hand-finished texture. The magic of Mackintosh's original building was coming to life again, as images taken days before the fire illustrate (*see* figs 4.34–4.38).

Overall, Mackintosh's plan – which was a value-added articulation of Newbery's vision – was a resounding success. It achieved the remit of 'a building with class rooms conveniently arranged and well lighted'. It was designed to be adaptable, with its movable partitions and basic provisions for artistic practice in every studio. It was easy to allow for shifting use and needs, which would become more pronounced over time. Artistic practice and pedagogy no longer fitted into discrete categories, and as disciplines bled into each other, so the art studio needed to be flexible, necessarily co-mingling with the technical studio.

But the flexibility of the Mack was not a product of Mackintosh being a 'modern' architect. It was based on practicalities and contemporary innovations, for he was an architect very much of his day. The mythology around the Mack as a proto-modernist building has been difficult to dismantle. Successful arguments against the notion that it was a building 'before its time' exist largely in more academic studies, such as George Cairns's 1992 PhD thesis, which was among the first to compare the Mack with contemporary building systems, particularly ventilation and heating systems, to illustrate how it was a project precisely of its time.[60]

FIG. 2.21 'Pavilion Corridor': interior of the loggia, photograph by Thomas Annan, *c.* 1910.

But Keppie himself informed us of the ubiquity of these systems, as Sharples notes:

> The original heating system was by hot air, forced through ducts by a fan in the basement. Large claims have been made for the supposedly innovative character of this system, but John Honeyman & Keppie themselves in their 'Description and Schedule of Contents' described it as 'almost too well known to require advocacy' and commented that it had already been 'applied with success to many well known buildings in Glasgow'.[61]

As for the Mack, Mackintosh included many technologies that, while not precisely 'new' for *c.* 1900, were the hallmarks of a contemporary building, from the lift shaft to electric lighting. Also Mackintosh did not design every single detail, a common misconception among fans. He ordered window handles from catalogues, and employed the latest available lighting and lifts he could acquire, even indicating on one rather beautiful section drawing from 1907 that the rooflights for the new basement studios were to be 'Hayward's Paving Lights', while the atrium over the museum was to be 'Pennycook's Patent Glazing' (*see* cat. 22).

The names of the highly skilled craftspeople who made the Mack – and most other buildings for that matter – are largely forgotten. Yet it is their work, in collaboration with the architect, that we have so admired. Recent digital research projects have enabled the study of these important firms. *Mackintosh Architecture* has made the Honeyman, Keppie & Mackintosh job books accessible to all, providing biographies of many of the contractors used and enabling further study into how these trades worked across the city, literally building Glasgow. Identifying makers who worked across several projects helps us to think more tangibly about previously elusive connections across Mackintosh projects, whether the roofing of a school or church or the glasswork in a tea room or private home. For example, several of the tradespeople who worked on the Mack were also involved in other Mackintosh-designed projects. John Anderson seems to have been a preferred slater, also working on the Glasgow Herald building (*c.* 1892), Martyrs' Public School (1895–7), Queen's Cross Church (1896–9) and the Daily Record building (1900–4), along with the private home Windyhill in Kilmacolm (1900–1). The plumbers Moses Spiers & Son were also used at both the Daily Record building and the Willow Tea Rooms. Perhaps the most notable of these contractors was McCulloch & Co. Hugh McCulloch studied stained glass with Daniel Cottier, then opened a glass- and tile-decorating business with fellow designer Charles Gow in the 1880s.[62] Together they had a very successful studio, including commissions for decorating the Banqueting Hall in Glasgow City Chambers, under the supervision of Leiper. Mackintosh himself worked closely with McCulloch, as evidenced in the wide range of commissions revealed in *Mackintosh Architecture*. Like Anderson, McCulloch & Co. worked on both the Glasgow Herald and the Daily Record buildings, and on some of Mackintosh's most important projects: glass at

FIG. 2.22 Wood panels recovered from first-floor north-west studios (originally architecture studios), stripped to reveal the original 'artistic green' stain.

Miss Cranston's Lunch and Tea Rooms, Ingram Street (*c.* 1900); paint and furnishings at the Willow Tea Rooms (*c.* 1903); and glass for the Dutch Kitchen addition at Miss Cranston's Argyle Street Tea Rooms (1905–6); along with work at The Hill House in Helensburgh for Walter Blackie (1902–4).

On completion of the school, the celebrations for its final opening on 20 December 1909 included the presentation to James Fleming of a silver casket, designed by Mackintosh and made by the silversmith Peter Wylie Davidson.[63] It contained an illuminated scroll created by another woman lost to time, Hilda M. Brodie, which was a gift to Fleming from the 'contractors, master craftsmen, wrights and artificers'. It states:

> [*We*] *offer to you this casket as a tribute of our veneration and esteem and in testimony of the pleasure we feel in having been associated in the provision of such a worthy institution for the use of the art students of Glasgow, and for the benefit of the citizens for all time.*

Their building was beloved by the city, transformed through time and attention, use and abuse, but the elegant artistry of these craftspeople is sadly but a memory now.

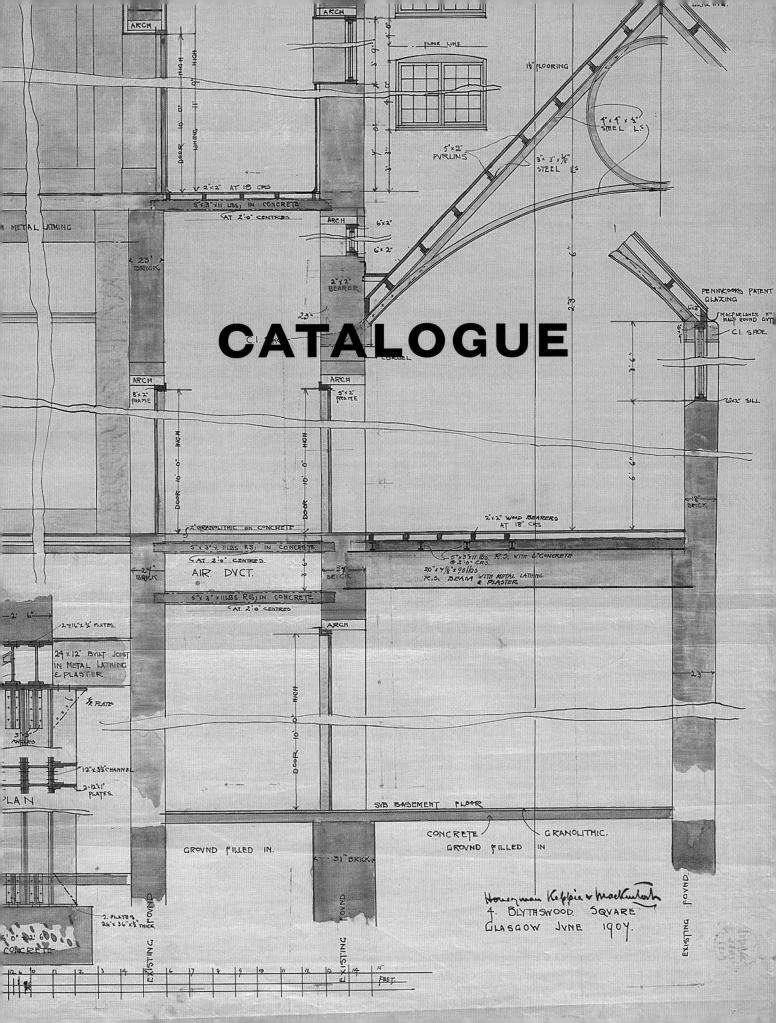

CATALOGUE

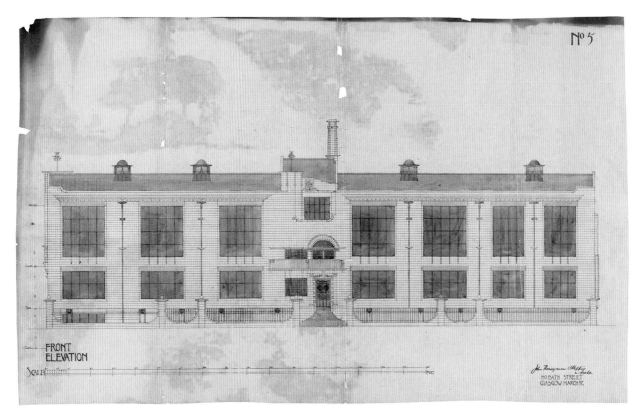

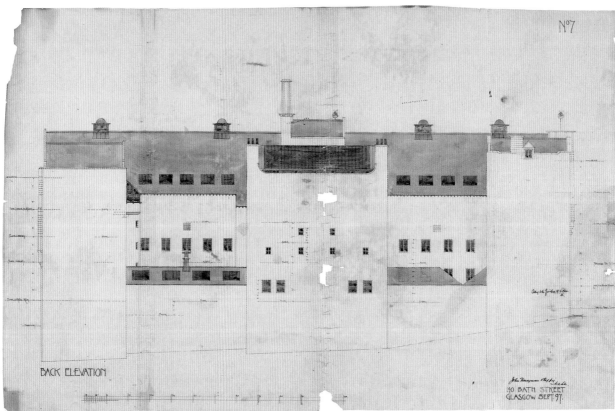

CAT. 1 North elevation, March 1897. Photo-mechanical reproduction and wash, 52.2 × 86 cm.

CAT. 2 South elevation, September 1897. Photo-mechanical reproduction and wash with ink inscriptions, 56.7 × 88.9 cm.

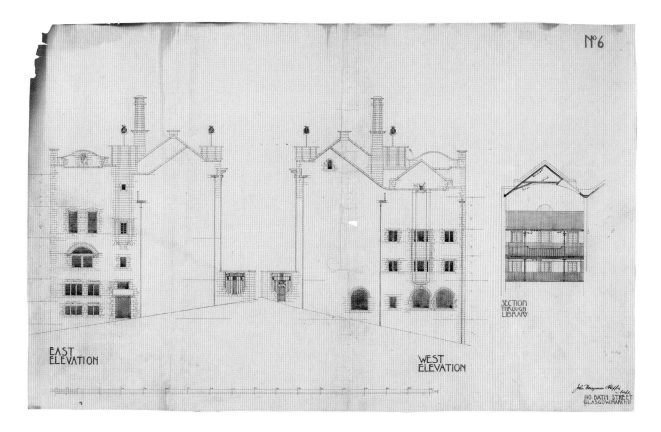

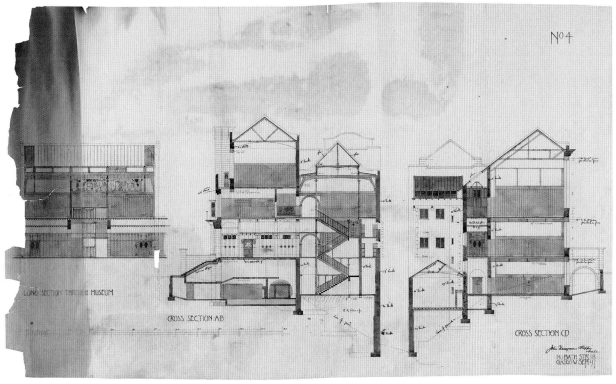

CAT. 3 East and west elevations, March 1897. Photo-mechanical reproduction, pencil and wash with ink inscriptions, 56.7 × 93.3 cm.

CAT. 4 Sections, September 1897. Photo-mechanical reproduction and wash with ink inscriptions, 53.8 × 90.8 cm.

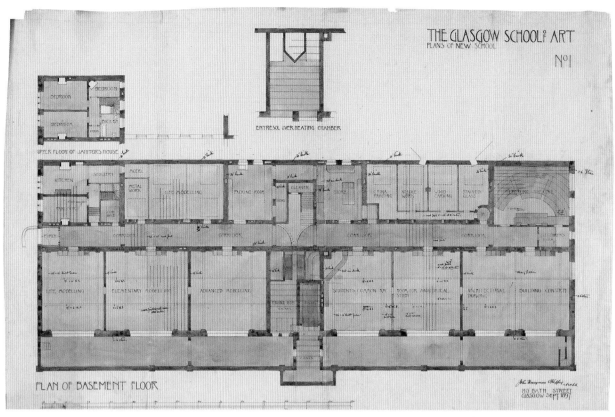

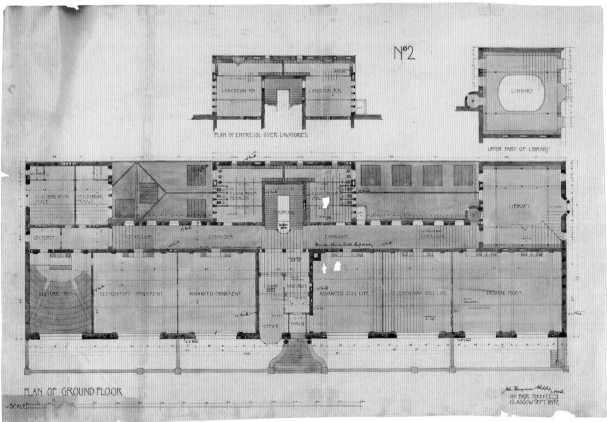

CAT. 5 Basement plan; plan of upper floor of janitor's house; plan of entresol over heating chamber, September 1897. Photo-mechanical reproduction and wash with ink inscriptions, 57.8 × 87.3 cm.

CAT. 6 Ground-floor plan; plan of entresol over lavatories; plan of upper part of library, September 1897. Photo-mechanical reproduction and wash with ink inscriptions, 56.7 × 86 cm.

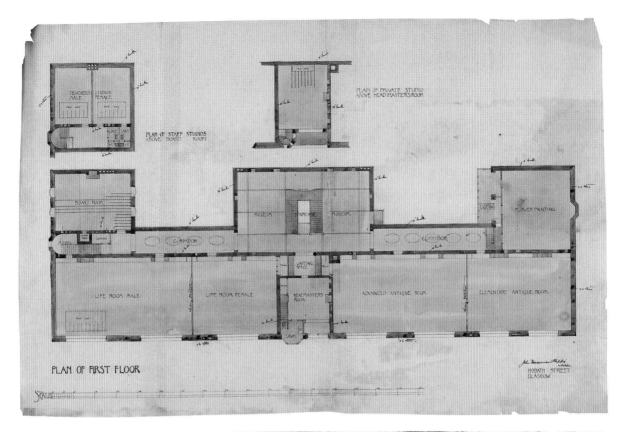

PLAN OF FIRST FLOOR

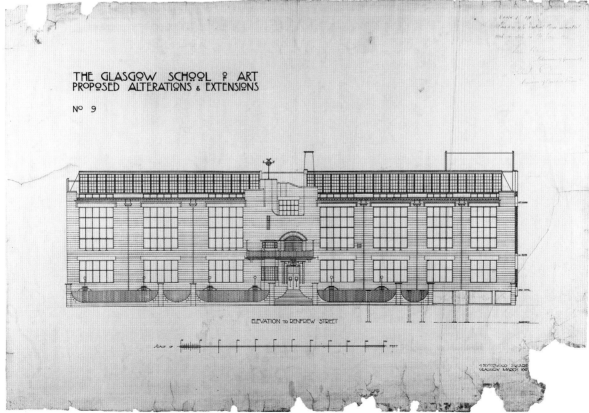

THE GLASGOW SCHOOL ⌖ ART
PROPOSED ALTERATIONS & EXTENSIONS

Nº 9

ELEVATION TO RENFREW STREET

CAT. 7 First-floor plan; plan of staff studios above board room; plan of headmaster's studio, 1897. Photo-mechanical reproduction and wash with ink inscriptions, 56.2 × 86.4 cm.

CAT. 8 North elevation, March 190[7]. Ink on paper, 68.6 × 100 cm.

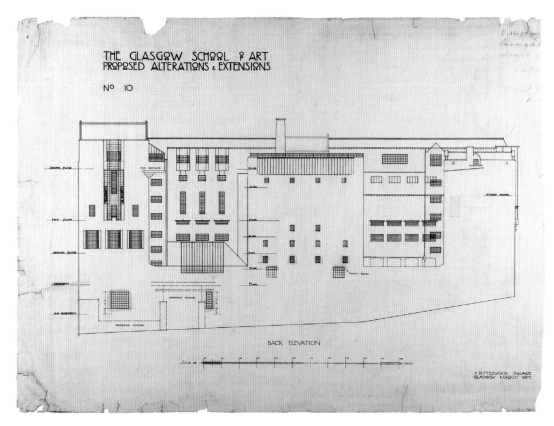

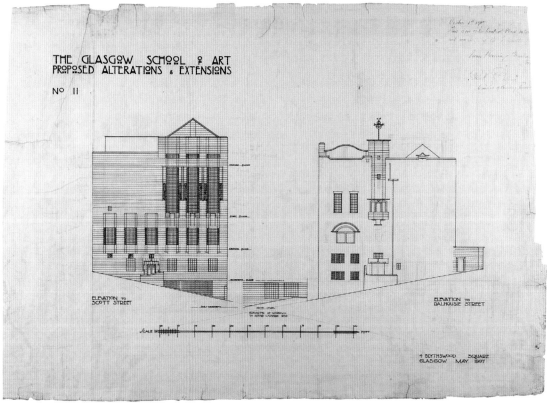

CAT. 9 South elevation, March 1907. Ink and wash on paper, 68 × 93.2 cm.

CAT. 10 The Glasgow School of Art, east and west elevations, May 1907. Ink and pencil on paper, 68.5 × 95 cm.

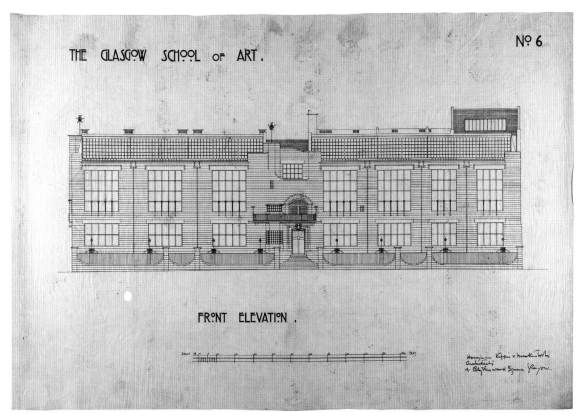

THE GLASGOW SCHOOL of ART.

FRONT ELEVATION .

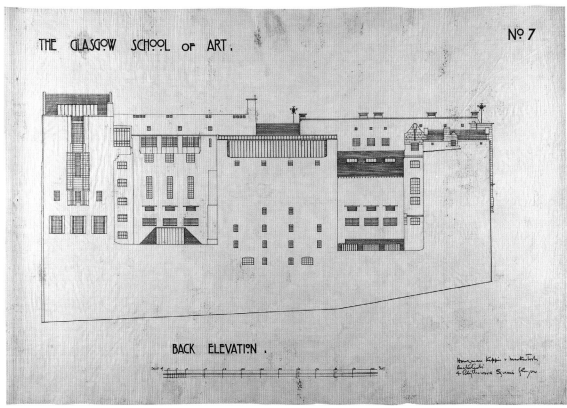

THE GLASGOW SCHOOL of ART.

BACK ELEVATION .

CAT. 11 North elevation, [1910]. Pencil and ink on linen paper, 66 × 95.9 cm.

CAT. 12 South elevation, [1910]. Pencil and ink on linen paper, 66 × 95.8 cm.

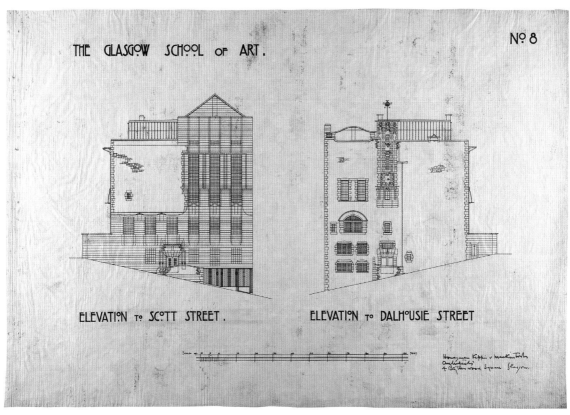

THE GLASGOW SCHOOL OF ART.

ELEVATION TO SCOTT STREET.

ELEVATION TO DALHOUSIE STREET

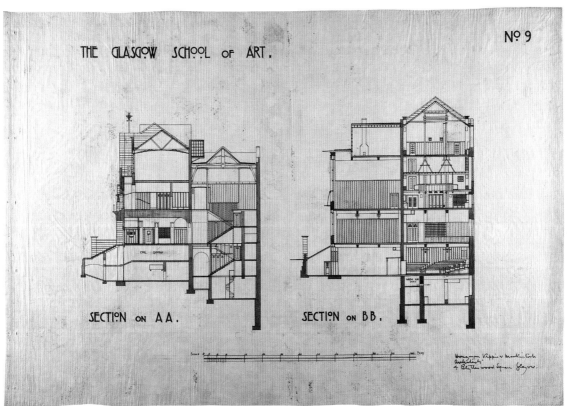

THE GLASGOW SCHOOL OF ART.

SECTION ON AA.

SECTION ON BB.

CAT. 13 East and west elevations, [1910]. Pencil and ink on linen paper, 66 × 95.7 cm.

CAT. 14 Sections AA and BB, [1910]. Pencil, ink and wash, 66.1 × 95.8 cm.

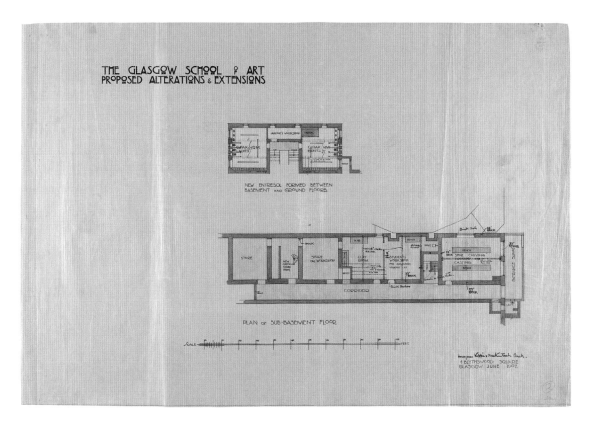

THE GLASGOW SCHOOL ⌀ ART
PROPOSED ALTERATIONS & EXTENSIONS

NEW ENTRESOL FORMED BETWEEN
BASEMENT AND GROUND FLOORS

PLAN OF SUB-BASEMENT FLOOR

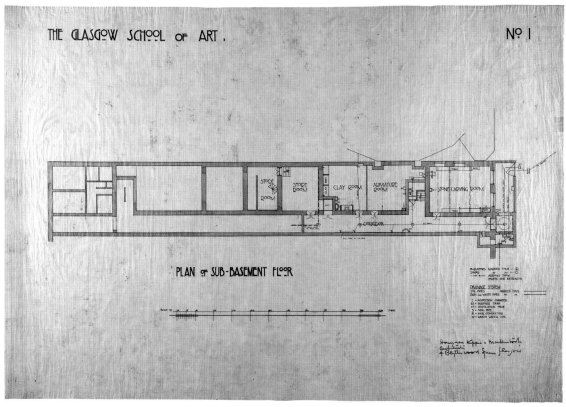

THE GLASGOW SCHOOL OF ART.   N⁰ I

PLAN OF SUB-BASEMENT FLOOR

CAT. 15 Sections CC and DD, [1910]. Pencil, ink and wash, 66 × 96.3 cm.

CAT. 16 Sub-basement plan, [1910]. Ink and wash on linen paper, 66 × 96.1 cm.

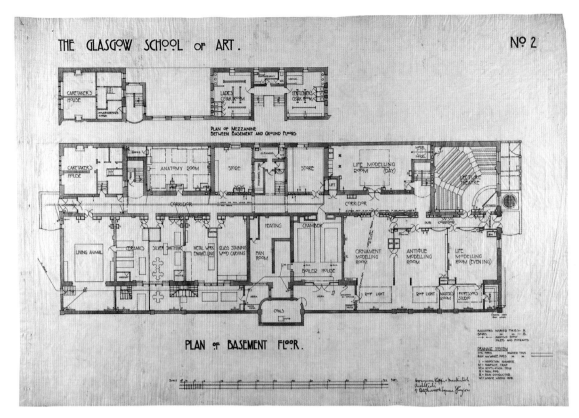

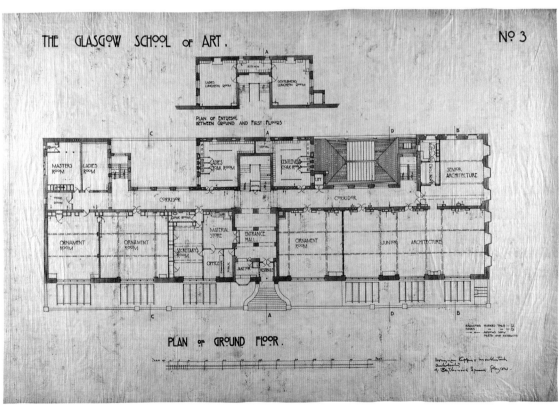

CAT. 17 Basement plan; plan of mezzanine between basement and ground floor, [1910]. Ink and wash on linen paper, 65.9 × 95.8 cm.

CAT. 18 Ground-floor plan; plan of entresol between ground and first floors, [1910]. Ink and wash, 66 × 96.4 cm.

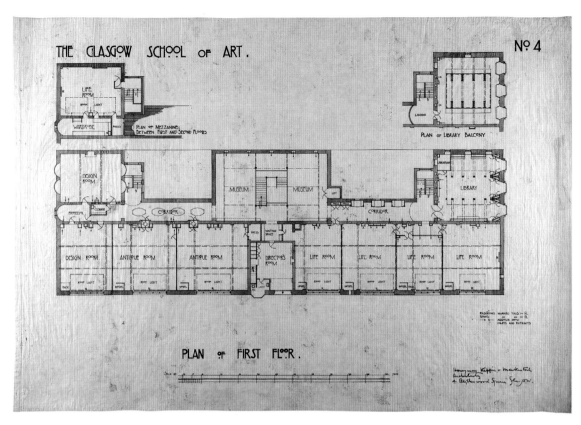

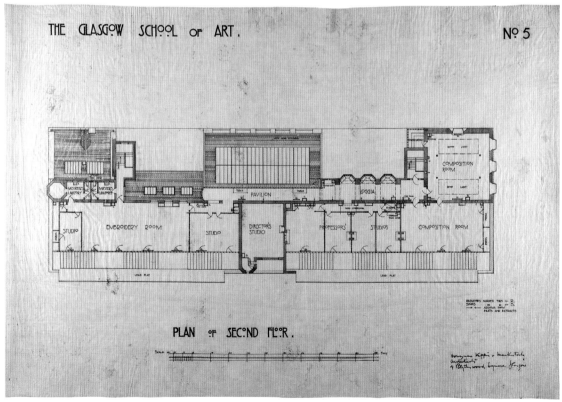

CAT. 19 First-floor plan; plan of mezzanine between first and second floors; plan of library balcony, [1910]. Ink and wash on linen paper, 65.9 × 95.7 cm.

CAT. 20 Second-floor plan, [1910]. Ink and wash on linen paper, 65.6 × 95.7 cm.

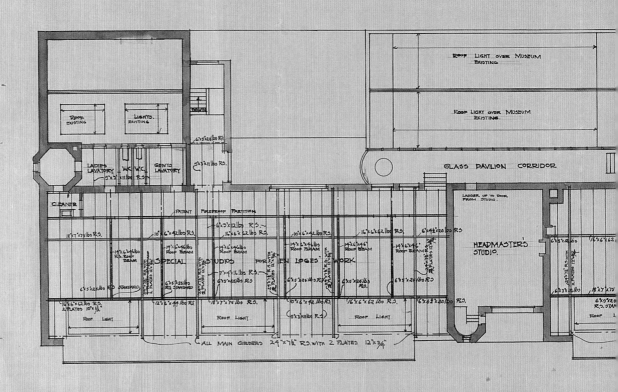

THE GLASGOW SCHOOL ᵒꜰ ART
PLAN SHEWING ALTERATION ᴏꜰ SECOND FLOOR
FROM WOOD CONSTRUCTION ᴛᴏ ᴛʜᴀᴛ ᴏꜰ STEEL ᴀɴᴅ CONCRETE.   Nᵒ 5

ROOF LIGHT OVER MUSEUM
EXISTING

ROOF LIGHT OVER MUSEUM
EXISTING.

GLASS PAVILION CORRIDOR

ROOF
EXISTING

LIGHTS.
EXISTING.

LADIES
LAVATORY   WC WC   GENTS
LAVATORY

CLEANER

PATENT FIREPROOF PARTITION

HEADMASTERS
STUDIO.

LADDER UP TO DOOR
FROM STUDIO.

SPECIAL   STUDIOS   FOR MEN LOGES   WORK

ROOF LIGHT   ROOF LIGHT   ROOF LIGHT   ROOF L

ALL MAIN GIRDERS 24"×7½" R.S. WITH 2 PLATES 12"×¾"

PLAN ᴏꜰ SECOND FLOOR

SCALE OF

CAT. 21 Second-floor plan showing alteration from wood to steel and
concrete, April 1908. Pencil, ink and wash, 64.2 × 100.9 cm.

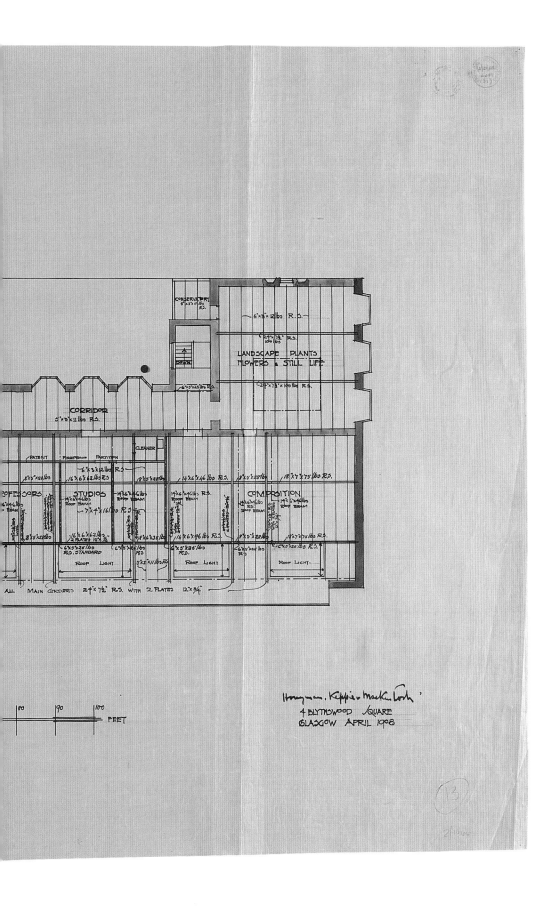

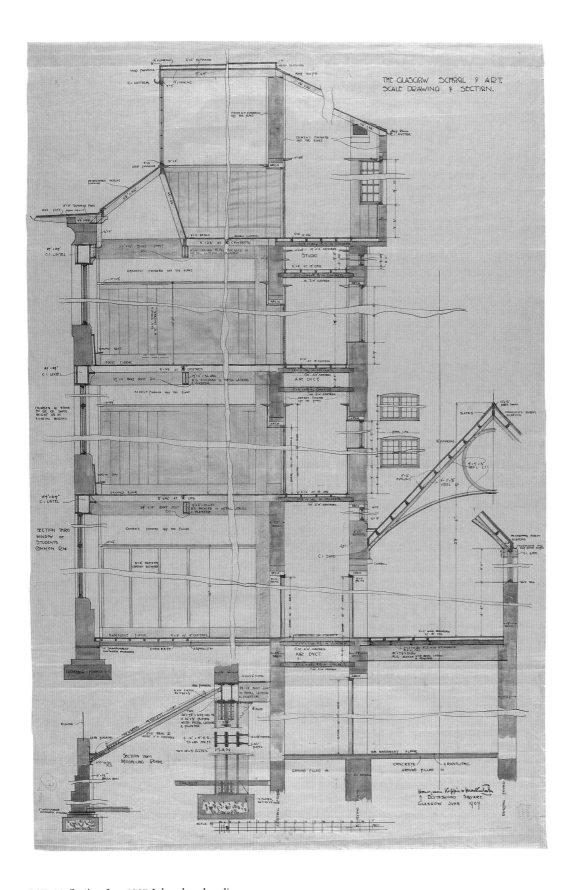

CAT. 22 Section, June 1907. Ink and wash on linen paper,
103.6 × 68.5 cm.

A PLAIN BUILDING

PREVIOUS PAGE (FIG. 3.1) The west entrance, early 20th century.

FIG. 3.2 The Mack from the north-west, early 20th century.

90 **THE MACK**

CHAPTER 3

A PLAIN BUILDING

We do not mean to imply that the School of Art is a cheap building, but it is a plain building, and the interior is refreshingly free from the modern architect's ruination, machine-run mouldings. Above all things, it is an interesting building, and this is the next best to being beautiful.

THE VISTA, 1909

It is not known whether the anonymous student who wrote this critique of the Mack on its completion in 1909 was aware of the governors' decree for a 'plain building', yet clearly the perception of austerity was one of its merits. This commentary in *The Vista*, the magazine of the Glasgow School of Architecture Club, highlights the building's virtues, even while struggling to find its beauty. The author observes:

When the School of Art was finished, we wondered if Mr Mackintosh felt forlorn or relieved at having this child of his imagination off his hands. Of course, that would depend on whether it was a child of joy or sorrow to him, a prodigy or a freak. In our opinion – but silence is the better part of discretion. There are, however, things which can be said about the child. The finest is, that it expresses what it professes to be. There are about it elements of mystery quite typical of the teaching of art, and it boggles the common man in the way all new art does, at the same time satisfying him, that though artists still study old masters, they are doing up to date work ... If Mr Mackintosh aimed at doing something bizarre, we would congratulate him on his success while condemning it on principle.

But we think better of him, and it may be that Mackintoshian ideals are not to be expressed in the ordinary language of architecture.[1]

Although damning with faint praise, the passage is also insightful. The writer is of the impression that the Mack is a reinterpretation of 'old masters', or historic architecture, but also offers something new and 'bizarre'. These critiques are not unlike those that labelled the artistic circle around The Four the 'Spook School' for their Beardsley-inspired figures. Rather than dismissing the Mack's unique qualities, there is recognition that this plain yet eccentric building is entirely appropriate for an art school. It is indeed these 'elements of mystery' that have made the Mack so compelling to countless visitors for over a century. In transcending the 'ordinary language of architecture', Mackintosh makes his plain building extraordinary.

OUTSIDE

From the outside the Mack is beguiling. To some anti-modernist critics, such as the architectural theorist Léon Krier, its lack of regularity is 'incoherent': 'I mean, if you stood in front of one elevation of his art school and were blindfolded and shown another elevation, you would never know it was the same building unless you knew the place.'[2] Referring to Mackintosh as a 'scatterbrain', his dismissal suggests a lack of looking closely: it might seem incohesive on a basic level, with each elevation wholly different from the next, but it is cleverly tied together through both its fabric and, more subtly, its decorative programme. It has been compared to a warehouse, but in material and even height it had sympathy with the tenements that surrounded it. Former Mack restoration project manager Sarah MacKinnon has spent more time looking closely at the building than most, having walked through and around it almost daily for nearly four years; she feels the variances in the design are down to Mackintosh being 'a bit of a magpie':

> He was absorbing vast quantities of detail from vernacular architecture, art, craft, etc. As a young architect in the first phase, he manipulated these designs to produce a unique composition of recognisable details. By the time he gets to the second phase, his confidence has grown and he can extract the essence of a detail or idea from somewhere else and apply that in an extraordinary way. So the two halves have a close relationship but the second phase is more abstract perhaps.[3]

The bulk of the structure is red brick faced with sandstone, with the south external elevation roughcast in a cement render that recalls Scottish 'harling'. Harling is a particularly hardy material that performs well in the Scottish climate. It has been used for centuries and is traditionally made of a slurry of coarse aggregate mortar (such as pebbles) and lime; later versions added cement. The stonework is traditionally cut and assembled but artistically crafted around windows and entrances with Mackintosh's molten flourishes. The construction is of 'snecked ashlar' (fig. 3.3). Ashlar refers to the square-cut regularity of the sandstone. Snecking is a Scottish building method using three different stone shapes: the largest stone is a 'riser'; the 'leveller' is about two-thirds the height of the riser with a length three times the height; and the 'sneck' is a similar length, with its height making up the difference between the leveller and the riser. By building these up in a strategic pattern, a strongly bonded surface is formed. It is also rather beautiful, especially with the blond sandstone, which came from two local stone bands according to analysis during the restoration project. The majority seems to come from the band known as 'Whitespot', a limestone coal formation characterised by flecks of black. It is of slightly lower

FIG. 3.3 The east elevation, post 2018 fire.

quality than the Giffnock stone used elsewhere in the building, an upper limestone formation that, due to its superiority, was often used to craft the elite villas of Glasgow's wealthier suburbs such as Pollokshields. An analysis of where each stone type lies in the building has not been completed. However, it may have been that the superior Giffnock stone was reserved for areas of interest such as the carved embellishments around doors, windows and parapets.[4]

It was not unusual to employ these building methods in Scotland, as Ranald MacInnes points out: 'The language of the stone mason's craft – snecked, random, bull-faced, or coursed rubble, stugged, broached or droved ashlar – was entirely embedded and codified within the architectural culture in which Mackintosh worked.'[5] These traditional methods, which Mackintosh would have studied throughout his training, were combined with more modern techniques, particularly in the structural steel and cement skeleton that lent internal support to the brickwork and, ultimately, spared the structure to a great extent during the two fires. Add to this the great expanses of glazing and ironwork, both functional and decorative, and we have a building that somehow in its very making bridges the past with the future. Each elevation is a new expression of 'Mackintoshian ideals' as they evolved from his early, more curvilinear style on the east to a more rectilinear approach on the west. Some might even view this as a move from Art Nouveau to Art Deco, though neither genre fits entirely comfortably here. The north is a unified, rhythmic face that only reveals its east–west differences in small details, while the south is an asynchronous sequence of volumes that express the shifting interior plan. Unusually, it is this 'back' façade that most people see first, walking up the hill from Sauchiehall Street.

SOUTH

Much like its front, the rear elevation of the Mack is difficult to view in its entirety (figs 3.4, 3.5). A single view is obscured by the sloping urban landscape of Garnethill. If one were to manage to glimpse over the rooftops from the adjacent Blythswood Hill to the south, one would get the impression of tall towers picturesquely arranged together. It has been compared to Fyvie Castle in Aberdeenshire (fig. 3.6), although in its current state it is reminiscent of a ruined castle like Linlithgow Palace (fig. 3.7). Mackintosh mentioned both in his 1891 lecture 'Scotch Baronial Architecture', calling Fyvie 'one of the finest and most characteristic castles in the Scottish style'.[6] Features that add interest are the glass screen of the pavilion or Hen Run, the window bays of the loggia and the cantilevered conservatory off Studio 58. The south elevation best shows how the exterior shell of the Mack is very much an expression of its interior plan, recalling Mackintosh's usurping of Leiper's adage that a building must not be an 'envelope without contents'.[7] While this approach is perhaps more obvious in his domestic works like The Hill House (1902–3), the irregularity of the south

FIG. 3.4 The south elevation, early 20th century.

FIG. 3.5 The south elevation, before 1965.

FIG. 3.6 Fyvie Castle, Aberdeenshire, *c.* 13th–19th centuries.

FIG. 3.7 Linlithgow Palace, *c.* 15th–16th centuries.

elevation exemplifies the way in which Mackintosh designed from the inside out. Viewing the south-western roofline ensemble from inside the building facing west, it was not dissimilar to that of The Hill House, especially the use of cement-based roughcast render on both projects (*see* fig. 5.3). The Hill House render has been notoriously problematic though, as the cement content in his formula was too high. It is presently covered with a large steel 'box' shelter to assist it with drying out from nearly a century of water ingress. The roughcast was better on the Mack but it still required periodic repair, which is to be expected with this material. This was done piecemeal as needed rather than in a costly full refurbishment, which over time resulted in a patchwork appearance. It was repaired with the help of experts from the Scottish Lime Centre, as former Senior Project Manager Elizabeth Davidson notes:

> I brought in the Scottish Lime Centre to advise on the spec of the repair mix as there had historically been issues with the harl cracking and bossing over time. The repair mix used the original aggregate (sand from [Isle of] Arran) but with the addition of a lime-based compound that allowed just a little more flexibility while setting as hard as the cement would have. So it was a sand/lime/cement mix for the repair with a unification coat added last to match up visually the colour between old and new – basically a watered down mix of the above.[8]

Against a typically grey sky the building might even have looked a bit careworn in recent years, but a few fine details, such as the soaring western oriole window with its pronounced stone casement, give the façade an almost medieval beauty. In the building's state of ruin, and with the render repaired, this impression is even more vivid (*see* fig. 5.1).

EAST

The only façade that is purely of the first 1896–9 building phase, the east elevation (figs 3.8, 3.9), is most often discussed in comparison to the later west elevation, which is often perceived as 'modern' (*see* fig. 3.11). However, taken on its own merits, the east elevation should not be dismissed as somehow immature. Mackintosh's historic interests are perhaps most strongly evident in this façade, seen when approaching the Mack via Dalhousie Street. It is a homage to the Scottish tower house style, and directly references several of the qualities mentioned in his 'Scotch Baronial Architecture' lecture of five years earlier. He makes this style's contemporary relevance plain:

> It is a matter of regret that we dont [sic] find any class of buildings but domestic in this style, whether the style can be developed beyond this or not is a point which our forefathers left for us to decide ... From some recent buildings which have been erected it is clearly evident that this style is

coming to life again and I only hope that it will not be strangled in its infancy by indiscriminating and unsympathetic people who copy the ancient examples without trying to make the style conform to modern requirements.[9]

The architectural historian Frank Arneil Walker found this passage particularly telling, for in suggesting the style be made to conform, Walker proposes that Mackintosh's intentions were distinct from the 'Modernist view that the form should be derived from the functional needs of activity, environment, structure or construction'.[10] He concludes that while Mackintosh is concerned with functionalism, what 'he seems to say is that things must work symbolically'. In other words, one can interpret a style and make it work for the requirements of a building; style need not be strictly dictated by function, nor must it be 'stuck' in its own past. It can be made flexible and suitable for the 'modern' building. The east elevation demonstrates Mackintosh's wresting of the Scots baronial style into the present. It is a showpiece that illustrates his views about 'the extraordinary facility of [the] style in decorating construction, and in converting structural and useful features into elements of beauty'.[11] In employing this style, he enshrines it as an undeniably Scottish building.

The composition is asymmetrical, divided by a cast iron drainpipe down the centre. To the south, or left, of the drainpipe is an eclectic composition of vertical windows, varied in size and style. No two sets of windows are alike; this is perhaps why the overall

FIG. 3.8 East elevation, view from the south-east, photograph by Thomas Annan, *c.* 1910.

FIG. 3.9 The east elevation, 2008.

effect feels historicist, as if the building grew and adapted over time. This is not just down to eccentricity on Mackintosh's part, but rather because he placed windows where they needed to be. All the elevations are articulations of the interior space; this is just less obvious where we find more regularity, such as the studio arrangements along the north side.

To the far left of the east elevation, at basement level, two sets of windows are arranged three and two, and articulate the split-level janitor's house inside. Above these is the most prominent window, the Dutch-inspired arched fenestration of the ground floor 'Masters' Room' (*see* fig. 3.56) and a small lavatory window to its left. At the top, two tall, narrow bow windows mark the original board room on the first floor. This whole arrangement is capped by a parapet with an elegantly arched crown.

The central portion of this elevation is demarcated with a central tower subtly emerging from the wall above the east basement entrance. A small rectangular window marks the first floor, and above this the base of the tower emerges from the stone in the form of an oriel window, above which is a tall thin arrowslit window; the glazing is set deep within each aperture. This arrangement is topped with a turret that, internally, has no function other than whimsy – inside it is a totally useless void that few ever saw – and is certainly a repudiation of arguments that everything Mackintosh did had functional purpose and that none of it was pure fancy. To the north or right-hand side of the pipe is an unrelieved wall of the snecked ashlar, which in its plainness is a celebration of the artistry in this building method. It was a practical decision of course; eastern windows would have ruined the even light of the north-facing studio within. Originally just one small window at the basement level punctuated this stark canvas; the larger window was a later addition and one Mackintosh didn't want, even going so far as to state that it would risk the structural integrity of what appeared as a fortification.

While the whole might seem historically inspired, the way in which the tower seems to grow organically from the surface of the building lends originality to this façade. This feature moves away from revivalism towards the Art Nouveau styles emerging on the continent; or perhaps it was inspired by another source: the recent writings of the American architect Louis Sullivan. His 1892 essay 'Ornament in Architecture' is resonant when thinking of Mackintosh's stone exteriors:

It must be manifest that an ornamental design will be more beautiful if it seems a part of the surface or substance that receives it, than if it looks 'stuck on', so to speak ... And this, I take it, is the preparatory basis of what may be called an organic system of ornamentation ... If now we bring ourselves to close and reflective observation, how evident it becomes that if we wish to insure an actual, a poetic unity, the ornament should appear, not as something receiving *the spirit of the structure, but as a thing* expressing *that spirit by virtue of differential growth.*[12]

This last sentence could describe Mackintosh's approach to stone ornamentation, especially the way in which forms emerge from the surface of the stone. They do not seem applied like cladding; they are drawn from the stone in the same manner Michelangelo described seeing his figures as 'trapped' within. The fluidity of this stonework and that on the rest of the building, even the west, creates Sullivan's sense of 'poetic unity'. There is no evidence that Mackintosh read Sullivan's essay when it was published in the *Engineering Magazine* just a few years earlier; the periodical was not part of the library collection but he may have seen it at Keppie's office. Many visitors and architectural historians have pondered the connection between Mackintosh and his direct contemporary Frank Lloyd Wright, but there is no tangible link. Sullivan, Wright's mentor and the only man he ever credited as having influenced him, provides an intriguing linchpin if Mackintosh was aware of his writing. As much as the east façade is a work of organic architecture, it would be exciting to know how much he was aware of the Chicago School when he redesigned his scheme for the west façade, with its tall windows of glass and steel.

WEST

The west elevation is the façade that has been most celebrated, housing the famous library (figs 3.10, 3.11). It was altered significantly from its original conception, which Howarth brutally described as 'dull and unimaginative', noting the 'diminutive windows' for the library and the 'pair of large, ugly, semi-circular headed windows which would have flooded the [lecture theatre] with light'.[13] The final design is by contrast bold and original; for Howarth in 1952, 'this elevation represents not a step forward of a mere decade, but a stride of twenty or thirty years in British architectural development'.

The western entrance, designed as the main entry for evening classes, is striking with the stepped 'Egyptian' style of the rather elaborate porch. It heralds Mackintosh's development towards more geometric motifs that would become popular a decade later, at the height of the jazz age. This entrance caused Mackintosh some trouble though. After a site visit, six of the governors sought out their friend Keppie at the Art Club, their usual haunt, to complain at the 'extravagance' of the stonework.[14] Mackintosh's design was apparently not what was drawn or approved. Mackintosh was asked to attend the 7 February 1908 meeting where this was discussed, but he was apparently 'still confined to bed'. The governors saw fit to write a formal complaint to the architects, reminding them of the clause in which the architects agreed not to make alterations without approval and that the governors would not bear the responsibility of increased costs.

The west elevation is subtly connected to the east façade by mirroring its companion in unrelieved snecked ashlar in the upper northern façade, unifying the overall composition. Below, however, three long windows on the ground floor set the rhythm for the even taller glass-and-steel fenestrations that grace the whole of the southern half of this façade. They project in three vertical stone bays, with the tallest set over the first floor, indicating the triple height of the library and book store above it. The windows themselves are on the theme of a grid and originally had square hoppers rather than the tall narrow ones added in the 1950s. It was hoped we would return to the squares when rebuilding these, but the expense was substantial. Flanking them are six stone pillars, one on either side of the windows, and altogether the composition reads as entirely 'modern', and to the contemporary eye looks forward to the glass-and-steel skyscrapers so familiar in our urban landscape.

But like so many other aspects of Mackintosh's work hailed as 'ahead of its time', it is not without precedent or relationship to contemporary work. Several scholars have pointed to the concurrent work of the English Arts and Crafts architect–designer Arthur Heygate Mackmurdo at 25 Cadogan Gardens in London's Chelsea (1893–4).[15] This house and studio, made for the artist and collector of Japanese art Mortimer Menpes, likewise used double-height windows and notably a triple bay over its northern façade. Mackintosh would have known this house as it was much discussed in architectural circles and published in a highly illustrated article in *The Studio* in 1899.

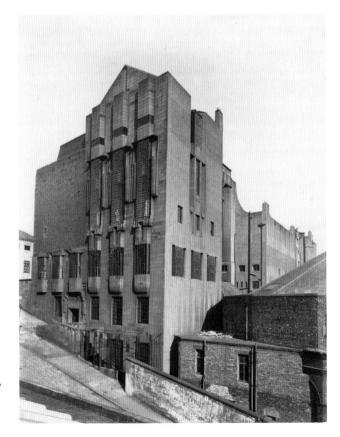

FIG. 3.1O The west elevation, early 20th century.

FIG. 3.11 OPPOSITE The west elevation, 2014.

Another possible source of inspiration is closer to home, however: Salmon, Son & Gillespie's Lion Chambers (1904–7; fig. 3.12), which was innovative in its use of Hennibique concrete technology that, sadly, has contributed to its dereliction.[16] It was originally designed as law offices but the client, William George Black, was also a member of the Glasgow Art Club and wished for artists' studios to be built on its top levels. The most desirable position for these is north-facing for the even light: the largest of the Mack's studios take advantage of this, as did Menpes's studio at Cadogan Gardens. The north elevation at Lion Chambers unfortunately faces a very narrow lane, near to the adjacent building. To capture as much light as possible, Salmon employed a triple bay of windows the length and width of the building above the ground floor, each bow framed by concrete bands over six levels. The

FIG. 3.12 Salmon, Son & Gillespie, Lion Chambers, 1904–7.

fenestration is a rhythmic grid, not unlike the Mack's west elevation.[17] The top floor where the artists' studios were located is different: each bay has three tall narrow windows, two panes across and six down, which in their verticality and evocation of a Japanese screen are not dissimilar to the Mack library windows. Each window is fully framed by concrete, unlike the adjoined sets below. While these windows are all single height, the overall effect is like both Cadogan Gardens and the Mack: a triple bay dominated by fenestration that is both functional in maximising light and aesthetically pleasing. How much more critical attention would James Salmon Jr's radical elevation have received if it did not face an unwelcoming Glasgow lane?

While Mackmurdo appears a more obvious source in the vertical expanse of glazing, Salmon's may have influenced Mackintosh in both the gridded arrangement and the unbroken, contiguous steel frames across the bow. But as 'modern' as Mackintosh's west windows now seem, they were designed to have traditional elements. The 1907 phase II drawings for this façade show that statuary was to be carved from the rounded pillars that flank each window on both the west and south elevations. The same year the *Glasgow Herald* reported that they were to be 'a series of emblematic figures, representing art, sculpture, architecture, and music', and on one version of the drawing, now in the GSA archives, we have notations in Mackintosh's hand that three of the figures were to be Andrea Palladio, Benvenuto Cellini and St Francis of Assisi (fig. 3.13). An odd combination on first impression, but Palladio and Cellini wrote critical texts on architecture and on metalwork and sculpture respectively, while St Francis was not only a poet but also the patron of nature as well as needleworkers. Art and nature? Or representative of the various arts and crafts? One wonders who the other three figures would have been. They were never realised; £1,000 was originally allocated to their production but was noted as removed from the budget in December 1908, according to the governors' minutes.[18] Presumably the money was required elsewhere, as Mackintosh was already requesting budget increases in other areas such as the library. If the sculptures had been

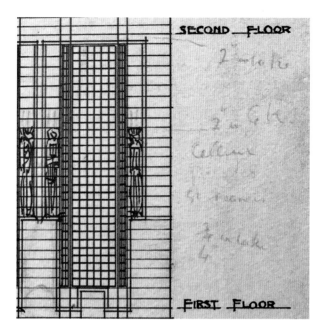

completed, the west façade would have looked a lot less 'modernist masterpiece' than 'Gothic cathedral'. Mackintosh is not usually associated with the popular Victorian Gothic Revival, but it is worth considering as an influence for the exaggerated, vertical elongation of forms and figures. Such designs manifest in work he did between phases I and II, notably his 1901–2 designs for Liverpool Cathedral (fig. 3.14) and interior renovations at Bridge of Allan Parish Church in 1903–4 (fig. 3.15). But the missing statuary effectively strips the otherwise obvious association with the past. This observation would move some to argue that the choice to leave the pillars uncarved was deliberate, but we have no evidence to prove that supposition. Could it be that the allocated funds were used to offset the increased cost of the west porch? And perhaps after designing

FIG. 3.13 ABOVE Charles Rennie Mackintosh for John Honeyman & Keppie, The Glasgow School of Art drawing for the east and west elevations (detail), May 1907. Inscribed by Mackintosh: 'Cellini' | 'Palladio' | 'St Francis'.

FIG. 3.14 BELOW Competition design for Liverpool Cathedral, south elevation, 1901 or 1902. Ink and wash, 62.3 × 91.6 cm. The Hunterian, University of Glasgow.

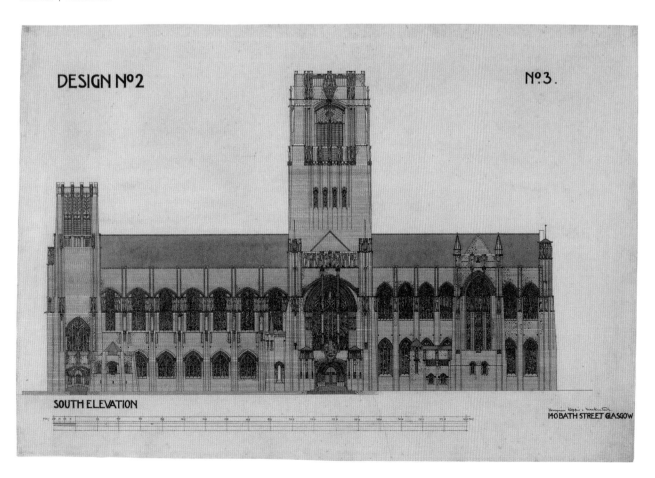

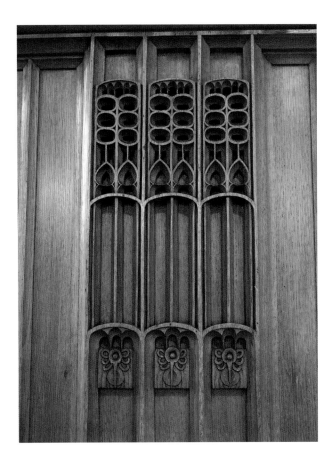

FIG. 3.15 Chancel furnishings, Bridge of Allan Parish Church, 1903–4.

FIG. 3.16 The north windows.

that 'extravagant' stonework Mackintosh had moved on stylistically from the Gothic-inspired statuary he initially envisioned.

The overall effect as completed looks beyond the continental Art Nouveau with which Mackintosh was hitherto associated and towards the bold geometry of his later work that points towards Art Deco. It is easy to see why this elevation has been read as proto-modern by so many, especially when the whole seems to be without historical precedence. But like the east, it is really an amalgam of influences and ideas – many with identifiable antecedents – uniquely combined. The complexity of the composition is not 'ahead of its time', but precisely 'of its time'.

NORTH

Standing on narrow Renfrew Street, it is impossible to view the entire north elevation in one glance (*see* fig. 0.8). The building appears symmetrical until one counts

the monumental window openings that dominate the whole of the front (fig. 3.16). There are three sets of these to the east and four to the west. The last two are slightly narrower – one pane's width less – giving the illusion of balance. At night the illuminated studios shone out across Renfrew Street. At the base of each of the larger first-floor windows, great ironwork brackets thrust forth from the wall, arching back towards the windows, meeting them above the first row of glazing in stylised wrought-iron blossoms. Four grace each of the larger windows, with three on the two smaller ones. Each set has a slightly different design to the 'flower', with the later western ones being slightly more delicate and elaborate than the heavier eastern versions.

The ironwork was made by George Adam & Son 'art metal works', a firm that also worked for Leiper.[19] They crafted an iron fence to guard the basement light well to

FIG. 3.17 The north fence rail.

FIG. 3.18 Charles Rennie Mackintosh for John Honeyman & Keppie, The Glasgow School of Art, north elevation (detail), March 1897.

FIG. 3.19 The north entrance, late 20th century.

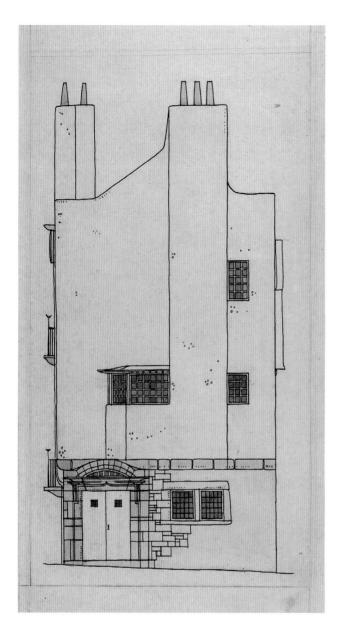

FIG. 3.20 Charles Rennie Mackintosh, Design for an artist's town house and studio, 1899–1900. Pencil, ink and wash.

the east and west of the main stairs (fig. 3.17); this was set within stone piers and matching walls that swept downward in wide curves. Atop the fence, tall ironwork grass bursts forth in intervals, from which lofty finials thrust upwards with stylised roundels of flora and fauna. Art historian Timothy Neat, who seeks out the esoteric, even occult, influences in Mackintosh's work, goes further, suggesting that the finials on the north

fence posts are symbols from 'Rosicrucian, Egyptian, Judaic/Christian traditions':

> When read from east to west: a dove with a chalice; an abstract image of unity, totality and completion; an Egyptian scarab beetle, a resurrection symbol; a sun and three stages in its rising, the Egyptian hieroglyph for bread; a bee, Egyptian emblem of Royalty.[20]

Buchanan, in response, simplifies these to 'bird, ladybird, scarab, ant, bee'.[21] Others have seen moths, butterflies, flowers, ladybirds, mushrooms. As we have seen, nature is a prevalent theme throughout Mackintosh's work. Organic motifs were always planned for the building, as suggested in his original 1897 drawings (fig. 3.18). The elaborate roof lanterns were never realised, but the two finials – his versions of the coat of arms – appear from the first. Amazingly they were barely touched by the 2018 fire. Were these the inspiration for the ironwork 'garden' across the northern front?

At the centre, the composition becomes almost domestic (fig. 3.19), with a layered roofline and diminutive doors reminiscent of his artist's townhouse design (fig. 3.20). This mostly articulates the director's office and studio above it, complete with a balcony from which one imagines they might address the students, though no evidence suggests this ever happened. Perhaps humorously, the attractive bay window is actually the director's private lavatory. At ground level, a spacious staircase narrows towards the entrance. The gently rounded edges of the bottom stair, which projected on to the pavement to welcome visitors, were buried by clumsy pavement works in 2014, another feature to restore in future. The overall effect of the north façade is an invitation: solid stone surrounding large expanses of glass that allow glimpses of activity within, and broad steps that seem to embrace the visitor, beguiling them and beckoning them inside.

THRESHOLD

At the threshold we are subtly introduced to the Mack's Symbolist decorative programme, which many over the years have sought to interpret. William Buchanan discussed the influence of Lethaby's *Architecture, Mysticism and Myth*, noting his pronouncement 'Portals must have Guardians', and suggested that the book's title page, which features simple line drawings of a circle and a square, might be the source for that motif as seen throughout the school.[22] These forms are also at the core of the visual art and material culture of Japan (*see* pp. 32–3), which was popularised through Aestheticism and equally had an important impact on Symbolism. Mackintosh also expressed his adherence to these sensibilities in an oft-quoted passage:

> *Art is the flower. Life is the green leaf. Let every artist strive to make his flower a beautiful living thing. You must offer real, living, beautifully coloured flowers that grow above the green leaf. You must offer the flowers of the art that is to you, the symbols of all that is noble and beautiful and inspiring. How beautiful the green leaf. How beautiful life often is, but think of the stupendous possibilities of the flower thus offered – of art.*[23]

This poetic artistic philosophy comes from his 1902 lecture entitled 'Seemliness'. Did it enable any sense of understanding to those who found their new (and as yet incomplete) building so bizarre? Mackintosh offers literal flowers in his garden façade, emblematic of the creative activity and growth within. Ascending the steps of the Mack, one is greeted by the liminal sculpture above the entrance (*see* fig. 0.6). It is Mackintosh's most elaborate design on the building, and the only one where we find recognisably human figures: two female sentinels that emerge spirit-like from the stone, flanking a rose bush at the centre. As noted in Chapter 1, the shape is that of a penannular brooch and it gives a decidedly Celtic Revival impression. As ever, Mackintosh left no description or clarification; it could be interpreted simply as just part of his art-as-nature Symbolism. Others have seen a more sexual image, the tree thrust between the half-moon figures. The more spiritual individual might see it as a guardian of sorts, especially now that it has survived a conflagration that consumed the entrance and doors below it: these stones remain wholly unscathed.

This entrance draws visitors up the narrowing steps and through the doors, which swing unusually from their centre post; at some point they were labelled 'In' on the left and 'Out' on the right, so students could more easily manoeuvre without collision, their arms full of projects and supplies. The architect Aldo van Eyck commented that the doors make one 'want to enter again and again, which is as it should be, surely'.[24]

INSIDE

For a 'plain building', the Mack interior defies a straightforward description. From the drawings discussed in Chapter 2, it might simply be described as a rectangular plan arranged over five levels, a central corridor dividing the north to south axis and the largest studios arranged along a north-facing frontage to maximise light, with smaller studios and offices to the south. East–west it appears as a symmetrical plan, with the wings separated by the central block of entrance hall, main staircase and museum.

Except it is not a simple design at all. The plan is a shallow E-shape rising from a rectangular foundation,[25] cleverly designed to maximise light access on the trickier south side of the building. While it was largely arranged over five levels, in actuality the Mack was a warren of mezzanines, entresols and half-landings, with smaller, cosier rooms for offices or lounging and hidden nooks for study, conversation, and even at times romance. Some areas appeared triple height, like the museum and studios, while others were divided into two or even three floors within a space, as in the combined library and book store. From the front arrangement of windows, it appears as a three-storey building although it is five; but when climbing the west tower stairs, one could stop on a total of seven levels, and were counted as ten in all (including service spaces and roof) by Page\Park Architects in their new plans for the 2014–18 restoration project. The arrangement could seem almost labyrinthine to the new visitor – even staff who spent years in the building might give pause and ask themselves 'what floor am I on now?' But rather than frustration, the deceptively complex plan felt adventurous, like there was always something new to discover. And usually there was.

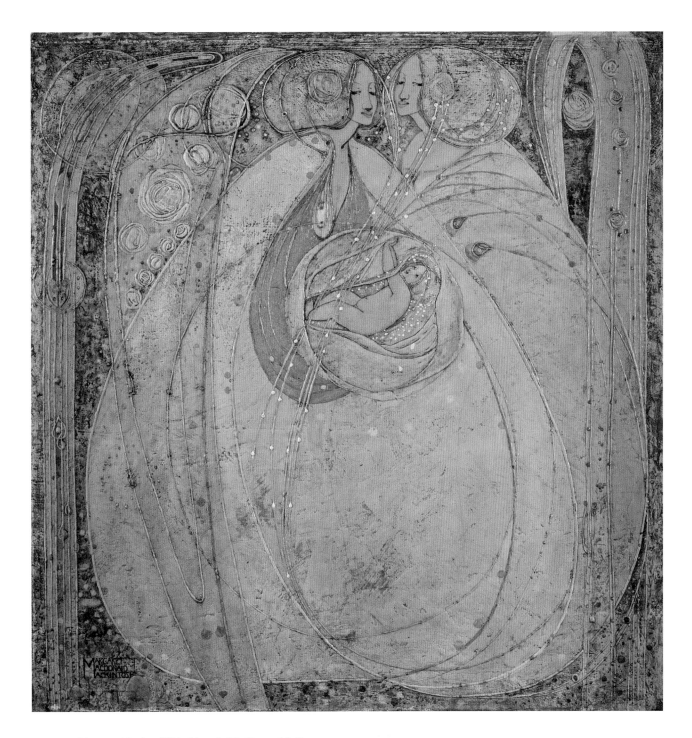

FIG. 3.21 Margaret Macdonald Mackintosh, *The Heart of the Rose*, 1902. Painted plaster-cast panel, 96.8 × 94 cm. During treatment after the 2014 fire, conservator Graciela Ainsworth confirmed that this was a plaster cast, not a gesso panel like others Macdonald made and as previously assumed.

Yet even in its complexity, there was a natural, easy flow to travelling through the Mack. Consider the route of the popular tours, led by knowledgeable students for several decades. Visitors entered at the east basement, went along the corridor to the central stair, up two flights to the museum on the first floor, turned right to briefly take in the Mackintosh Room and the furniture housed there, then reversed down the west corridor to the library at the opposite end. Here they paused, looking up to the balconies but never visiting them. Out again and up two flights of the west stairs and out through the loggia, along the Hen Run for breathtaking views, and then back down to the very basement into a furniture gallery (fig. 3.22) where they could admire selected Mackintosh furniture and Margaret Macdonald's exquisite gesso panel *The Heart of the Rose* (fig. 3.21), before exiting through the gift shop (in the former animal room). The tours travelled up, across, up, across, and down again. A simple plan, a plain building. No art studios to be seen.

This was *not* the Mack as the staff and students have known it, but probably the one that most recent visitors understood, as public access had shifted over the decades from casual and unmonitored to controlled visitation through exhibitions and tourism. GSA's Exhibitions Director Jenny Brownrigg reflected on her own occupation of the Mack, when she was a student there from 1990 to 1994:

FIG. 3.22 The furniture gallery (originally the 'Ornament Room') after the 2008 Conservation & Access project.

I studied Drawing and Painting in the Mackintosh building, beginning in the year that Glasgow was European City of Culture. My route through the building was ascension through the floors of studios, as I moved through second, third and fourth year. It was a specific daily route too, up the stairs and straight to the studio, for long days. On breaks I would make a beeline for the studios that friends were in. Studio culture was exciting. When tutors allocated space at the start of the academic year, it often put you next to students who you initially did not know well, which meant you were in direct contact with totally different ways of working.[26]

Inside, the Mack was a largely timber interior, fitted over a plaster skin and embedded on a brick, steel and, in places, cement skeleton. Ornamentation was largely abstract, found in the patterns created by the arrangement of joinery, lighting fixtures, the artistic finishing of steelwork, tiling in the stairwells and, perhaps most subtly and potently, in the light that constantly shifted throughout the internal spaces and through the day. When asked about his memories of the building, Alastair Macdonald, GSA Professor of Design and former student from 1973 to 1977, offered this impression:

I was conscious of the very different levels of light – from the dark corridors to the brilliantly lit studios – someone once described this in terms of a conscious phototrophic design, and how these changed significantly depending on the time of day or night, or the season. It had much more variety of light than most other buildings I have experienced.[27]

This kaleidoscopic aspect is the one most frequently commented on by those who worked in the building, followed closely by its sound and smell: creaking floors, banging doors, paint and musty old books. The Mack, as its community of users remember it, is often fondly romanticised these days, so it is worth an interjection that the building had problems commensurate with its age. While regular maintenance and repair happened throughout the years, the first major conservation project was in 2008 (funded by Historic Environment Scotland and the Heritage Lottery Fund and led by Page\Park Architects), which offered valuable information for the restoration project. As recently as 1991, a visit to the Mack could be shambolic, as remembered by Bruce Peter, Professor of Design History and Theory and former student from 1992 to 1996, when he attended the GSA open day:

I can honestly say that my first visit to the Mack was a disappointment … the studios were out of bounds due to teaching being in progress and the library similarly was locked and so my first 'tour', such as it was, was of corridors and stairways that were very run down, with smokers loitering and huge numbers of cigarette ends strewn everywhere. The Hen Run, similarly, was water-stained and dilapidated with several smashed windows and cold draughts howling through (I later discovered that male painting students sometimes played football in there, with disastrous consequences for the glazing). In the toilets, though, I recall being immensely impressed by the sheer imagination, extremely grotesque vulgarity – and artistic excellence – of the graffiti … But overall first impressions were … disappointment – and that wasn't because I hadn't tried to like it; I just hadn't learned what I should be looking for or appreciating – yet – nor had I been allowed the opportunity to view the most visually and spatially impressive areas.[28]

The Mack had certainly improved in recent history, but it was still layered with the sights, sounds and smells of decades, which enliven our memories. It is an icon of architectural heritage, but it should be remembered that it was also a living and working art school. A mere textual 'tour' of the building can never replace the actual experience of exploring it; and a discussion of its component parts (wood, metal, glass, brick, stone) disrupts the symphony of the whole. Instead, a review of the interior through spatial typologies allows consideration of materials, environment and atmospheric effect across the whole of the building.

FIG. 3.24 The main stairwell from the ground floor, with the janitor's cupboard in use, mid-20th century.

FIG. 3.25 Basement corridor with plaster cast storage, photograph by Harry Bedford Lemere, *c.* 1909.

CIRCULATION SPACE

The arteries of the school mostly comprise the circulation spaces – corridors and entrances – and also the areas that helped the estate function. These are the 'serendipitous' spaces in the school, where one might bump into friends and colleagues in passing. But in a few key areas, Mackintosh provided more than just a passage: he purposely created opportunity for pause and conversation, as well as quiet contemplation. For Aldo van Eyck these were 'certainly no corridors, but streets with *interior urbanity* along which the school's various localities are gathered and all and sundry occurs'.[29] These 'streets' begin at the front doors, where the entrance hallway was largely a thoroughfare but with plenty of space to loiter (fig. 3.23). This area was home to the janitors and reception, with simple benches for lingering students or waiting guests, and at one

FIG. 3.23 OPPOSITE Entrance foyer, 2003.

point had an art supply shop at the east side. A vacant janitor's box in front of the grand central stairwell (fig. 3.24), with space for just one person, was a reminder that not all the school's fittings remained fit for purpose.

The basement and ground-floor corridors were largely functional (figs 3.25, 3.26), but both provided ample space to pause and, especially in the case of the basement, sketch the plaster casts on display there. From the west entrance, through the exotic stepped architrave, Mackintosh carried the design through to the interior by installing a series of glass-fronted cabinets and a curved recess with a bench outside the lecture theatre (fig. 3.27). It was stained very dark and painted black in recent memory.

In the first-floor western corridor, two floors above, were the famous window seats that Mackintosh perhaps included to compensate for the lack of a 'School of Art Club' space, which had been sacrificed in the final design (figs 3.28, 3.29). Cosy nooks were a feature in many

FIG. 3.26 Ground-floor corridor looking east, photograph by T. & R. Annan, *c.* 1910.

FIG. 3.27 West basement entrance corridor, 2003.

FIG. 3.28 West corridor, first floor, photograph by T. & R. Annan, *c.* 1910.

FIG. 3.29 West corridor, first floor, window seat, *c.* 1960s.

FIG. 3.30 The Hen Run, 2002.

of his buildings, especially in domestic spaces, often designed around a hearth. One of the great pleasures of being part of the GSA community was the privilege of enjoying these intimate alcoves as a place to sketch, chat, or simply take a quiet break from the day's work. I have a distinct memory of sitting in one of those snugs with a colleague during an exhibition opening, glasses of fizz in our hands, and thinking how lucky I was to work in such a place. Their frequent use was evidenced in the decades of initials carved into the dark-stained wood benches. It is these traces of memory that are among the most painful losses.

Mackintosh's command of these fluid spaces led the architect Hans Hollein to call him 'a master of circulation, not in the functional sense like a factory, where something comes in and goes out as a product, but as a creator of shifting experiences as you move through his buildings.'[30] This is perhaps best exemplified in the corridor formed by the Hen Run and loggia at the top of the building (fig. 3.30). Hollein specifically referred to the Hen Run as 'an

exciting spatial experience' through which Mackintosh offered 'understanding of how life in such a building could be'.[31] This corridor was not merely an innovative solution for east–west access through the divided second-floor plan. In the most practical sense, the Hen Run and adjoining loggia (fig. 3.33) were places to work when stronger light was needed, especially on rainy days (and latterly students continued to set up their easels there, regardless of the daily trail of tourists ambling through). Mackintosh even provided services such as sinks in this area to help facilitate it as a flexible working space. The Hen Run was also used for critiques, the students pinning up their drawings on the walls. The southern position offered vistas across the city that begged to be sketched. To this end, Mackintosh provided bespoke furniture in the form of folding drawing desks in the loggia bays (fig. 3.34), and devised gridded window frames that could cleverly be used to map out the city beyond the glass.

FIG. 3.31 The rebuilt Hen Run, early 2018.

But research from the restoration project has revealed unique, tangible ways in which Mackintosh may have intended this passage to be used as an extension of the teaching studio. In living memory, the Hen Run roof was made from translucent panels set at a pitched angle that allowed for occluded light. This seems to have always leaked, given Glasgow's often inclement weather. It had been repaired many times, with a rebuild in 1977 and major conservation by Page\Park in 2008–10. After the 2014 fire, research on photos in the GSA archives (fig. 3.32) revealed that originally the roof was a gridded glass screen, level, not pitched – just like the walls of the glass pavilion. This leads to a further hypothesis about the Hen Run roof, inspired by an early drawing by the Page\Park restoration team that restored the glass grid roof. I observed that the shadows cast inside the structure when the sun was at its zenith could have generated a 360-degree illusion of orthogonals rushing towards a vanishing point in the centre of the arched entrance to the passage (fig. 3.31). Combined with the loggia desks, the glass pavilion could have itself facilitated instruction on perspective.

FIG. 3.32 Students in the Hen Run, *c.* 1914.

FIG. 3.33 TOP Loggia, photograph by Harry Bedford Lemere, *c.* 1909.   **FIG. 3.34** The loggia windows, with collapsible desks, 2004.

FIG. 3.35 Top of the west staircase with 'cage', 2004. The Masters' Room desk, now lost, sits somewhat forlornly on the landing.

FIG. 3.36 East stairwell, 2003.

Could this entire corridor be a teaching tool for drawing principles embedded in the very fabric of the building? It was decided to restore it to its original condition, and the work had just been completed before the second fire. The full effect was observed, but untested.

Stairwells comprised the vertical access of the building, although one rather claustrophobic lift was also available for most floors (though not some of the entresols, which was being rectified in the restoration). The central, main stair was the only one extant during phase I, and it was a showpiece (*see* fig. 3.24). The palpable experience of ascending the central stair and arriving at the soaring museum is eloquently described by Christopher Platt:

> *The familiarity of its exterior makes the surprise and delight of its interior even more powerful. I still recall that first sequence of climb, threshold, vaulted hallway and arrival at the first-floor museum – a sequence of being spatially squeezed, then released – of light, dark, then light again.*[32]

There was little room for pause along the narrower west and east stairs (figs 3.35, 3.36), although many have lingered to consider whether the varying patterns of coloured tile on each landing had any special significance (fig. 3.37). Also puzzling to many are the two steel 'cages' that crowned each of the stairs (figs 3.35, 3.38) – an open circle atop the east and a gridded square at the west. Many a visitor has joked that they were prison cells for the students; they also call to mind iron portcullises and other architectural defences. Bruce Peter has suggested that 'more prosaically, it could be that the cages were an inexpensive, lightweight and safe solution to the problem of enclosing landings high in the structure.'[33] It has also been proposed that, along with the tiles, they form a wayfinding device, but just how this might work has never been adequately explained.[34] Both were installed during phase II: is this merely a continuation of the circle/square motif? After spending a great deal of time working on the restoration of the Mack, architect John Brown of

Page\Park departed from his initial scepticism about any symbolic programme in the buildings towards devising an interpretation of his own, inspired partially by conversations with the firm's principal architect David Page. Slight shifts in the decorative programme from phase I to phase II made him consider how it might be expressing Mackintosh's shifting perception of life:

I think there is stuff that is quite obvious in the building – on the external there's the pollinators on the ironwork, the seeds and the flowers in the ironwork ... I think even if that is someone's reading, it's a very convincing reading ... [In looking inside the building] ... all the symbolism I read in the east wing is about rebirth and optimism, and I think if you read the west wing,

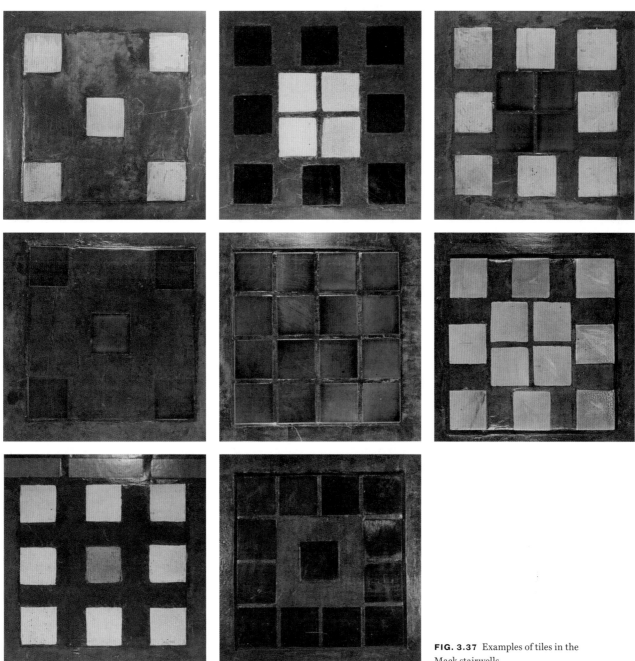

FIG. 3.37 Examples of tiles in the Mack stairwells.

FIG. 3.38 Top of east stairwell with ironwork 'cage'.

FIG. 3.39 Charles Rennie Mackintosh, coat of arms sculpture above the central stairwell (destroyed in the 2018 fire, fragments recovered).

you come up against something that reads as a pessimism in life. That rebirth isn't guaranteed, that things don't necessarily flourish ... Maybe it's about a more complex reading of life, actually, in the west ... had he lost his optimism of youth?[35]

It is an intriguing observation developed from Brown's extremely close and purposeful study, cataloguing the doors and project-managing much of the building restoration for Page\Park. Other symbolism in the circulation areas was more obvious. Crowning the central stair was another, rather abstracted, version of the Glasgow coat of arms: the bell, the bird, the fish, the tree (figs 3.39, 3.40). Along the ground-floor corridor, the stained glass in the doors featured roses and other flora (fig. 3.41), including the rare figural decoration, a stylised female very much like those seen in his tea-room schemes, in the stained glass of the ground-floor studio doors and both female and male toilets.

The fluidity of the circulation spaces was tied together by the decorative programme: the repetition of stained-glass motifs and door designs across the east–west corridors,[36] the organic details of stone, timber and plaster framing doors, windows and hearths; the repetition of squares and circles on doors and even the chequerboard clocks (fig. 3.42), keeping the rhythm of the whole school. This system of 20 clocks, each with a similar but minutely different face (one was painted directly onto a wall), ran on a network controlled by a 'master' clock. They all survive (except the one on the wall), asynchronous designs that kept the school literally synchronised across space and time.

FIG. 3.40 Surviving bell from the coat of arms.

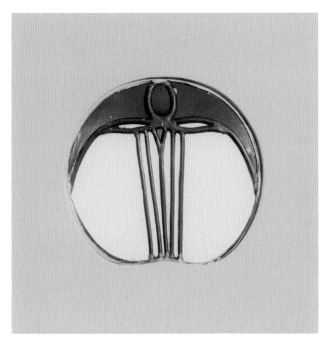

FIG. 3.41 Examples of glass and door fixtures in the building.

FIG. 3.42 One of the clocks from the circuit. Each was painted with a different pattern, and one was painted directly on the wall. The surviving clocks had been undergoing conservation and so escaped the 2018 fire.

COLLECTIVE SPACE

Some of the most extraordinary spaces in the school were those created to bring people together more formally for group activities such as lectures, meetings and exhibitions. The lecture theatre on the ground floor was much beloved despite – or perhaps even, endearingly, due to – its notorious discomfort (figs 3.43, 3.44). Three sections of raked benches faced a small proscenium stage adjacent to the west wall. The back entrance used in recent memory was a mid-century addition to improve fire access; originally there were just two entrances, both inside the western access to the school: the double doors that the students would use and a smaller, more exclusive door to the 'Lecturer's Room', a small 'backstage' area that had more recently been blocked off by a large projection screen. When this screen was removed during the restoration, the original sliding chalk boards were found in situ, complete with decades-old architecture lessons still inscribed on them. Indeed, as technology evolved, so too did the room: the back row centre benches were removed for a projection and sound booth some time mid-century, and a semicircular sectional desk was also permanently

removed from the foot of the stage to make room for a new lectern and digital equipment. A ramp with a raised floor to accommodate accessibility regulations was added during the *c.* 2008–10 Conservation & Access Project. What always remained though were the back-breaking benches, which even the addition of slippery vinyl padding in the 1970s could not improve. Above the seating and the desk, elliptical pendant light fittings provided soft illumination, enabling the more engaged audience members to take notes.

Acoustics were also a long-standing problem, and one which even inspired a plea for help in 1966 from then Director Harry Jefferson Barnes to Geoffrey Wimpenny of Keppie Henderson & Partners – who the school continued to work with exclusively until the 1980s – regarding the highly embarrassing 'fantastic noises' coming from the ventilation system due to the still-extant vacuum steam boiler. Alastair Macdonald recalled that in the 1970s, 'as the soundproofing was so poor, we could always hear people coming in and out, the basement corridor and studio doors swinging and banging as well as the doors into the lecture theatre itself, and sometimes sounds from the wood workshop extractor fan or circular saw in the sub-basement below.'[37] Frances Robertson, Reader in Design History and Theory and former student from 1997 to 2000, was also not a fan of the space:

FIG. 3.43 Lecture theatre, 2003.

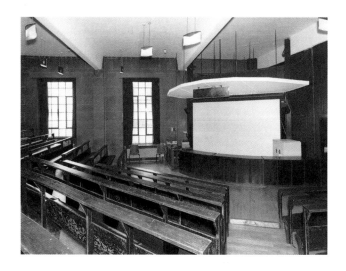

The Mack lecture theatre was very oppressive, and it had a gothic anatomy theatre presence, as I say very challenging physically to endure a lecture in it. But maybe that ghastly House of Usher feel was part of the pride we felt in the Mack, a grim dungeon for testing artists.[38]

For many others though, myself included, it was a most exciting place to teach. Perhaps it appealed to those of us with a fondness for the 'Spook School' element in Mackintosh. Likewise, the noise of the school added to this atmosphere. In fact, when people were asked to share their memories of the Mack with the restoration team, it was its sensory aspects that were most often recalled: the fall of the light, the smell of age and art materials, and the sound of creaking floors and swinging doors. Such sounds were literal music for former student Scott Hutchison of indie band Frightened Rabbit, who studied illustration in the Mack from 2000 to 2004.[39] He wrote and performed an exquisite art school-inspired ballad for the 2009

FIG. 3.44 Lecture theatre, photograph by Harry Bedford Lemere, *c.* 1909.

BBC documentary *Mackintosh's Masterpiece*, using the metronome-like swish and bang of the doors as a percussion track to 'get the building talking', and his vocals were its voice:

I've always liked the idea that inanimate objects have emotions and personalities and this building, more than any other that I've ever been in, has such a unique personality … it's like an old dandy kind of man who likes to hang around young people just because they keep him young, and it remains hip in spite of its age.[40]

In contrast to its darker, moodier spaces, an altogether lighter experience was to be had in the Mackintosh Room, which in recent years had been used as a flexible space for teaching and meetings (figs 3.45, 3.46). It occupied the south-east end of the first floor, and it is part of the school's oral history that the governors were

not comfortable conducting their very serious business in this bright, 'feminine' room. This may be apocryphal, as since only half the building was delivered in phase I it is just as likely that a room such as this would have been ideal for coveted studio space – and it was already listed as the Design Room in phase II drawings in 1908. It became the Mackintosh Room in 1947, displaying the school's growing collection of Mackintosh furniture. Later the room display included original light fittings from Windyhill, which to some visitors most glaringly did not belong in the space, especially when compared to early photographs showing the original, austere and practical cone chandelier system designed by Osborne & Hunter. It was spacious and bright, illuminated by double bow windows to east and west, although the western window would become a curiosity when it was enclosed in the phase II eastern stairwell addition (fig. 3.48). The most prominent feature in the room was the carved stone Arts and Crafts-style hearth, framed in timber with flanking square pillars that align with the panelling that cladded the lower portion of the walls. Light permeated the space, bouncing off the white panelling, giving the overall effect of a bright, airy salon.

FIG. 3.48 East stairwell outside the Mackintosh Room, 2008.

In comparison the small dark-panelled board room that was eventually built on the ground floor felt more like a gentlemen's smoking lounge (fig. 3.47). On plan Mackintosh called it the 'Secretary's Room' and it was designed to be the office of John Groundwater, who was employed full-time as Secretary (a role that was akin to an assistant director or registrar) in 1908.[41] It was also the original archive for the school – hence the useful walk-in closets behind the panelled walls – and

FIG. 3.45 OPPOSITE TOP
Design Room (later Mackintosh Room), photograph by T. & R. Annan, *c.* 1910.

FIG. 3.46 OPPOSITE
Mackintosh Room, 2014.

FIG. 3.47 Board room (Secretary's Room), photograph by Harry Bedford Lemere, *c.* 1909.

the main meeting space for official governors' business. Smaller and more private than the original design for the Mackintosh Room, it more readily suited the needs of running the school. It may have been a consideration of Mackintosh's design that those visiting the secretary and treasurer in the early twentieth century would have included public officials, financiers, lawyers and other professionals. But its deep 'oak' panelling (actually tulipwood, like the library) and playful nods to classicism in the abstract fluted columns have been interpreted as Mackintosh poking fun at the governors, creating an overtly 'masculine' space for the men who found the upstairs room too 'feminine'. It is easy to assume a gendered reading that this room was preferable to the all-male board of governors' tastes, particularly in its unusual 'classical' ornamentation.[42]

The perception of the Secretary's Room as being a 'man's room' was perhaps reinforced by the 1913 painting by Newbery of the building committee gathered there, which also hung on its wall (fig. 3.49). The painting was removed after the 2014 fire and has thus survived, along with light fittings that had been

removed for conservation. Originally it portrayed just the group of those governors who saw the building to completion. A middle-aged Mackintosh, grasping his building plans, was added as an afterthought before Newbery gifted the painting to the school in 1914. This was no slight by Newbery, but some have interpreted the way in which Mackintosh seems at odds with the rest of the group as a sign of his disfavour. For our purposes it is as much a portrait of the room, and perhaps the group have coloured the perception of this space as exuding traditional masculine gravitas. For example, Sarah Smith, Head of Research, recalls attending meetings there when it was the deputy director's office (in many ways, a return to its original function):

> *The formality of certain 'high ranking' rooms was something I was never overly fond of. All those portraits of men … felt very exclusive and excluding when I first attended meetings in that space.*[43]

Although it is easy to understand why such perceptions have arisen, looking at the board room from a more formal, analytical perspective, it was as distinctive as the famous library upstairs (and crafted around the same time, as a renovation of an extant studio space). While its dark tonality might seem redolent of officialdom,

FIG. 3.49 Francis Newbery, *The Building Committee, Glasgow School of Art*, 1909–14. Oil on canvas, 132 × 170 cm.

FIG. 3.50 Detail of relief carving in the board room, 2017.

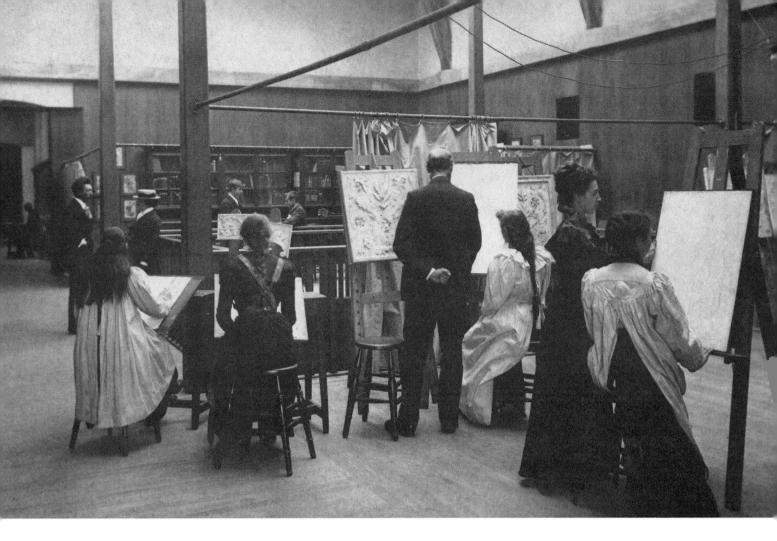

FIG. 3.51 Students in the museum during a painting class, *c.* 1900.

FIG. 3.52 Elizabeth Anderson, *Museum, Glasgow School of Art*, 1900. Oil on canvas, 76.2 × 55.5 cm. Lost in the 2014 fire.

the board room was also artful in the way in which Mackintosh turned seemingly conventional elements into what might arguably be called modern design. The eight pilasters initially seem of Ionic order, but each was carved with a unique flat pattern of squares that, to the contemporary eye, looks 'pixelated' (fig. 3.50). But it might also be argued that this room, designed around 1908, was the next iteration in Mackintosh's exploration of essential forms. Lethaby's Symbolist architecture comes to life with the artistic arrangement of circles (light fixtures, the table, the pierced work on the chairs) and squares (the panelling, the glass, the chairs, the ceiling, the light fixture again, the columns). The total effect reflects all the departments of the school: classical elements of architecture, designed through an exploration of emerging forms of artistic

representation, and rendered skilfully in handcrafted low-relief sculpture. Perhaps because of its exclusivity, it was in the best condition of all the rooms in the school – even to the extent that the interiors of the cupboards, virtually untouched by exposure to light or use, gave the best indicator of what the tones of the wood used in the library and elsewhere originally looked like. The loss of this undervalued interior may be one of the most tragic in the entire building.

The museum was arguably the most 'Arts and Crafts' space in the building (figs. 3.51, 3.52), largely due to the mammoth hand-crafted roof trusses, rough-hewn, untidily stained, with prominent pegged joinery. Mackintosh used these exposed roof structures in other designs of this period, such as at the Helensburgh Conservative Club (1894–5) and Ruchill Free Church Halls (1899), but the Mack trusses are his most artistic composition (fig. 3.53). The four main trusses comprised coupled timber rafters, straight and curved, tied at the centre with two sturdy posts, and a tie beam across the bottom. The posts were mirrored in form with a large notch at the top and a point at the bottom, suggesting that each set was carved puzzle-like from the same enormous log. Towards the bottom of these ties was what appeared to be a hole when viewed from a distance, but on closer inspection contained a

FIG. 3.53 The museum during the 2014–18 restoration project.

FIG. 3.54 3D scan of the museum with the *Nike of Samothrace* plaster cast, 2014. Photogrammetry. Terrestrial laser scanning, Al Rawlinson.

curved wisp of carving, another *mon*-style design like those elsewhere in the building. The tops were pierced with two heart shapes somewhat incongruous with the rest of the decorative programme, a perhaps too obvious signifier that the museum was the 'heart' of the building and likely part of Mackintosh's original, more decorative vision for the space. Previous scholars have suggested Mackintosh took inspiration for this motif from C.F.A. Voysey,[44] which may be true, but hearts were a common feature in Victorian Arts and Crafts decoration and in the Celtic Revival.

Designed to exhibit students' work, the museum was a highly flexible space. It always housed some of the more monumental plaster casts, including statuary from the door of Chartres Cathedral, which framed the vestibule of the director's suite opposite the stair landing, and a monumental plaster cast of the *Nike of Samothrace*. These were too difficult to remove from the building and, along with several other plaster casts, have now perished, but they were captured digitally when the building was scanned (fig. 3.54). During phase I the museum space was both library and teaching studio, and after the building was completed was used for student and staff exhibition space for most of its life. More recently it served as a contemporary art gallery with a programme of exhibitions beyond those of the school community. Jenny Brownrigg, the most recent custodian of the museum, reflected:

> It always struck me that the art school was a porous and collective enterprise. The Mackintosh museum in particular felt like Plato's cave, with the flickering shadows of all the forebears in past staff and students resonating in the space. Taking time to feel this weight of histories, and to understand that I was a caretaker in my role, felt an important act.[45]

The museum was an active and popular part of Glasgow's thriving art scene that was open free to the public seven days a week. Lively exhibit previews welcomed the wider public, adding another dimension to the Mack experience. It was the open studio of the collective spaces within the school, welcoming to all.

CREATIVE SPACE

Most of the internal area of the Mack was dedicated to the working spaces of the school, studios and offices, though arguably the whole building was designed for creative activity. The entresols of the main stairs, originally comprising dining rooms and staff lounges, were long ago turned over to first studio then office space (fig. 3.55). They had interesting 'Mackintosh' features, such as hearths and built-in cabinetry, but few visitors saw beyond the stained-glass inset of their closed doors. The warren of rooms in the east basement that was originally the janitor's flat was also made into offices. Above this on the ground floor was what Mackintosh originally called the Masters' Room, a staff room designed for the male teachers (fig. 3.56). In recent history, having been converted into an administrative office, this room was seldom seen even by staff and students, and did not form part of the tour, to the extent that it was never properly photographed. It was a plain room, apart from two prominent features. The first was the divided-arch window, reminiscent of those at Martyrs' School; from the exterior it was one of the lovelier windows in the diverse composition of the east façade. Inside it was a prominent feature for such a seemingly inconsequential room, flooding light into the diminutive space. The second surprise was a small screen at the rear of the room separating the area for coat storage and the WC entrance from the rest of the

FIG. 3.55 Staff office, 2003.

FIG. 3.56 TOP Masters' Room, photographed in 2015.

FIG. 3.57 RIGHT Screen in the Masters' Room, photographed in 2015.

FIG. 3.58 Writing desk for the Masters' Room, 1910. Ebonised cypress and leather, 117 × 211 × 75.7 cm. Lost in the 2014 fire.

FIG. 3.59 Sculpture studio, photograph by T. & R. Annan, c. 1910.

room (fig. 3.57). From straight on it looked like little more than four wooden slats supported by two upright posts, but from the side view they were topped with a tulip shape, mirrored in the blue leaded glass of the WC door. It was a much simpler expression of the kinds of open screen Mackintosh would use to partition spaces in, for example, the Ingram Street Tea Room. There is

FIG. 3.60 Ground-floor studio during a degree show, mid-20th century.

also evidence that this room was originally painted in the same 'artistic green' found elsewhere in the building, and there was bespoke furniture designed for both this room and the female staff room next door.[46] Mackintosh designed a large ebonised cypress desk with space for three occupants (figs 3.35, 3.58). It had subtly sloped surfaces for reading and was clever, but perhaps his clunkiest piece of furniture. It was shuffled around the Mack for many years, at times simply sitting in dark corners of hallways. Nonetheless it was one of the losses of the 2014 fire, as it was a unique original piece made for the school. It was overlooked, much like the simple but striking room for which it was designed.

Ironically the most vital spaces in the school were the ones about which the least might be said: the studios. Overall they were bright, austere workspaces that functioned as they should. Many had subtle 'Mackintosh' details such as screens and carved flourishes, particularly in doors and cabinetry. In recent times they were repeatedly painted white after degree shows to provide a 'blank canvas' for new students. A handful of studios, mostly built in phase II, are worth noting specifically for their architectural features (figs 3.61, 3.62). In the basement workshops we find

FIG. 3.61 West basement studio, photograph by
Harry Bedford Lemere, *c.* 1909.

FIG. 3.62 West basement studio with later mezzanine
by Keppie Henderson.

projected from the vertiginous back wall of the Mack
was a great place to take a break, looking south over the
city centre'.[47] It seemed like the one place you wouldn't
want to be in a fire, and yet its structure has twice
survived relatively unscathed.

By mid-century the studio spaces were rapidly
outgrown by the student body, requiring the school's
expansion into other buildings. Keppie Henderson &
Partners designed mezzanines for some of the studios in
1966–8 to increase capacity. In consequence many areas
were darker and more crowded than originally intended.
These were being removed in the restoration, though one
– Studio 45 on the north-west corner of the first floor –
was being preserved as part of the building's history.
Overall, the experience of working in the studios is
perhaps best described through the memories of artists
like Alison Watt, who studied there from 1983 to 1988:

> *From the moment you walked into the Mackintosh
> building, there was an irresistible urge to look up.
> What filled your vision was a glorious network
> of oak beams which framed the light and drew
> you up the main staircase to some of the most
> extraordinary painting studios anywhere. (On the
> way to them you would pass a row of booths, which
> I liked to hide in.) The studios were magnificent,*

artfully twisted terminations on the exposed steel
beams of the ceiling, which have even survived the
latest conflagration, though now somewhat battered
(fig. 3.63). Studio 11, the former life modelling studio,
had lovely skylights and wooden trusses (fig. 3.64). It
was designated to be reinstated 'back to 1910' during
the restoration project, complete with its original
lighting scheme as a historic showpiece. But perhaps
most memorable was Studio 58, atop the building,
with its Japanese-inspired post and lintels – made
from mammoth Douglas fir – that supported the
west gable end (*see* fig. 0.12). This is the room from
which the cantilevered conservatory was suspended;
Alastair Macdonald remembered 'the plant room which

FIG 3.63 The ends of the steel beams in Studio 11 had each been turned
to a unique flower-like shape. Photograph post-2018 fire.

often cited as the best in Europe, if not the world. Mackintosh's use of light was exceptional and with their immense north-facing windows they were shaped with beauty around practical considerations. A rare thing. To this day they are (I find it hard to use the past tense here) the finest studios I've ever worked in ... I still dream about the art school. I imagine myself walking through its corridors, touching its walls and entering my old studio. I can still smell it.[48]

Watt's emotional recollection is shared by many, but not all. For some students the studios were simply great spaces to work in. For others they were problematic,

FIG 3.64 Studio 11, photograph by Harry Bedford Lemere, *c.* 1909.

especially as changes in artistic approach required new technologies (there were never enough electrical sockets). Not all studios were for students though. The top of the building contained cosy professors' studios (fig. 3.66), well suited for many gatherings (reportedly whisky-fuelled in previous days), attendance at which felt like an exclusive rite of passage to some former students.[49] For most of their history these were used as workspaces for painting professors and as tutorial spaces to facilitate the atelier system that Newbery had set up a century before.

The director's office and studio that Mackintosh designed for Newbery was also a rather distinctive

FIG 3.65 Director's office, photograph by Harry Bedford Lemere, *c.* 1909.

FIG 3.66 Professor's studio, photograph by Harry Bedford Lemere, *c.* 1909.

space, full of characteristic details in the stained glass and bird-like motifs of the cabinetry (fig. 3.65). It seems closest to fulfilling the decorative programme envisioned in the first phase of the building. The suite of furniture Mackintosh designed was only partially carried out: a meeting table and chairs were made, but not a desk he designed for Newbery. There is little evidence of the original configuration of the private toilet, but it was 'refurbished' with a historically inspired but rather postmodern shower by the architect Edward Cullinan in 1990. It remained an object that generated mixed feelings, but after the 2014 fire it was decided it would stay as an interesting relic of the school's more recent history; however, it too was lost in 2018. A clever aspect of the director's suite was the private studio, accessible only via a narrow set of stairs inside the office. Mackintosh designed a hatch in the floor through which paintings could be raised from or lowered to the office vestibule. The last director to use the upper studio to paint was Dugald Cameron (1991–9),

and the office was somewhat controversially made redundant when a new directorate suite was built in the Reid building across the street. The former director Tom Inns (2013–18) was planning to reinstate the office in the original space as a renewed appreciation for it was cultivated after the 2014 fire.

In some ways though, the most stimulating creative space in the building was one that had lost its primary purpose over the last few decades: the library (figs 3.67, 3.68). Its function was to support creative practice in housing research materials for study and inspiration. It served this purpose for many years but by the 1960s, as the campus grew, there was a need for expansion. The reading collection first stretched into the first-floor architecture studio next door (many current staff who were former students remember it there), and then moved entirely into the 'new' Bourdon building when it was completed in 1979. The library continued to

FIG 3.67 The library.

FIG 3.69 Library lights, detail.

house the more historic special collections, and access remained fairly open until the Mack's fame grew as a tourist attraction in the 1980s. Library opening times increasingly became limited to hours between the tour schedule, then ultimately, due to staffing difficulties, doors remained locked most of the time. Although staff could still 'borrow the key' from janitors – providing visits were courteously arranged around tours – the library became in many people's eyes a 'museum' space. It was no longer openly accessible to students, though many staff arranged teaching sessions there. Still, it was no longer the space that was remembered by some of the school's most august alumni, as told to members of the restoration team at an afternoon tea hosted in December 2017 to collect their memories of the Mack. Former student Anne Ferguson recounted to me that the reason for her and her friends' frequent visits in 1946 was, 'The *Vogue* is in! We never went for the books.' Another former student, Barbara Dryburgh, had a more reverent view of the space from when she was a student assistant librarian in 1957. She remembers sitting in the 'booth' (the corner office), and although she wasn't allowed to check out books, she could check them in. She strongly recalls feeling that it was 'a real privilege to be in the space' and that it felt 'dark and cosy'.[50] More recent

FIG 3.68 OPPOSITE The library from the south-west corner.

librarians provide some of the most eloquent visions of the space. Former Librarian David Buri recalls:

To enter through the library's double doors was always to enter a different world, even from the rest of the Mack building. It had its own distinct mood and atmosphere – sombre, silent and studious, but never forbidding or 'dead'. The timbers creaked as the building warmed up or the sun came out, the light changed as the day progressed, and the sounds of the city faintly drifted up from Sauchiehall Street below. The library had its own smells too: I recall a musky, slightly sweet smell from the thousands of books, overlaid with the scent of the polish used by the cleaners on the floor and the brass fingerplates and numerals of the entrance doors.[51]

Librarian Duncan Chappell poetically described the experience of working there:

It did have a certain ambience to it, I mean, the times I remember working there really strongly are when we had a typical day of Glasgow weather, very dark, rainy, windy, and it's such an exposed

FIG 3.70 Mezzanine balustrade.

site there as well that I remember being in there when the gales were howling and the wind was rattling the panes in the windows and … it was very very dark, it was a dark space anyway, and even if you had all the lights on it was still quite sombre in atmosphere, which kind of worked I think in terms of the study space, the students seemed to quite like that.[52]

The library appeared a smallish square space, double height at the centre with tall timber posts supporting a mezzanine that wrapped the entire way round its perimeter. This second floor was originally only accessible via an exterior door on the west stair entresol (which itself had a balcony from which to peer down at the corridor and its niche seating), but an interior stair was added for convenience in 1945. At its centre a cluster of pendant lights fell at varying heights from a square grid above, casting a gentle warm light over the

space (fig. 3.69). The library had the confounding effect of feeling both open and airy and contained and intimate at the same time. Mackintosh's ability to give one experience entirely opposing sensations simultaneously was a mark of his creative power as a designer.

Probably since the library doors opened in late 1909, visitors have been trying to interpret its decorative programme. The atmospheric space had been repeatedly described as reminiscent of a clearing in a forest.[53] There is a consensus that the coloured notches on the mezzanine balustrades – red, green, blue, white – refer to the elements, and perhaps by association can be interpreted as Mackintosh referencing the seasons (fig. 3.70). But the features that most baffled visitors, staff and students were the beautiful carved wooden pendants that dropped like heraldic banners from the mezzanine. There were 20 of these decorative panels set into the balcony: three each to the north and south, five each to the east and west, with four smaller corner panels. Mackintosh resisted a symmetrical arrangement of four panels per side, adding interest to the otherwise square space. It is an asymmetry that echoes the arrangement of the north façade windows flanking the main entrance of the building. Each panel is pierced with a series of hand-carved naturalistic oval holes and slits arranged in even rows: four rows on the corner pieces and six

FIG 3.71 Carved pendant 'BACCAB'.

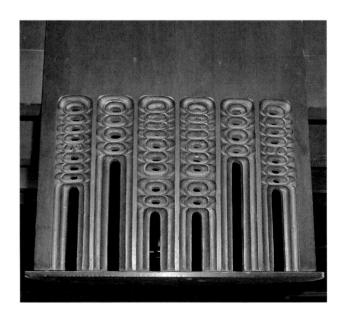

on the rest. The enigmatic patterns of these carvings – similar to those found on the table legs throughout the room – seemed to demand further investigation.

In fact after the 2014 fire there was a brief moment of worry regarding whether good enough documentation existed to recreate the unique design of each individual panel. A complete set of photos was ultimately discovered, but in that short period of uncertainty questions about the nature of their meaning were directed to me, as Mackintosh Research Fellow, in the event that their design needed to be reinvented: did the numbers of notches have any special significance; was there a code to be 'cracked'? My initial response was offered through the perspective of Symbolist design theory: there was not necessarily a specific meaning, although sometimes Mackintosh works did have identifiable literary or narrative references, such as the Rossetti-inspired theme of the Salon de Luxe at the Willow Tea Rooms (*see* fig. 5.4).[54] But other ornamentation was devised to engage the viewer, allowing them the pleasure of suggestion and contemplation to engage their physical and intellectual senses. Much of the belief that there was a secret meaning to these pendants was down to past interpretations. Many scholars have agreed with Buchanan's suggestion that the carvings in the pendants represent seedpods or possibly even corn cobs – plant life, in any case.[55] However visitors and users over the years have pondered different possibilities, wondering whether the patterns could be a system for cataloguing the books or even represent musical notes. Such discussions were always fun intellectual acrobatics, never with a need for a particularly firm answer.

Rather than wholly dismiss the notion that there was a hidden meaning, however, I gathered what images were available, including film footage of the library, and began sketching the design for myself. Quickly I realised there *was* a pattern in a literal, rather than symbolic, sense. The rows on each pendant comprise just three different designs (let's call them 'A', 'B' and 'C') of carved oval patterns pierced through to make a hole void at centre, arranged vertically over a pierced slit (figs 3.71, 3.72). 'A' comprises four ovals above a long slit. 'B' is an arrangement of four ovals, then one oval with two smaller adjacent holes, which is again over three more ovals and then a medium slit. 'C' is simply nine ovals over the shortest slit. These three patterns are then arranged in various combinations to make a design that evokes rows of seeds or perhaps even something resembling an abacus. The corner panels all contain the same four-pattern arrangement (fig. 3.73): CC BB, but the remaining sixteen are each unique variations, such as BACCAB or AABBCC.

FIG 3.72 Carved pendant 'AABBCC'.

FIG 3.73 Carved corner pendant.

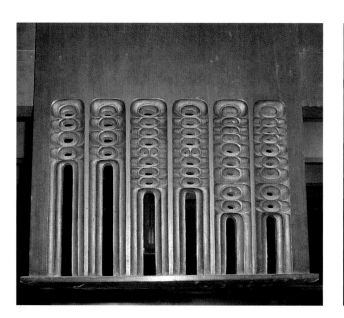

There is no obvious reason why these particular permutations were selected to be carved, but they do indicate something of the process: that Mackintosh must have made these three patterns, then arranged them in different variations to make the 20 designs to be carved. It is not known to what extent the joiners participated in this plan; perhaps he left them to it, but it seems unlikely. However, through this close study, I came to a realisation about the pendants, and the library itself: that for a century these designs, and the space in its entirety, enlivened the mental faculties of its visitors. Contemplating the scheme, they have mused on what Mackintosh meant with his decorative programme, and in so doing they were setting their minds to a particular kind of thinking, a querying mode of action perfectly suited to the key activity of the space they were in: a library. The interior scheme sets the tone for its use, inviting us to question, to search, to think critically and creatively and seek knowledge and understanding. The material composition works in concert to create these intangible experiences. Did Mackintosh subtly embed similar suggestions elsewhere in the building?

THE GESAMTKUNSTWERK

While some want to see in the Mack a full Symbolic narrative, others feel that it is merely a functional and at times quixotic building. Perhaps the truth lies in the murky middle: in the fabric of his building Mackintosh has provided cues for its use. In the smallest spaces we focus and go about the business of running the school; in the studios we are given the space and light to settle into creative practice; in the Hen Run and loggia we are inspired by the structure to practise the foundational principles of line drawing; in the corridor nooks we are encouraged to pause, rest, gather, discuss; and in the library we contemplate, study and reflect. Whether one believes the building is a symbol of life or nature, or just a lovely and sometimes idiosyncratic edifice, Mackintosh's message is the same throughout: create. Let Glasgow flourish.

In art and architectural writing we often discuss the 'overall effect' of a work. But Mackintosh, like so many great architect-designers, was very much interested in the 'overall *affect*'. How does the combination of materials, the symphony of materiality, come together to work on our senses, to inform us on spatial use and to create environmental poetry? All of these come together to produce a *Gesamtkunstwerk*, a 'total work of art'. Therefore rebuilding just part of the Mack would never have worked. Even built in two phases, the building fitted as a whole, as Davidson observed:

> *the genius of it is … when asked to complete the second half a decade later and fit so much more into it – he was able to extend (mainly upwards) without either destroying the overall concept design or undermining the original design for the first phase – quite simply it just looked as if it had been designed that way from the start … I cannot think of another architectural masterpiece that was so amended mid-stream and still hangs together as one coherent design!*[56]

Over time the Mack became a palimpsest of physical accretions and the spectres of its inhabitants. It told us a story, if we took the time to listen. This is powerfully expressed by Chappell:

> *Buildings always talk to you! They have to talk to you … I mean it is an extraordinary thing about buildings, isn't it? And … I think the reason historic buildings are fundamentally interesting is that they are constructs of human activity and then they are constructed for us to occupy and so the older a building gets, the more that timeline of occupation becomes kind of enticing to human beings.*

Those traces went up in smoke, literally, but the Mack has never stopped speaking to us – even now, in its most dramatic and tragic chapter.

ASHES TO ASHES

CHAPTER 4

ASHES TO ASHES

*I would like to see the Mack be reinvested with the
status, the regard and the brilliance it deserves.
And to do that the school has to build upon what
has survived. Not just the physical ruins but also
metaphysically through its still intact identity
and ambition – to create a symbol of its resurgence.*

**ELIZABETH DAVIDSON, FORMER SENIOR PROJECT
MANAGER, MACKINTOSH RESTORATION**[1]

On 23 May 2014 the Mack caught fire (fig. 4.1). The
international reaction was overwhelmingly one of
heartbreak and sympathy. This was very different to the
predominant outrage on 15 June 2018 when, just as a
full restoration was nearing completion, the building
was consumed by a second fire. What happened to the
Mack in the intervening years? What was learned, and
is there yet hope that this significant monument can
live again? The recovery and restoration of the Mack
is worthy of its own text, and no doubt one will be
forthcoming in some future when the building is rebuilt,
in whatever form that takes. An all too brief overview
of this extraordinary, and ultimately tragic, story is
presented here in the meantime.

THE MACK AS 'FIREPROOF' BUILDING

In 1892 revisions in Scottish building legislation
included increased attention to fire safety, notably

the regulation that 'the construction of external
and party walls, supporting structure, and internal
partitions around passages and stairs was required to
be of incombustible materials, such as stone or brick'.[2]
Mackintosh had experience of planning for fireproofing
through consideration of materials designed to stop or
slow fire spread, as well as including fire suppression
systems in his designs when requested. As noted in
Chapter 1, Mackintosh's iconic 'Lighthouse' tower at
the Glasgow Herald building (*see* figs 1.21, 1.22) was
in fact a tank to feed the 'roof-drenchers', 'perforated,
galvanised iron tubes running along the roof ridges
and window tops, capable of supplying "a flowing
shield of water" against flying sparks'.[3] The impetus for
these may have been several notorious fires in nearby
Buchanan Street, which had placed the Herald premises
in jeopardy in the preceding years, and the fact that
newspaper offices were filled with oily machines, paper
and chain-smoking journalists. Such suppression systems
were slowly being installed in commercial and industrial
premises but not yet educational or cultural institutions,
reflecting the perceived level of risk. The Mack did
have fire risks in the way of hearths in the Mackintosh
Room, professors' studios and offices, including that
of the director, but these were common at the time
for the important functions of providing warmth and
keeping damp out of the building. The reality is that such
systems were not required by law – and still aren't in
many buildings even today.[4] The Mack was by no means
unusual for not having a suppression system; fireproofing
was usually implemented through detection systems,
compartmentalisation and exit strategies to provide
protection for property and human life.

PREVIOUS PAGE (FIG. 4.1) The May 2014 fire.

FIG. 4.2 Volunteer conservators inspect textiles for damage,
May 2014. Conservation efforts were supported by experts from
Historic Environment Scotland, Glasgow Museums and the
University of Glasgow.

Fire risk at the Glasgow School of Art was originally mitigated through building standards and compartmentalisation strategies. In 1896 concerns were raised by municipal inspectors: 'in consideration of the system of flooring being adopted in the corridor the Master of Works had foregone his objection made previous to the meeting of the Dean of Guild Court to the corridors not being fireproof.'[5] In phase II insurers were concerned and requested alterations such as not using timber-framed windows, especially in the areas near Hengler's Circus (later the ABC Theatre). Fire regulations had strengthened in the city and a strategy was taken to use fireproof materials as necessary, including expanded metal lath and fire-resistant render on structural steel elements.[6]

And yet many small fires erupted in the Mack throughout its history. In general, the building and its internal system of watchfulness worked, largely because there was always someone on the premises, including a live-in janitor for many years. But even in its earliest days the timber-heavy Mack was perceived as high-risk, as recent research by Glasgow Museums curator Alison Brown has revealed. While preparing a 2018 Charles Rennie Mackintosh exhibit, Brown discovered a loan agreement in the V&A archives from 1913 for teaching objects (part of the South Kensington system Circulation Collections programme). An inspector visited the school and remarked on the fire risk, noting the amount of wood, the heating system and concluding: 'I am however of opinion that if a fire once started the premises would rapidly be gutted.' Consequently, the insurance rate was doubled.[7]

Real concern began growing in the mid-twentieth century as an awareness of the building's age – and its significance – caused increasing risk to become apparent. In 1964 a small fire began in a first-floor studio, caused by a 'movable black heater' that no longer met regulations.[8] This prompted a thorough inspection by the fire service. In assessing the Mack, the report notes that the amount of timber, which had dried out for more than half a century by then, made the fire load of the building 'very high', and the age created a great risk 'that fire could very rapidly spread throughout the entire building'. The fire inspector, J. Swanson, also expressed

deep concern for 'housekeeping', as the accumulation of materials increased the fire load. For example: 'In the wardrobe, east stairs, it was noted that there are old mattresses, and it is suggested that if these have served their purpose they should be disposed of.' Other hazards noted were recent partitions with no fire resistance, hazards in the shop, unused gas cylinders and stored cellulose paint that was 'subject to licensing conditions under the Petroleum (Consolidation) Act of 1928'. A key recommendation was simply that 'It is necessary that all holes in ceilings and walls through which fire may spread easily should be made good'.

This report was carried out during the directorship of Harry Jefferson Barnes (1964–80). After Swanson's report, Barnes acted quickly to secure £6,207 from the Scottish Education Department to instal a smoke detection system in August 1964. But the recommendation of a sprinkler system came with a hefty price tag of £20,000–22,000 for installation, not including 'building work required which will be extensive in a building of this nature'. This work was not carried out, nor was anything done about the 'holes in ceilings and walls' – the now infamous voids – that Firemaster Swanson cautioned should be seen to. It is unfortunate that the funds were not located to instal a sprinkler during the fireproofing works of 1964–6, which included the installation of fire doors designed by Keppie Henderson and also the relocation of various Mackintosh doors throughout the building.[9] But as already noted, sprinklers are not legally required even now and fireproofing is still focused on prevention and detection rather than suppression, even in A-listed buildings.

Over the years other worries regarding fire risk in the Mack were noted. Most of these appeared in the journal of the Charles Rennie Mackintosh Society, including building updates in the 1970s and 80s with references to the ducts and voids. But fire-prevention solutions were not fully addressed again until the mid-2000s, under the directorship of Seona Reid (1999–2013). The GSA commissioned two studies from the fire engineering consultancy Buro Happold FEDRA, a Fire Protection Strategy Options Study in 2006 and a Property Protection Feasibility Study in 2008. At the outset the 2006 report makes clear: 'Due to the historic nature and value of the property and many of its contents, a fire poses a great threat.'[10] It outlines the positive prevention strategies already in place: automatic fire detection in 'certain locations', CCTV in 'certain areas', building occupation on a 24/7 basis and provision of security staff. It notes that these had prevented two previous fires that were detected quickly and extinguished before taking hold. The list of cons, however, is much lengthier. It discusses the structural problems, fire load and detection issues already highlighted, and includes new issues such as the presence of ignition sources, that the detection system was not 'full coverage' and that there was no formalised fire safety management plan or risk-assessment procedure set in place. Finally it outlines a straightforward strategy of improvement to take the building from high to low risk. This included policies for controlling combustible materials and firefighting and awareness training for staff.[11] The 2008 report, commissioned in service to the £8.7 million Mackintosh Conservation and Access Project supported by the Heritage Lottery Fund and Historic Scotland, is much more detailed in terms of offering strategies to take forward. While the building was always compliant with statutory regulations, as a result of this report it was finally decided that a mist suppression system was feasible.[12]

So why was this not carried out before 2014? Our built heritage is very complicated and expensive to maintain. Historic buildings are not subject to the same regulations as new builds, and just a few site visits – including to Mackintosh properties such as Queen's Cross Church, the headquarters of the Charles Rennie Mackintosh Society – will reveal that very few have any form of fire suppression system, although they will have robust fire prevention controls and detection systems. Historic buildings are full of voids and accretions, which only add to the fire load of ageing structures. The funding GSA received in 2008 was from a scheme designed to provide improved access for tourism and for the building and its collections as a heritage site. The school cleverly used this programme to complete much-needed restoration works, mainly around the conservation of interiors such as the library and main staircase; to update some of the collections storage; for a new visitor centre, furniture gallery and gift shop;

and for new (replacement) fire suppression doors on the ground, first and second floors. A new fire suppression system could not be included because the public funds received by the project would not allow for it; Historic Scotland (now Historic Environment Scotland) specifically stated that 'they were only empowered to provide grant aid for repairs to listed buildings, not improvements'.[13] In July 2009 GSA and Page\Park, who had been appointed as lead architects on these works, jointly advocated directly to Historic Scotland and the Scottish Government for a change in policy to include fire suppression systems within their Building Repair Grant scheme, writing:

> In view of all of that research and technical awareness, it does seem inconsistent that fire suppression systems addressing what is the major risk to some of our most important buildings and collections cannot be grant-aided, even though this can be achieved for heating systems.[14]

The paper suggested that one way forward might be for the Mackintosh building to be considered as a model or case study, with policy consideration being the underlying objective in terms of where Historic Scotland's limited resources could best be applied in relation to our national built and cultural heritage. The Glasgow School of Art and its professional advisers were more than willing to collaborate on such a project on the basis that this was a matter of national importance and not just specific to the Mackintosh building.

No changes in policy were forthcoming, and it was to take another five years to get the £520,000 funding, design and statutory consents for this project in place. In 2013–14 a continuous phase of work began on the installation of a more advanced mist suppression system throughout the building. The fact that this was never completed was the worst luck imaginable.

THE 2014 FIRE

After the expansion of the campus to new buildings in the 1960s and 70s, the Mack was largely occupied by the School of Fine Art (fig. 4.3). As artistic practice changed in the twentieth century, the building seemed to lend

FIG. 4.3 Fine Art Painting and Printmaking Studio, west wing, 2006. Photographed from balcony level, the window shows the Newbery Tower building across Renfrew Street before it was demolished to build the Reid.

itself naturally to the study and practice of what were increasingly regarded as more traditional media, namely painting and printmaking. But during the annual degree show of the graduating class, the Mack became a magnificent multi-disciplinary art gallery in which to exhibit painting, printmaking, sculpture, environmental art and photography together. Displays were never divided by medium: one might find clothing, textiles, video, performance and participatory installations, plus myriad other creative experiences that reflected the inter-disciplinary approaches of late twentieth- and early twenty-first-century artistic practice.

In May 2014 just such an artwork was being installed in Studio 19 in the north-east basement by a final-year student. Students were to complete risk assessments for their projects, including disclosures and permissions for the use of flammable materials, which would then be approved by their department and sent to GSA Estates for any further action or support.[15] The student proposal form at the time of the fire included a very general list of items to seek advice on, including fumes, gas and electricity.[16] Rachael Purse, who wrote

her PhD thesis on best practices in the restoration of heritage buildings damaged by fire, notes:

The GSA did not appear to have a list that explicitly banned any materials or substances in 2014 … The onus [to discern] if these items are involved in their work is on the student themselves, they must seek 'advice' from their 'School/Department'. This approach, hoping that students will act sensibly and responsibly, places the crucial decisions to be made about health and safety into the hands of individuals who have not been trained to make them.[17]

In this case the exhibit was to be a video projection inside a room made from temporary MDF walls, sprayed all over with expanding foam that is typically used for insulation and expelled by a propellant of three highly flammable gases: propane, isobutene and dimethyl ether.[18] The walls themselves were made outside the Mack but assembled in the studio using more of this foam to fill the gaps between the wall panels. The video projector, which was loaned to the student by GSA and so would have been PAT-tested as being in good working order, had been left on for two to three hours while the foam was expelled. According to the Scottish Fire and Rescue Service (SFRS) report, the likely cause of the fire was the ignition of these gases by a spark from within the projector, drawn into the machine through its fan.[19] This in turn set alight all the highly flammable panels, which burned quickly and fiercely.

At 12.27 pm, the SFRS received an automated alert from the school's smoke detection system; three appliances were on site by 12.31 pm, just a minute after they received the first public call about the fire. On site the evacuation was already underway, protocols having been followed by staff who, having expelled fire extinguishers unsuccessfully, recognised the severity of the situation. Firefighters entered the building from the east and quickly extinguished the original source of the fire by 12.45 pm. However, heavy black smoke indicated that the fire had spread, and a team made their way through increasingly dim conditions up the east stair to the top of the building, where a well-developed fire could be seen through studio doors.

What might have been an isolated incident turned into a disaster through ill-fated circumstances. First, work on the new mist suppression system that was being fitted in the building had been put on hold in its final stages due to the discovery of asbestos in the entrance hallway of the school. In line with strict government health and safety regulations, work could not be completed until the asbestos was professionally removed, which would have to be done in a closed school immediately after the degree show. So while the school had a warning system, it still had no working fire suppression system.

Second, there was an unsealed ventilation duct right next to the area where the highly flammable exhibit was installed. Ironically this had been left open because it was where part of the mist suppression system was to be routed. The duct opened onto a ventilation shaft, one

of the huge vertical voids throughout the building that were no longer used for the original warm-air heating system Mackintosh had designed. These shafts had been useful for routing cabling and pipes over the years. As Elizabeth Davidson observed:

It is important to note that the voids, service ducts are not in themselves a fire hazard. The vast majority of buildings built during the Victorian and Edwardian times incorporated routes through their fabric for the routing of services – water, gas and later electricity. In the case of the Mackintosh Building the ducts were part of its designed structure – taking these services and also heated, dehumidified air conditioning around the building. The Mack had at least 12 fireplaces and chimney flues in use for much of its history and smoking was allowed well into the last century – so the presence of ducts in this and thousands of other still extant buildings is not in itself a cause of fire – but they can of course add to the spread of fire if unprotected/stopped.[20]

The open shaft in Studio 19 acted as a chimney, encouraging the fire to spread beyond the ceiling of the basement, jumping across to other studios in the east and burning up through to the top floor, across the Hen Run to Studio 58, then down through the book store and into the library, which was a tinderbox. Timber, books and furniture were just kindling. The book store was a rather lovely storage room 'hung' into place with large industrial iron brackets (fig. 4.6). In 1981 this space was turned into the furniture gallery for tours and remained so until the 2008 Conservation & Access Project. Unfortunately, when the new gallery was built on the east end ground floor, this room continued to be used as storage for the furniture and paintings collection. It remains unclear why this decision was made when so much effort had been put into creating a new and appropriate space for the rest of the collection (textiles, design objects, works on paper, etc.) and the archives in the sub-basement.[21] This new dedicated archival space not only functioned but survived virtually unscathed through both the 2014 fire and the

FIG. 4.4 The Hen Run, May 2014.

FIG. 4.5 Studio 58.

far worse one in 2018. The items kept in the book store all perished in the 2014 fire: 139 pieces of furniture, nearly all by Mackintosh and including some unique items (fig. 4.8), and 92 paintings by many former GSA students and staff, including the likes of Joan Eardley and even Francis Newbery.[22] This was a huge loss, about which – according to some critics including Roger Billcliffe – too little concern has been expressed by the school in the ensuing years, with no effort to replace any of the lost collection despite an insurance pay-out.[23]

By 1.56 pm the building was 30 per cent alight, and a decision was made by Fire Chief A.C.O. Goodhew that to save this beloved building the SFRS would fight the fire from inside as well as out, forming a defensive barrier along the central stair to keep the flames contained to the west. Just over an hour later they were able to make a break in the roof as well and fight the fire downwards. The building was becoming flooded and there was growing concern for the collection in the sub-basement. The archives salvage plan was enacted and by 3.06 pm light pumps were brought in to clear water while teams began rescuing items from the lower floors. This went on through the night. The fire was not declared extinguished until 10.20 am the following morning, but appliances remained on site until 30 May to put out any small new fires that might have started in lingering hot spots. They left the building to the sound of bagpipes and cheers from hundreds of students and staff who gathered in thanks to see them off.

Although the scale of the destruction was massive and many precious items were lost, the building was rescued by the bravery of the fire service. Because the staff and students had been evacuated, the SFRS were only mandated to fight the fire from the outside. But they made the choice to fight from within as well, increasing the risks to their own safety to save the building that for so many is at the heart of Glasgow. In doing so, they helped make the school's decision to rebuild a very easy one.

How this decision was made, though, was a matter of some criticism. When interviewed on the street on the day of the fire, the former Chair of Governors

FIG. 4.6 The 'book store', used as a furniture gallery from 1981 until the purpose-built gallery was created in 2008. The iron hanger/bracket is visible in the centre.

FIG. 4.7 The library, June 2014.

Muriel Gray made a bold statement: 'We will rebuild, and we will rebuild well.'[24] And that seemed to set the tone; it was barely questioned whether this was the correct way forward. Some critics found this rash: how could such a decision be made without a full consultation? For many the loss was irreplaceable; the Mack was a masterpiece destroyed. Arguments against reconstruction are entrenched in ideals around materiality (see pp. 20–22). The SPAB (Society for the Protection of Ancient Buildings) manifesto tells us 'Fabric is precious', a notion at least partly rooted in the phenomenology of memory and our interaction with

FIG. 4.8 Charles Rennie Mackintosh, Square table for Hous'hill, 1904. Oak, varnished, 75.7 × 66 × 64.6 mm. Lost in the 2014 fire.

the physical. Opinions that the Mack will never again be what it was are not without validity, and are perhaps more relevant now that the entirety of the interior is lost. Yet there is still the design. Gray's declaration that the Mack would be rebuilt was perhaps premature, but it had a galvanising effect on staff and students at a time when hope was needed. And in the end she was right: it could be done and done well.

RECOVERY 2014–15

The staff of the GSA rallied on the Monday after the fire to begin recovery efforts. Along with conservation colleagues from HES and the University of Glasgow, among others, people pulled together to begin to decant the building, especially the collections, much of which survived (fig. 4.9). Everything was removed, and a priority was placed on retrieving the archives and collection that survived and whatever student artwork could be salvaged. This material was decanted to nearby buildings: the vacant McLellan Gallery – home of the school when Mackintosh was a student – was 'borrowed' from the city, while the newly opened Reid across the way from the Mack was ideal for unrolling wet textiles in its vast, nearly empty spaces (fig. 4.2). For the staff it was all hands on deck, and the positive effect of being able to participate in the post-fire recovery was perhaps only truly appreciated in 2018 when we, along with all of Garnethill, were essentially barred from the site for months due to dangerous conditions.

As much as there was heartbreak about the Mack, there was also great concern about the students whose degree show was affected, and especially those who lost their work inside the building. This loss was deepened by the fact that these students would miss the opportunity provided by the degree show to launch professional careers. The Phoenix Bursary programme was set up to provide them with funded and sponsored residencies, both locally and internationally, to rebuild their practice. This was backed by a £750,000 grant from the Scottish Government and was in the end a hugely successful enterprise: it would be wonderful if such opportunities could be provided without requiring a disaster. Their exhibition was held in the Reid building in July 2015 to huge acclaim.[25]

FIG. 4.9 Surviving plaster casts are wrapped and moved to safety in the east studios after the 2014 fire. Unfortunately, most of these perished in the 2018 fire.

FIG. 4.10 Remains of the periodicals table recovered from library debris.

Meanwhile the GSA released a statement of intent about the building:

> *our ambition is to achieve an exemplary restoration of the Mackintosh Building, using meticulous and detailed conservation, traditional craftsmanship and construction skills combined with technology, design innovation and robust functionality ... Above all our commitment to the restoration must focus on the very highest standards of safety for the GSA's community while operating as a working art school, visitor attraction and jewel in Glasgow's architectural heritage ... [Former] Director Tom Inns neatly summarised our intent thus: 'What the eye sees will be Mackintosh. What Mackintosh sees will be the 21st century.*[26]

This was a lovely sentiment, and one most of the community were happy to get behind. However, it is also indicative of an approach that has ultimately led to some of the school's biggest troubles in the press: communication through statements that to some are carefully constructed and polished messages that keep GSA 'on brand'. This may not be a fair assessment of the intention or sincerity of these media releases, but for many they smacked of distance and a lack of engagement with stakeholders and the wider community. The positive and optimistic Tom Inns had succeeded Reid as director mere months before the new School of Design building

(named for Reid) had opened. He oversaw a 'normal' campus for about six months before the first fire, then he was forced to be at the helm of what was essentially a building project for the rest of his tenure, until late 2018.[27]

Inside the building initial work was delayed by all the administrative complications to be expected in such a circumstance, such as the fire investigation and insurance reconciliations. This process meant that it took several months to get a roof over the west wing, and rain fell periodically inside the building. Clearance was done as far as possible in areas that had either suffered minimal damage or had been severely damaged and which had no items of significance to look for: the Hen Run, for example, was severely destroyed but had no 'Mackintosh' lighting or fixtures to speak of. The library, of course, was a very different case and it was decided that a methodical excavation was needed to recover as much material as possible from the metre-deep debris that had collapsed onto the floor (fig. 4.7). Paul Clarke, Professor of Architectural Design at the University of Ulster, described it poetically:

> *Voids agape in stonework, where once fine metal grids held shimmering pockets of sky; dark wooden floors misted grey with a moon dust of fallen plaster; once elegant columns scorched into an elephant skin of charcoal and standing like sentinels outwith gravity, shadows of Callinish. At the centre of this landscape of wreckage, the*

FIG. 4.11 Fragments of library lights.

burnt remains of the library are piled high, like a bonfire that has fallen from the sky.[28]

Kirkdale Archaeology in partnership with AOC Conservation were enlisted to perform a systematic excavation and recording of the debris and an archaeological standing building record of the library site.[29] This was performed just as for any excavation, and the process uncovered a lot of valuable information about how the fire affected the room, as well as recovering items needed for the restoration to study – if not use – such as stone fragments, timber (roof structures and joinery were particularly useful) and even larger items of Mackintosh furniture, like the remains of the periodicals table (fig. 4.10), which is still in the collection for study. The process proved fascinating and fruitful in salvaging not only a small number of surviving books but all kinds of fragments of items that would be useful for the restoration project, very specifically over six hundred fragments of brass that were once part of the famous lights, from all over the room (fig. 4.11). As we will see, this was invaluable for the reconstruction. As the extent of the loss became known, offers of book donations began flooding in and GSA librarians Duncan Chappell and David Buri began a project to rebuild the library special collections that had been lost.

During this period, a complete 3D laser scan of the building was made by a joint collaborative team from the GSA School of Simulation and Visualisation (now the School of Innovation + Technology) and HES. The team used photogrammetry to make 360-degree scans (figs 4.12,

FIG. 4.12 3D scan of Mack exterior, 2014. Terrestrial laser scanning, Al Rawlinson and Lyn Wilson.

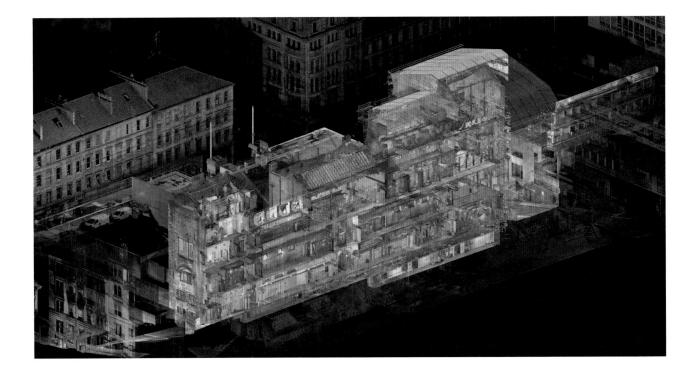

4.13) and simultaneously high-resolution photographs to record the building in its entirety, including services and voids. Other data such as thermal and moisture readings can be added to inform building condition and conservation approach.[30] HES's Head of Digital Innovation and Learning Alastair Rawlinson observed:

> *By using this cutting-edge technology, the architectural beauty of the Mackintosh is seen in ways never before possible. It allows new visual perspectives to be gained, while the 3D data is providing tangible, practical benefits for the restoration process.*[31]

It is unfortunate that a complete scan of the Mack was not made before the 2014 fire; an external one was completed, however, and it was vital in proving that the west gable was not in danger of collapse (fig. 4.14). It was used to persuade Glasgow City Council's Building Control department that outward movement was in fact minimal. But both the west and east gables of Studio 58 were still dismantled for repair, the stone from which was numbered and stored offsite by HES and largely reinstated in the reconstruction. These scans were valuable in that they almost immediately

FIG. 4.13 3D scan of Mack interior elevation, 2014. Terrestrial laser scanning, Al Rawlinson and Adam Frost.

FIG. 4.14 3D scan of Mack interior section, 2014. Terrestrial laser scanning, Al Rawlinson and Adam Frost.

FIG. 4.15 Film still from *A Beautiful Living Thing [Part 2]: Improvisation #1*, 2016. Conceived and directed by Ross Birrell, filmed in collaboration with Hugh Watt and co-produced by Jo Crotch. In this still, harpist Catriona McKay of the Glasgow Improvisers Orchestra is pictured in a studio surrounded by recovered burnt fragments of the Mack library.

informed us on the condition of the building, a process that continued to be used in the 2018 salvage operation.

Throughout this period, and the whole of the restoration project, the Mack continued to be a site of creative activity and response.[32] After ensuring the building was safe through minimal stabilising works and clearance of debris, limited access was granted for artistic activity and several GSA staff took up the opportunity. The GSA choir recorded 'Light Through Tall Windows' in the library, a choral work composed by former architecture student and choir director Jamie Sansbury and choir member Muriel Gray. Artist Ross Birrell created a series of films entitled *A Beautiful Living Thing*, inspired by Mackintosh's 'Seemliness' lecture. The atmospheric and moving films included performances by musicians and dancers filmed inside the Mack in the aftermath of the 2014 fire (fig. 4.15). The films were co-produced by Joanna Crotch of the Mackintosh School of Architecture, who also began a 'Mack Memories' project, collecting people's reactions and reminiscences from the building.[33]

Similar kinds of activities continued throughout the project; some were driven by the students themselves

and others even raised funds for the restoration, such as 2017's 'Ash to Art' project in which 26 internationally renowned artists were invited to make work from a piece of burned wood – now charcoal – from the library.[34] According to the participating artist Chantal Joffe: 'Receiving the box was quite upsetting, like receiving the ashes of a dead friend. The charcoal was softer than I'm used to, it was hard to get an edge. As I drew, it released the smell of the fire.'[35] Creative engagement also extended to educational opportunities, between site visits for staff, students, heritage professionals and other specialist groups for whom seeing the Mack as a 'work in progress' had great value. A handful of PhDs have arisen from this event too, including two creative practice-based projects by Dawn Worsley (2019) and Carolyn Alexander (2021), which investigated the material remains of the building, and Rachael Purse's study (2020) examining how we might better care for built heritage.[36] I taught an undergraduate course myself, 'Rediscovering Mackintosh', on the restoration project from 2016 to 2021.[37] Until 2018 these classes were held inside the building, in the site office that was the converted shop and furniture gallery inside the east entrance, allowing a close study of the project. They were the last classes ever to have taken place inside the original building. Traditional skills apprenticeships took place within the project too, with young women and men learning stonemasonry, plastering, joinery and other valuable crafts needed to maintain our built heritage. These were the many ways in which the Mack was still very much a 'beautiful living thing' – offering creative lessons and artistic inspiration for the GSA community and beyond.

THE FIRST MACK RESTORATION PROJECT (MRP1)

Meanwhile appointments were made for the team that would see the project to fruition, with respected heritage and building experts Elizabeth Davidson and Sarah MacKinnon appointed as Project Managers for GSA.[38] An extensive brief, written by Davidson, was developed for the design team, with the following key principles to inform the restoration methodology:

1. *Flexibility and Adaptability – the ability of the building design to embrace future change and adopt new ways of working without major remodelling.*
2. *Future Proofing – the ability of the building design to take account of technological and operational developments.*
3. *Quality – the restoration, repairs, reconstruction and new design interventions will ALL require to be of an exemplary standard of design, material and fabrication excellence.*
4. *Accessibility – the Building should be as open as possible for its users but consider means by which the enhanced security and safety of its occupants are unobtrusively integrated to the works.*
5. *Connectivity – the disruption of the fire introduces the opportunity to integrate services and new technologies sensitively into the design of the internal spaces.*
6. *Innovation – the School has a global reputation for invention and unconventionality – these should [be] reflected if possible in the Project particularly in the use of or exploration of new technology and product design.*
7. *Sustainability – both the design process, the site construction works and the final product should champion sustainable means of procurement,*

delivery, operational experience and the life cycle maintenance of the Building.
8. *Accountability – every member of the team – both consultants and client bodies are responsible for acting with the highest standards of integrity, transparency and ethical considerations.*[39]

By April 2015 a competition was launched for the architects, won by Page\Park. David Page and Brian Park knew the building well, having worked on the Hen Run conservation in 1994 and then the 2008 Conservation & Access Project, as well as the successful and sensitive transformation of the Glasgow Herald building into the Lighthouse Centre for Design in 1999. Park was also one of two key architects who conducted a buildings survey project for the Charles Rennie Mackintosh Society, so their expert credentials in this field are well established. By mid-2015 the rest of the design team was assembled, including Gardiner & Theobald Management Services, electrical and mechanical engineers Harley Haddow and civil and structural engineers David Narro Associates. Kier Construction (Scotland) was appointed to carry out the reconstruction in mid-2016, at which time they took over possession of the site as per Scottish Standard Building Contract law. Work towards rebuilding could properly commence.

The reconstruction effort was an enormous research project. Luckily GSA holds a vast archive, arguably one of the largest of its kind. Early administrators seemingly never disposed of any papers, and the archives contain not just meeting minutes, but invoices, bills, photographs and a host of other documents that provided detailed information about how the school was built. This research was used in concert with a forensic study of the building itself, including scientific analysis of materials taken from the debris (destructive testing of wood, for example), paint surfaces, metalwork, glazing, lighting, render, plaster and stone. The 3D laser scan was also invaluable, providing the basis for the Building Information Model (BIM) that would house the diversity of data in a multi-layered plan accessible across the design and construction teams. Although BIM technologies have been developed since the 1970s, it is only in the last decade that they have been applied to heritage management. The Mack restoration project was one of the first to utilise BIM in a hybrid way, as a tool for conservation planning and 'new build' purposes. It might have been a heritage project, but it was also state of the art.

Page\Park's methodology for reconstruction was presented as an 'Atlas', which reflected the philosophical approach of treating the building in an almost topographic way: the 'Building as a Whole', 'Room by Room' and 'Piece by Piece'. This method was clever in that it reflected both an understanding of the way in which Mackintosh approached his own work, especially in thinking about the building as a *Gesamtkunstwerk*, but also, as the Atlas states, due to the range of damage and repair: '[t]here is no single charter, principle, or philosophy which is applicable to every aspect of the Mackintosh Building.'[40] The Atlas laid out ten principles that encompassed the Page\Park methodology:

1. *Art School – first and foremost, the Mackintosh Building is an Art School for all – the user and visitor should experience this as the primary function.*

2. *Room and Space – a return to the original two typologies of space – the formal room (for example, studio) and the fluid space (for example, Loggia).*

3. *Use – these rooms and spaces facilitating uses, rather than uses resulting in the need for significant change.*

4. *Access – the Mackintosh Building 'belongs' to all.*

5. *Nurture – pioneering the collaborative learning environment was the building's role on completion and should continue.*

6. *Catalyst – Mackintosh and his legacy as a creative tool in education.*

7. *Light – understanding how light is used in the building.*

8. *Enhancing the Building Performance – working with the building to optimise and improve its long term sustainability.*

9. *Imperceptibility – reinstating the original intention of the architecture, its aesthetic and its functionality.*

10. *Functionality through Furniture – in the spirit of Mackintosh and in lieu of building fabric alteration and addition.*[41]

The principle of 'access' expressed by Page\Park was particularly important as prior to the fire, key areas of the Mack such as the library were seen by many to have become a museum rather than a school. It was intended that the renewed Mack could be enjoyed more fully by all, especially students. In service of this a decision was made that the building was to be used by first-year students from across the school, to ensure that every undergraduate had an experience of the building at the start of their studies.

The Page\Park division of spatial typologies is like those presented in the previous chapter, although this book attempts to distinguish the 'formal' spaces meant for social/collective activity from those designed for work/creative practice. But we have seen how the beauty of the Mack is that the building as a whole has a fluidity to it, with certain spaces not easily defined by form or function. A reconsideration of studio arrangements was made by looking carefully at planned use requirements. All incoming students would launch their studies inside a collaborative environment with Mackintosh's (but really Newbery's) building as a guiding principle for practice. This links directly with the 'nurture' and 'catalyst' principles in the Atlas, which describes the 'fertile environment for creative activity' that must be preserved:

> *Mackintosh brilliantly exploited the creative potential of the room and the extrusion of space in proportion, decoration and construction such that he embraced the potential of all things, and for any young or older person inhabiting the space, empowered their thinking rather than conditioned it.*[42]

The final four principles are practical ones for any building but show particular attention to these as special qualities for the Mack. We have examined the importance of light and its clever manipulation and issues around building performance – certainly an area for improvement in any older structure. 'Imperceptibility', though, is a more complex principle and one that ultimately became a possible point of criticism. On the surface it seems like good conservation practice: they were keen that this would look like the Mackintosh building, not a Page\Park one.

But there were certain areas of the building that really needed a fresh eye and some rethinking in terms of their functionality. These were not the 'key' rooms but areas like entresols, offices and even toilets. Perhaps there were opportunities for bolder solutions, which the Page\Park team approached more tentatively, even unimaginatively at times, for example offering 'catalogue' proposals for the toilets. However, they offered imaginative plans for the entresol outside the old book store above the library. Rather than returning it to inadequate furniture and painting storage, this would become a special collections research and study room. It was to have a more contemporary interpretation of the 'nooks' below to offer further study space, and even a break area for visiting researchers to have a snack or use the phone.

The way in which all these ideas were ultimately carried out has been sadly destroyed. The untold stories of the craftspeople who translated and improved this project through their traditional skills and expertise are another disappointing loss. We can catch a glimpse of what might have been by taking a more detailed look at the rebuilding of the library, as well as imagining what is possible for the future of the Mack.

THE MACKINTOSH LIBRARY RESTORATION

I can remember where the scratches were on the cabinets because, obviously, over the years it had taken a real beating, that space, with students dragging books out and looking at them, and ... in recent years there was a bit more of a kind of preciousness about that space, but still it was a workable space and still people did use it as a kind of working building, so there were scratches in the surfaces and I can still remember the sort of 'patternation' of all of those cabinets, in my mind's eye, I can imagine ... I can remember going from cabinet one to cabinet two to cabinet three and I know exactly where all those scratches are ... and of course, when it all comes back those scratches won't be there anymore, so it'll be very different.

DUNCAN CHAPPELL, LIBRARIAN[43]

The Mackintosh library is an interior of exceptional significance for architectural and design heritage. In a spectacular building it was the showstopper, and no photos can do justice to the experience of being inside its jewel-box atmosphere. Therefore, the decision to rebuild it as close as possible to its original design was overall received positively. The project was not 'taking it back to 1910', as was sometimes stated in the press, but was removing unsympathetic additions and alterations that were not part of the original design. For example, just before the school officially opened, the librarian reported that it was far too cold – students were already complaining – which also put the books at risk.[44] On 18 February 1910 the building committee noted that Mackintosh 'expressed regret' that radiators would be installed in the window bays.[45] In the restoration project, the addition of a contemporary underfloor heating system alleviated the need for radiators, leaving the bays clear as per Mackintosh's vision. Improvements were also made to the timber structure, notably a slight alteration of the encasements for the steel roof beams where the earlier design had cracked and failed. Both interventions were essentially invisible but nonetheless characterise an approach that balances an adherence to original aesthetics with practical improvements.

The research for reconstructing the library was methodically approached in a manner accounting for the mixed reliability of sources. Achieving an accurate representation of what was lost was a complex task, full of expectation and scrutiny. Authenticity – in this case recreating an honest reconstruction based on the original design, rather than trying to replicate the room as it was in 2014 – could only really be achieved with a thorough understanding of the materials, techniques and conditions in which the original was made, and there was an acceptance that this would never be an exact replica, nor should it be.

Natalia Burakowska was an intern when she first worked on the Mackintosh library, but she had mostly seen it from the external scaffold: 'I was on an apprenticeship to Page\Park when they were working on the windows [in early 2014]. I only went inside once when I snuck in "illegally" with my friend who was a student at GSA.'[46] She could hardly imagine

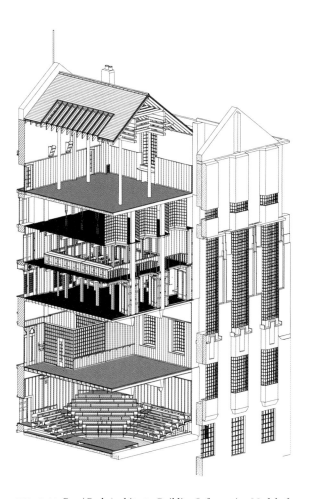

FIG. 4.16 Page\Park Architects, Building Information Model of west tower, 2016.

FIG. 4.17 Library bay prototype, Laurence McIntosh, 2017.

that one day in the not too distant future, it would be her responsibility to mastermind the reconstruction of the destroyed library. She was as surprised as anyone when David Page and Brian Park put their faith in her, as a young heritage consultant working for the firm, to lead such a task. Burakowska's investigation was painstaking, supported by researchers at Page\Park, GSA and many other expert consultants. For example, a library condition survey was made during the 2008 project by conservator Sarah Gerrish, who provided advice and consultation alongside the useful material in her report. The *Mackintosh Architecture* project provided a chronology of changes and repairs in the building up to 2014 and an excellent springboard for sourcing drawings, images and reference material. Besides Mackintosh's 'final' 1910 drawings, the photographs taken by Harry Bedford Lemere in late

1909 were also critical, and access was given to study the original glass plate negatives, now at the National Record of the Historic Environment in Edinburgh, which had many fine details that were indistinct in printed images.[47] There were even a handful of student dissertations about the library that proved helpful for providing measured drawings of doors and furniture. But perhaps most valuable for piecing together what none of this other research could was the extant material from the library itself: timbers that had survived the fire. Burakowska notes:

> They were divided into categories in terms of
> reliability of dimensions that we could take
> from them. Others, even if badly charred, told us
> how things were put together. I think it is quite
> important as it was primary evidence.[48]

From all this prototypes were built from the digital to actual size (figs 4.16, 4.17). In essence, the library reconstruction was based on all extant evidence of the scheme as finished in 1909–10.[49]

DRAWINGS

A detailed set of drawings of the library made in 1993 by Paul Clarke (fig. 4.18), a member of the expert panel for the restoration project, was key to Burakowska's research.[50] In a recent essay Clarke highlighted that the few Mackintosh drawings we have, mostly drawings made for civic approval processes, are inaccurate in relation to the 'as built' works.[51] The sundry, day-to-day drawings made for craftspeople are largely lost, like those for the work done by George Ferguson & Sons as indicated on invoices (*see* fig. 4.25). Clarke, who had measured and drawn the library by hand 'from life', advised Burakowska as she investigated debris and analysed photographs to create accurate reconstruction drawings 'from death'. This, in combination with modelmaking and testing, helped craft a measured drawing of a room that was not nearly as symmetrical or regular as it appeared.

These reconstruction drawings were prepared using Building Information Modelling (BIM) technology; however, it was discovered that despite the advanced technology of this process, some of the fine detail of the room, such as the carved pendants and balustrades, lacked the regularity that is usually seen in contemporary building. As such the digital process was insufficient to model these pieces, and so hand drawing is still at the heart of the library reconstruction. Burakowska notes: 'I think this process also allowed us to know the building much more intimately. Hand drawings make you study chisel marks – BIM would never catch that.'[52]

STRUCTURE

The first step in rebuilding the library was to ensure that the structure was sound. It was, after clearance, a large open void through to the lost book store above, with a hole in the south-west corner floor. Most critically there was severely damaged stonework around the west windows. These needed to be entirely dismantled and rebuilt, a project overseen by Dominic Echlin of David Narro Associates Engineers, someone

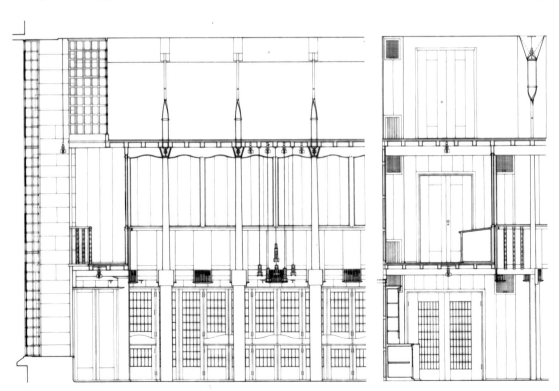

FIG. 4.18 Paul Clarke, full library section, Glasgow School of Art, 1993.

who would become instrumental in rescuing the building remains in 2018, precisely because he was able to learn exactly how the building materials performed under the extreme heat and rapid cooling of water from fighting the fire. The stone around windows and doors on the west elevation, which were essentially masonry and mortar, shattered and cracked. They were left with the obvious blackening of the fire and spalling of the surfaces. The piers supported the steel windows, which became structurally compromised when the windows failed, their iron expanding into the stone and helping to thrust it out of position. The piers were dismantled and stones that were salvageable were sent for repairs. This process enabled us to learn about the way in which these were built to make the shapes of the columns and niches surrounding the windows. They were originally carved on site, and some red chalk plumb lines were still visible on dismantled stones. Stones were replaced only where they could not be repaired through consolidation or partial replacement. This micro project has now become vital, for it is exemplary of what has happened all over the building and gives insight into the daunting task of what it will take to repair the external fabric.

The other aspect of the structure to be considered was the reinstatement of elements that were for some contentious. The internal stairs, which were built in 1945, were precarious and made a disruptive intervention in the balcony floor. It was decided that they would not be rebuilt; instead balcony access was to be returned to the entresol one floor up. The second was the 'librarian's box', an office in the south-east downstairs corner (an area that had burned through the floor), which had essentially become storage. The debate over this 'box' was insightful for the ways in which we must weigh interpretation against evidence when doing research for reconstruction. At one design team meeting, which included the expert panel of architects advising on the project, there was a suggestion that the box somehow ruined the aesthetic flow of the space.[53] An opinion was also argued that the box was not something Mackintosh wanted, because it had been moved into that position at the request of the librarian for better light (it had originally been designed at the centre of the east wall). Furthermore it was suggested

that the reason it didn't appear in the Bedford Lemere photos was because Mackintosh didn't like it (fig. 4.19). However, this point is incorrect, as the photos were taken before the box was built. As per invoices in the GSA archives (*see* fig. 4.25), the librarian's box was delivered on 27 October, so it simply wasn't there yet.[54] Another objection to its reinstatement came from the former Head of Learning Services, who stated that the library wouldn't be used in the same way and therefore it wasn't needed. My own opinion on this was the same as most of the design team: it should return because, in the end, Mackintosh designed it and it was there from the time the building opened, for the life of the library. Reinstatement seemed to be the course decided on at the time of the second fire.

Burakowska's research into the structure even revealed some amusing overlooked details about Mackintosh's design process and the lengths to which he would go to keep to his vision. In January 1909 members of the building committee objected to his design for the balcony crossing in front of the west windows, thinking it would obstruct valuable light. The librarian 'did not think it would be of any special service' and so they asked Mackintosh 'to omit this portion of the balcony from the proposed Library Fittings'.[55] Mackintosh objected:

> *If the balcony across the western windows is omitted there will be a considerable increase of cost as the whole construction of the side balconies would need to be altered. We are of [the] opinion that to take away this balcony would to a great extent spoil the proportions and design of this room.*[56]

Through her research, Burakowska has shown that Mackintosh may have been stretching the truth in order to carry out his vision:

> *Knowing the construction of the library intimately we can uncover Mackintosh's intentions: he cared hugely about the integrity of the design while the excuse of increasing costs was just false. This part of the balcony could be easily removed as the other*

three sides of the balcony are supported by joists resting on the 8 no posts; 4 against north and 4 to south elevation.[57]

There was also a vast amount of research done into the bookcases, which – ironically – were some of the most overlooked items in the library. Most visitors were so enchanted by the space itself and its decorative details that the most functional and arguably important elements of the room faded into the background, as Mackintosh perhaps intended. Thus they were some of the most challenging items to research.

TIMBERS AND FINISHES

One of the surprises of the reconstructed library was its tonality: it was much lighter and warmer than any living memories recall. The visibility of wood grain is perhaps startling when contemplating how dark nearly every extant image of the original space is. But close study of the 1909 Bedford Lemere glass negatives revealed surface details not easily seen in printed photographs: the texture of hand-finished plaster, the shiny patina of unpainted metalwork lights and the smooth-stained grain of the timbers all became apparent. This grain was visible in the library to a careful observer, a mere suggestion when a rare sunbeam struck the wood just so, appearing as a pentimento might in a painting.

The wood too was a revelation. Even in recent publications, the library has been described as being made from oak.[58] It is what Mackintosh wanted, but the budget didn't stretch that far, and there was a rumour among some experts consulted that it was made of kauri pine. This was the assumption the team was originally working on, which was worrying because kauri pine is now a protected species. But an analysis of wood fragments had surprising results: the library and board room were largely made from tulipwood, a North American yellow poplar that was quite popular in the period,[59] noted for its ability to be stained to look like other woods, as we are told in a contemporary joiners' handbook:

It is one of the largest trees of the Atlantic forests, 80 to 150 feet high, with a trunk up to about 13 feet in diameter. The wood is of fine texture, of a pale canary colour … as it is easily worked, its uses are illimitable for interior finish, mouldings, and furniture. It should not, however, be applied to constructive purposes, as it is not adapted to carry heavy loads. Owing to the fine grain it possesses, it is capable of either being polished in its natural colour, or made to imitate any other wood, such as mahogany or walnut.[60]

How the change in materials came about remains unclear. George Ferguson & Sons were the joiners appointed to the second phase of construction and they may have been responsible for the procurement of materials. Certainly, the decision to use tulipwood was made in consultation with Mackintosh, if not under his direction. He had written about the treatment of timber in 1892, especially in relation to staining it to make it appear like other wood:

I suppose that none are taken in by 'oak' or 'walnut' doors so plentiful in our houses … doors & all woodwork must certainly be preserved, and if it must be by painting then it should be in even tint – if the yellowish tone of oak grained doors – or the dark brown of the walnut fraud be liked – then the same effect may be obtained in a rational manner by harmonious arrangement; a still better way is to use stains which permit the true grain of the wood to be seen.[61]

It is likely that as long as he remained within approved budget, the governors would not fuss if he selected a similar wood to do the job. Archival records support what the restoration project technical studies revealed: sales ledgers for Robinson Dunn & Co. Timber Importers and Sawmillers show that tulipwood was purchased by Fergusons 24 times between 1907 and October 1909. Listed as 'Canary Wood' in the Robinson Dunn & Co. sales ledgers, Ferguson bought the timber in various states: as 'dressed boards', 'boards', 'split boards', 'planks' and 'finishings'.[62]

FIG. 4.19 The library, photograph by Harry Bedford Lemere, *c.* 1909. The tables and periodical rack for the large desk have not been delivered, and the librarian's box in the south-east corner has not been built.

FIG. 4.20 The Oak Room (1907–9), rebuilt at V&A Dundee, photo 2023.

FIG. 4.21 Queen's Cross Church (1896–9), balcony pendant, photo 2024.

While this wood was inexpensive and available in 'great widths' at the turn of the twentieth century, this was due to it being taken from the plentiful 'old growth' forests throughout eastern North America. Today most tulipwood is new growth, which posed an interesting challenge for the project, as this wood seemed to be unavailable in sizes wide enough for the facing planks of the prominent columns. In the end the tulipwood was procured from Europe. Other wood was finished more conventionally: the interior posts of the columns were spruce, floorboards were maple and the ceiling was Douglas fir.[63] Floors in the library – and throughout – were made from maple, another change as the original floors were of pine, which ultimately was not as strong or sustainable.

Evidence-based research revealed finishes that seemed drastically different to the expected dark tones. Ian and Michael Crick-Smith, experts in architectural paint research and analysis, revealed that the 'stain' Mackintosh used was a blend of a highly pigmented oil-based paint and beeswax.[64] Such a solution might have been commercially available in 1909 but could have been

mixed on site in batches suited to the project. Finding the correct 'original' finish would always be guesswork to some extent, and the scientific investigation included a study of similar interiors, including the Oak Room of Miss Cranston's Ingram Street Tea Rooms, which had just been conserved and installed at the newly opened V&A Dundee (fig. 4.20). Also examined were the drop panels at Queen's Cross Church (fig. 4.21) and the Mack board room, especially cabinet interiors, which had been virtually untouched by light. These will all have darkened with age in any case, so the warmth of the finished prototype and what we were seeing of the installed library was astonishing (figs 4.22, 4.23). The final stain was made from a 3:1 ratio of raw umber to burnt umber of artists' oil paint, earthy and rich.

The only paint colour found in the library was on the notches of the balustrade spindles. Although fragments of these survived, they were damaged to a degree that meant the paint colour could not be determined, only that it was lead-based. A similar painstaking research and testing process was carried out for these, and here Gerrish's conservation report was invaluable.

FIG. 4.22 Prototype carved pendants (detail), Laurence McIntosh, 2017.

FIG. 4.23 Prototype (detail) showing original colours and tone of wood.

CARVED PENDANTS AND JOINERY

From my study of the pendants, described in the previous chapter, and examining video footage of the library, I was able to confirm the order of the patterns on all the pendants and their arrangement around the room.[65] However, the real work to recreate the pendants, and all the exquisite joinery of the library, was accomplished by Burakowska alongside the craftspeople at Laurence McIntosh, the company that won the contract to rebuild the library. Interestingly Laurence McIntosh are not strictly specialists in the heritage field: their portfolio includes everything from bespoke cabinetry to new-build country houses to Edinburgh's Scotch Whisky Experience tourist attraction. What they possess in spades, though, is spectacular attention to detail and – most important for this project – the willingness to remake the library using traditional methods rather than using modern techniques and machinery.

This decision, which was backed unanimously by the project team, was met with exasperation by some. The team was accused, for example, of being 'fetishistic' for

choosing to use the same hand-cut nails – sourced from the original company, which had relocated to the USA – rather than using local 'off the shelf' nails to do the job.[66] Yet from building prototypes, it was observed that not only do these 'heritage' nails have technical superiority in the way they fastened the facing pieces of timber to their supports, but they also had an aesthetic quality that commercially available nails lack. Their smooth, flat heads married beautifully with the surface of the tulipwood, producing a visually faithful 'arts and crafts' reconstruction.

To begin reconstruction of the pendants, a dedicated study was made of photographic details, in which Burakowska determined that, due to variances in carving, they were made by several different hands. But with all the pendants having perished entirely, details such as measurements and depth of the carving were difficult to determine. Almost miraculously GSA had been contacted about an unusual artefact that was then loaned to the project: two small casts made of two of the carved 'notches' (fig. 4.24).[67] This small but critical object allowed for a detailed reconstruction of the dimensions of these details. Prototypes were made and work was carried out in traditional methods by master craftsmen Angus Johnston and Martin Cirulis.

Similar methods were undertaken for the rest of the room, including for the coloured balustrades (*see* fig. 3.70), and a painstaking survey of the ceiling joists, which it turns out lacked regularity in their width, based on study of surviving wood fragments. Predicated on all this research, a full-scale prototype of a library bay was unveiled on 8 September 2017 (fig. 4.17). Seeing it was like meeting a long-lost friend.

FURNITURE

Mackintosh designed a complete suite of furniture that was executed by George Ferguson & Sons. It is one of the few areas where we have detailed records for the interiors, as there are itemised invoices for the work. Fergusons built the majority of the interior in phase II, including alterations to existing fabric and other plainer items of furniture such as the tables for the architecture studio. But obviously their craftsmanship was to a very high level, for they were able to beautifully execute Mackintosh's intricate library. Reviewing the invoices (fig. 4.25), we can see exactly what items were made for the library and when they were delivered:

> 7 August 1909: 'Table for Library' (bill date
> 20 September 1909)
> 22 October 1909: 9 cypress tables
> 27 October 1909: librarian's office (bill date
> 8 January 1910)
> 7 November 1909: rack on library table

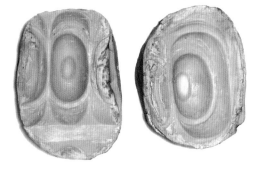

FIG. 4.24 Casts of library pendant notches.

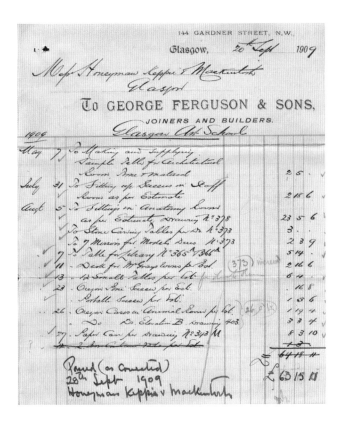

FIG. 4.25 Invoice from George Ferguson & Sons joiners, detailing delivery of fittings including the main library table.

> 25 November 1909: 'To removing old tables from
> Library and setting new ones Time 5 Hours'
> 28 November 1909: 'To fitting Shelf in Library room'
> 2 December 1909: portfolio case in library
> 8 December 1909: fittings in librarian's office

The furniture package made by Fergusons, comprising the central periodicals desk, its magazine rack and the nine tables (*see* fig. 3.67), was to be remade following a process like that used for the pendants. As noted above, the 'librarian's box' was still open for debate. To consult on the completion of the furniture programme, a meeting of experts was scheduled for 26 June 2018, just a week after the second fire;[68] this was of course cancelled and so this part of the project remained unfinished. But there was already a difficult internal debate brewing at GSA about the library chairs.

In adhering to the approach already laid out for the library, 40 Windsor chairs (fig. 4.26) should have been recreated: four for each of the nine tables and six for the periodical desk at the centre. However, these were *not* the chairs in the library at the time of the fire. What was being used – and had been used since the 1950s – was a set of sturdier chairs from the Oak Room of the Ingram Street Tea Room, which had been gifted to the school by the Glasgow Corporation when they acquired its contents (fig. 4.27).[69] While the original Windsor chairs had served their purpose for decades, by the 1950s their structure had weakened, their delicate spindles snapping. At the time of the fire only nine of the original 40 remained in the collection, out of use, having been roped off many years ago. These all perished, except for a lone survivor that had been broken several decades before and was heading for the skip, but instead a student kept the broken parts and fixed it for themselves. It was loaned to the project for study, and we were very grateful for their sleekit ingenuity in saving it!

Why, then, would we not make a full set of Windsor chairs – a typology that has its roots in the vernacular furniture of the west of Scotland and was often used in libraries – just as Mackintosh had intended? As much as it is joked that Mackintosh furniture is largely

uncomfortable, these chairs were not – if you can fit in them. The chairs are diminutive by contemporary standards. They are low to the ground, and while reportedly comfortable to a person of a small to medium stature, they are not suited to larger users in either height or width, nor would they be usable by many with mobility issues. They are simply not ergonomically suitable for certain bodies, certain physical limitations and possibly not for extended use. In a culture where we strive to be more attuned to a diversity of user needs, reinstating these chairs – and *only* these chairs – would have been problematic. Yet this was the decision the Mackintosh Building Committee – the governors' panel that oversaw final decisions – was staunchly advocating. It created a dilemma as GSA wanted the rebuilt library to be used for a variety of purposes to honour both the public and academic interests of their stakeholders. The space had to be appropriate for visitor audiences while also enabling it for sustained use as a study space for our students and staff. If the original chair design was unsuitable for some, should it be the only one reinstated? And if not, how do we recreate

FIG. 4.26 Charles Rennie Mackintosh, Windsor chair for the library, Glasgow School of Art, 1910.

FIG. 4.27 Charles Rennie Mackintosh, Chair for Ingram Street Tea Rooms, 1907.

the furniture set for the library in such a way that we do not compromise the original design, but which also provides a practical seating scheme for users? These questions remain unanswered and will need to be addressed in future. At least now there is time to give them due consideration.

LIGHTS

The conservation of the library lights is one of the great successes of the first Mackintosh restoration project (MRP1). They are remarkable survivors of the 2014 fire, their solder melting in the heat, causing them to fall to pieces even before the library was consumed. This aided their survival, surprisingly, as a great deal of debris collapsed on them, protecting the fragments. Although these lampshades are iconic Mackintosh designs (often copied and produced commercially, though as poorly made replicas), they were never accessioned as part of the 'collection', because they were fixtures, attached to the building. In fact, no items that were 'attached' to the building – doors, lights, door number plates, etc. – were ever fully catalogued. This was fortuitous for the project, as they could be treated more quickly as part of the building repair works.[70]

According to Mackintosh's 1909 drawings (figs 4.28, 4.29), 53 lights were originally commissioned, but there were just 48 in the library at the time of the fire, plus two more in storage in the book store above, with the furniture collection. One light survived as it was on loan to the Lighthouse, although some small differences in its details (the gauge of the metal) made us question whether it was an early replica or even a prototype. The 'Lighthouse light' was critically important in helping to create a blueprint for how the rather architectural lights were puzzled together, alongside one rather damaged 'survivor' that has been retained as is for the GSA collection (fig. 4.30). There were three different types of lights too: large and small pendants, which hung in a cluster at the centre, and canisters, which were fixed to the ceiling around the balcony on both levels. They were made from 19, 18 or 14 pieces respectively, and were set with mottled pink, purple and blue glass. From the Kirkdale archaeological excavation, over six hundred pieces of metal were recovered and numbered.[71]

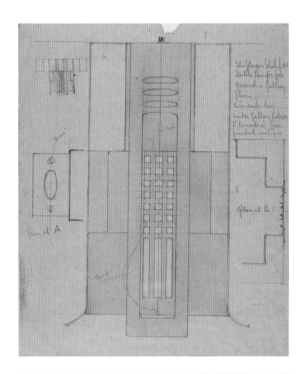

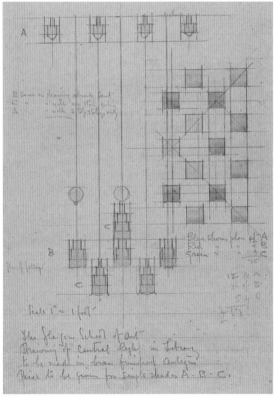

FIG. 4.28 Charles Rennie Mackintosh, Design for library light fitting, 1909. Pencil and watercolour on paper.

FIG. 4.29 Charles Rennie Mackintosh, Design for library light fitting, 1909. Pencil and watercolour on paper.

FIG. 4.30 Library light recovered from the fire.

FIG. 4.31 Restored light, 2017.

FIG. 4.32 A 'kit' of lights from recovered fragments.

FIG. 4.33 Rodney French of Lonsdale & Dutch, Edinburgh, works to restore a light.

While many were recognisable as 'Mackintosh', many more were simply structural bits without any particular character.

Initial workshops were arranged with conservation experts to determine the feasibility of repair and restoration. Fragments were tested and found to be robust, if worse for wear. A methodology was then worked out based on the meticulous reports made by Kirkdale. Because the pieces were numbered, Archives & Collection Recovery Project lead Polly Christie was able to create a system to map where each fell in the room. While this meant the bulk came from the centre, there were only two in each zone of the balcony area. Assisting Christie with sorting these pieces, we began grouping them into areas, to see if we might be able to put together a complete light (or two) from one of these zones. We understood from the outset that we would never be able to completely reassemble a light exactly as it had been, but it was a good exercise to see what might be possible.

From this process 'kits' of lights were created (fig. 4.32), literally putting all the pieces to make a light into a plastic bag. A selection of materials was sent to the Edinburgh studio of master craftsman Rodney French at Lonsdale & Dutch (fig. 4.33). French, who took over the studio from Arthur Dutch in 1997, is an expert on historic lanterns, using traditional methods and equipment in his practice. It was a painstaking process of repairing each fragment, then working out and replicating the exact techniques that were used originally. Part of this was trying to understand what the finish should be.

In all living memory, these lights were painted black. But in the Bedford Lemere photographs, a close inspection reveals that they were not black but had a metallic finish. Mackintosh's original drawings show the three different sizes and their dimensions. A note on the drawings states 'to be made in brass finished antique' and that there are to be 53 made – at £1 apiece! Like the tone of the wood, this was again achieved through educated guesswork. French understood the term and the result is a surprising deep copper (fig. 4.31). Between these rather sparkling lights and the warmer wood tones, the library was shaping up to be a much brighter space than anyone would have imagined. The original lights were of mixed quality up close, though they look magnificent when viewed from below. The first light French reconstructed has been saved for the GSA collection. From the remaining usable fragments, French was able to make 28 reconstructed lights from wholly original material, 15 new lights, and 11 that were made from mixed original and new material. All new fragments have been given a Lonsdale & Dutch maker's mark, and all have now been accessioned into the collection – survivors of both fires now. A selection of them were temporarily hung in the Reid building in 2021, in one of Steven Holl's signature voids. One hopes they will return to their intended home in future.

Each of the projects described above necessarily examined material forensically, but also inspired philosophical enquiries on issues of materiality, particularly when faced with the problem of loss of fabric, and consequently loss of atmosphere. That word 'patina' often rears its head in such considerations, the evidence of time, which we know we cannot recreate but which we hope to honour and acknowledge through research, considerable sensitivity and a deepened understanding of Mackintosh's approach to materials and materiality. The library is a symbol of what the school was, and what it could be again. The story of its reconstruction after the 2014 fire is exemplary of the painstaking attention to detail the previous restoration team employed, and the possibility for the rebuilding of the Mack in the near future. The reconstructed library would have been a working space again. Generous donations, some from other libraries, led to a rebuilt collection, possibly even more impressive than before. Volumes were being prepared to populate the shelves. The library was becoming what it was from the start – a handcrafted, magnificent, total work of art, from top to bottom – ready to excite and inspire a new generation of artists.

THE 2018 FIRE AND SALVAGE (MRP2)

On 13 June 2018 GSA PhD student Rachael Purse made one of her periodic research walks through the Mack, unknowingly capturing some of the last images of the building as it neared completion (figs 4.34–4.38).[72] Her documentary photos show evidence of a flurry of activity: the beautiful lath-and-plasterwork

ceilings were being 'finished off the float' (as per Mackintosh's original direction); the Hen Run was fully reconstructed; and paint swatches throughout gave evidence to final finishes under debate. Even the most monumental of micro projects were coming near fruition. The immense posts of Studio 58 had been sourced from an old mill being dismantled in the United States, its North American yellow pine of a similar age and quality to the originals (see fig. 0.12). In the end these had issues in the way they were being finished as the stain was applied after the Japanese-inspired construction was complete, and natural movement meant that gaps were showing where the wood was unstained – something to be learned for future reconstruction. The library was also largely installed (fig. 4.36), though thankfully the bespoke carved details – panels and balustrades – were still being completed and had not yet made the trip from Edinburgh. The team were also about to embark on another consultation on the completion of the library furniture package, having already solicited prototypes for chairs. Although much was left to be completed, one could already see that the experience of walking around the restored Mackintosh building would have been spectacular.

Friday 15 June 2018 was graduation day at the Glasgow School of Art. The weather was glorious, and while ceremonies always take place in the Neo-Gothic Bute Hall of the University of Glasgow, celebrations eventually end up at The Art School, the long-standing nightclub in the student union, across from the Mack. And so it was that among the first people to smell smoke and see flames flickering behind the north-east windows of the Mack was a celebrant who stepped outside for a cigarette. This is curious, as by all accounts no detection system went off. There were even alarms on the scaffolding that went off when Glaswegians who had perhaps had 'one too many' attempted to go exploring. Why were these systems apparently silent on 15 June?

According to the 2022 SFRS Fire Report, at approximately 23.10 pm the night watchman heard a series of noises that he thought may have been an intruder on the scaffolding.[73] He exited the building and saw nothing untoward, then returned to his desk

FIG. 4.34 ABOVE Lecture theatre, 13 June 2018.

FIG. 4.35 ABOVE RIGHT Corridor seating, 13 June 2018.

FIG. 4.36 Library mezzanine, 13 June 2018.

FIG. 4.37 Professor's studio, 13 June 2018.

FIG. 4.38 LEFT The Hen Run, 13 June 2018.

FIG. 4.39 The Mack on fire early in the morning of 16 June 2018, viewed from north-west. At bottom left is Stow College (Whyte & Galloway architects, 1932), which GSA purchased in 2016 and is now home to the School of Fine Art.

just inside the east entrance of the building (where the site offices were located). Within minutes, he heard more noise inside the building, so proceeded up the east stairwell. Up two flights, on the main floor of the building, he observed fire and sparks coming from 'a crawl space' or 'duct' near the ceiling. Following protocol, he immediately called emergency services while exiting the building at 23.19 pm. Around the same time, a passer-by took a photo of the east elevation, with the 'tower' window just outside the Mackintosh Room already alight with a terrible glow. The first SFRS appliances arrived within six minutes and the advance investigative team accessed the Mack through the main entrance. They turned left down the east corridor and 'observed a well-developed fire that was located directly above them'.[74] All these facts, along with subsequent investigation, place the source of the fire somewhere between levels five and seven of the eastern end of the building – that is, somewhere outside the Mackintosh

Room and/or the mezzanine levels above and below these areas.

By midnight half the building was well alight from the basement to the roof (fig. 4.39). By 1.45 am the police were evacuating nearby properties – homes on Dalhousie Street and bars and restaurants on Sauchiehall Street – due to the fire spread and fears that the Mack would actually collapse and tumble down the steep hill. Near 3.00 am the fire finally broke through the roof of the adjacent ABC Theatre, destroying the Victorian dome of Hengler's Circus still hidden inside. The immediate area had already been evacuated and the exclusion zone was extended to include another three streets down the hill and one on either side. This cordon stayed in place for months.[75]

Ultimately, there were over a hundred firefighters with 17 rescue pumps and five aerial appliances battling the hellish conflagration, which was burning so fiercely that the water supply in Garnethill was eventually exhausted, and more had to be pumped from the River Clyde. It travelled furiously – some reported loud bangs, which could have been any number of things – electrical transformers, canisters of paint stripper – inside the building. These sounds fuelled initial conspiracy that the cause was arson, or even a bomb. But what did cause this terrible event?

The final report from Watch Commander and Lead Fire Investigator Peter Allardice was, disappointingly, inconclusive:

> *Due to the extensive damage throughout the entire site, post fire indicators were not available to support the investigation by indication of a possible origin or cause area. Directional indicators did not exist on the remaining structure as surface finishes had either spalled or been consumed in the fire, window lintel blackening, although visible, was present on multiple apertures as the fire progressed through the building … Having considered the available evidence and the possible origin and cause hypotheses, in the absence of any further information, I conclude that the cause of the fire to be recorded as Undetermined.*[76]

In essence any potential clues were destroyed, sometimes crumbling to dust even as they were recovered. The report, which took over two years to complete (and the Covid-19 pandemic only set this back a few months), is incredibly thorough in discussing the methods of the forensic investigation. It proposes 'three broad hypotheses', none of which could ultimately be discounted: wilful fire-raising (arson); fault or failure of electrical appliances or distribution systems; and accidental ignition (not electrical). Each of these is discussed in depth, with individual investigations that are fascinating reads worthy of Agatha Christie or Ian Rankin.

Arson is unlikely, despite reports of a 'shadowy figure' watching from a nearby carpark, but because the intruder warning systems seemed to have failed that night it cannot be ruled out entirely. Non-electrical accidental ignition is also doubtful, given that the only hot works done in the building were much earlier in the day and not in the right location for the fire source, and smoking was strictly prohibited, which security was fastidious about. Although the report does not offer any conclusion, the unspoken message is that the most likely culprit was an electrical fault:

> *It is certain that transformers on all levels at the east side of the Mackintosh Building were energised, offering a viable ignition source. However, due to extensive fire damage, inspection of the remains of the transformers, supply cables and 110 volt trailing leads and festoon lighting has provided no evidence that would indicate a fault condition or mechanical damage … Taking these factors in to account, ignition by electrical transformers, portable appliances or a fault in a cable cannot be fully discounted, as mains voltage supplies and 110 volt equipment were known to be present throughout the building and energised in the area where fire was first observed.*[77]

In the immediate aftermath of the fire, it was unclear what – if any – of the building could be saved. On 19 June limited supervised access to the site was allowed to a small team that included Dominic Echlin of David Narro Associates. By this time it would not be an exaggeration to say that no one knew this building better than Echlin in terms of its material, and especially how it performed in the extremities of a fire event. Drones were used to assess damage at high level, which from the street didn't look 'that bad' – the fact that the finials were standing intact offered a sign of hope. However, through closer inspection it became rapidly clear just how severe the damage was (figs 4.40, 4.41), with a great deal of fractured stone at high level, multiple large cracks and some shearing of the east façade: the building was literally coming apart at the north-east corner (fig. 4.42). Most worrying of all, the east stairwell, part of phase II and so added to the building rather than built integrally with it, seemed to be pulling away entirely. There was fear that if it collapsed, it would result in much wider damage and impact on the buildings below it in Sauchiehall Street. The team, which also included Ranald MacInnes of HES, needed to work up a plan to save what remained of the building (fig. 4.43). On 20 June, following consultation with the GSA and building engineers, Glasgow City Council Building Control applied a Dangerous Buildings Notice to the site due to the potential for partial or full building collapse. Glasgow

FIG. 4.40 TOP Mackintosh Room with visible paint test panels, 13 June 2018.

FIG. 4.41 Mackintosh Room hearth remains. Drone still, June 2018.

FIG. 4.42 North-east façade, fractures and shearing of corner visible. June 2018.

City Council gave the team a short window to prove they could make the building safe; just 48 hours by some reports, though in the end time was a bit more generous. The alternative was total and rapid demolition.

New 3D scans were made to compare with the originals, more drone footage was taken, and a crane was brought in for high-level investigation (figs 4.44, 4.45). Emergency measures were taken in removing some of the more precarious stone on the east stair gable; the only safe method of doing this was knocking it into the building. It was also determined early on that the phase II concrete slab that Mackintosh designed for the new top level was, in fact, helping to hold the building together. The Mack was stable.

Armed with as much information as possible, a stabilisation and salvage plan was put together that showed both how the building could be made safe, and highlighted the areas of significance that every attempt should be made to salvage, the stonework on the east elevation in particular. This included an incredible work of engineering by Echlin's team, who rapidly designed

a cantilevered brace that would help to support the horrifically damaged west tower (fig. 4.46). It perhaps goes without saying that the nearly completed library and Studio 58 were gone, but amazingly those industrial brackets in the book store weathered a second fire!

The plan was approved, and by 27 June 2018 down-taking work commenced. Approximately the top third of the building was removed, and the Mack was braced by over seven hundred tons of scaffolding. The fire investigation was dependent on the clearance of the building, which was filled with debris, to a height of ten metres in some areas. It was also imperative to be as painstaking as possible to uncover any evidence of the fire's cause, but also to recover any objects of significance that had still been inside the building. The doors, it was sure, were a lost cause. But some metalwork was miraculously recovered, including the mangled remains of the coat of arms that graced the main stairs; one hopes Rodney French will be called on to work the same magic he did with the library lights.

In late 2020 the school finally began a consultation programme to decide the building's future, and in October 2021 published a Strategic Outline Business Case, which was led by an external agency.[78] It concludes:

Through extensive consultation and robust economic analysis, this preliminary strategic business case demonstrates that the best value option is to undertake a faithful reinstatement, within the practical constraints of the current regulatory environment while innovating to ensure that technology and sustainability are at the building's heart.[79]

It is interesting to consider how, after the 2014 fire, it was passion for the building and for Mackintosh heritage that drove an immediate decision to undertake a faithful reinstatement, seen as hasty by some. The slow, painstaking and expensive exercise of creating a Strategic Business Case, while a necessity given the calamity of the fire, reached the exact same conclusion.

On 25 January 2022 the Scottish Fire and Rescue Service published their report on the cause of the second fire, which enabled the school to begin the process of finding a new project team to rebuild the Mack. A focus of the project going forward seems to be sustainability, which is a good thing, especially given the increased materials costs associated with present global strife. How this will be implemented remains to be seen, but in late January 2023 the GSA made a brief press statement that rebuilding works would soon commence, to be completed by 2030, and that the renewed Mack would become the home of the graduate school.[80] This latter decision is very welcome – colleagues including myself advocated for this in 2016. The Mack is ideal for postgraduate studio space, which the school sorely lacks.

This statement also reported that 'in excess of 5,500 of tonnes of fire damaged material have been removed from the site' and that the school was 'committed

FIG. 4.43 Salvage recovery plan illustrating areas of special significance to be saved if possible. Elevation drawing by Page\Park.

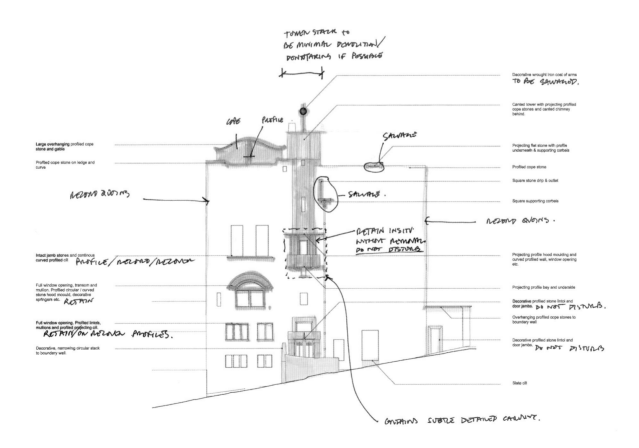

FIG. 4.45 3D scan of Mack exterior, 2018. Terrestrial laser scanning by Jared Benjamin.

to reinstating the building through retention of as much of the original fabric as possible'. This enabled a second phase of works to begin, to stabilise the internal structure and erect a temporary roof.

But who will lead the project? In addition to an internal project board comprising various senior managers across the school, an external project steering group was appointed by the board of governors.[81] The key remit of the project governance was to appoint the new professional team, the tender for which was circulated in March 2022, shortly after the SFRS report was published. The brief outlined that the team would comprise three separate appointments: project management, cost consultants and an architect-led full design team. The appointment was expected to be announced in October 2022, but there was still no word in the January 2023 statement.

Then on 1 March 2023 GSA delivered a depressing update:

> *The Glasgow School of Art announced today that the procurement exercise for the Architect-led*

Design Team for the Mackintosh Building Project will be closed and no appointment will be made. This follows the identification of a technical error in the scoring matrix used in the procurement process … The procurement process will now be thoroughly reviewed prior to a new invitation to tender being announced in due course. We wish to thank the companies who submitted tenders and hope that they will consider submitting proposals again.[82]

Some interpretation of this statement was offered in the *Architects' Journal* the following day, with the chief executive of the Royal Institute of Architects Scotland (RIAS) stating: 'design procurement in Scotland is broken, and the latest sad twist in the ongoing saga of the Mackintosh Building Project is symptomatic of a system that is in deep trouble.'[83] Glasgow MSP Paul Sweeney, a heritage advocate, added:

> *Unfortunately this is just the latest in a long line of setbacks that have befallen the rebuild of Glasgow School of Art's Mackintosh Building, but*

FIG. 4.44 OPPOSITE Threshold of the Mack with laser scanning equipment used as part of the salvage, August 2018.

it's not one that was entirely unforeseen ... The rebuild has been an unmitigated disaster from the outset and has been afforded nowhere near the level of financial support that it merits. Given the significance of the Mackintosh Building to Glasgow and Scotland's architectural heritage this should have been a national project overseen by the Scottish Government, in the same vein as the efforts to rebuild Notre Dame Cathedral.[84]

The GSA statement lacks clarity, and perhaps leaves too much room for speculation. And that, in essence, has perhaps been the GSA's optics problem all along. There is a perceived lack of transparency that has engendered a feeling of extreme distrust in both internal and external stakeholders in the GSA community, and the public more widely. The constant dependence on succinct messaging may be the smart decision for an institution fearing litigation, and recent history has shown that detailed information will largely function as ammunition for further backlash. But this approach also sets the narrative in the hands of people not only lacking information but with absence of faith in the institution. In such minds, documents that were redacted to protect privacy, for example (as in the case of the 2014 fire report, to protect the student who accidentally started the fire), become 'hidden documents' and demand a 'public enquiry'. Such communications are misguided, but communications could surely improve – tell the people what 'a technical error in the scoring matrix actually means, for example, to avoid confusion and further public ire?

What risk does this create for the future of the project in terms of trust? Which of the architects – who will have spent untold sums on their bids – will wish to try again? In hindsight, this quagmire makes the 'procurement error' of 1896 – the miscalculated budget and the consequent fuss kicked up by the shortlisted architects – seem charming.

At a recent lecture, Pritzker Prize-winning architect Sir David Chipperfield was asked what he would do with the Mack, given the opportunity. He replied: 'Cutting to the chase, I think a rebuild.' He stated how his project at the Neues Museum in Berlin had 'status

FIG. 4.46 The Mack west tower, June 2018.

as a ruin' for over fifty years, but that the Mack 'has no status as a ruin as a burnt out shell'. Chipperfield fervently agrees that the Mack can be rebuilt as a very 'high class copy' due to all extant evidence and previous research, but suggests finding someone with 'very deep pockets' as the question of rebuilding is 'not technical, it's financial', and it is difficult to justify in the current economic and political climate in Scotland. An initial estimate of £62 million was given by GSA for faithful reinstatement, but with ongoing delays and continued soaring of costs of materials, that figure could easily approach £100 million or more before we see a renewed Mackintosh building.[85]

By the time this book is published, there will have been ten years of students who have never known the Mack. By the time the building is reinstated, it might even be a whole generation. To the outsider, the Mack has sat in silence since 2014. Inside, though, work to clear and stabilise has kept pace all along, even through Covid-19. In June 2023 a 'building wrap' was put in place to help the Mack dry out from the initial drenching after the fire and subsequent years of exposure to the blustery Scottish climate. It is hoped that when work begins to rebuild, the new team will have an equal amount of passion as the previous one (and that some of them, at least, will have once been inside it). There are surely lessons to be learned from the disaster that befell Mackintosh's masterpiece. But there is a lot of building left, and standing inside its wreckage, the Mack is still a beautiful living thing.

THE EPHEMERAL SCHOOL OF ART

Mackintosh didn't build an art school. He didn't carve the stone or glaze the windows. Tradespeople, craft-folk build an art school. What went up in flames, again, was the work of roofers and joiners, masons, and tilers ... Memories went up in flames too, again. Mackintosh didn't build them either ... Mackintosh built plans and elevations, built designs and decorations. They, for the most part, didn't burn down. So, build them again. Hundreds of times if you want. Someone else's memories will follow.

NEIL BICKERTON, ARTIST AND GSA ALUMNUS[1]

The original version of this epilogue was entitled 'What Does the Mack Mean?', a question that was intended to neatly summarise – and celebrate – the completion of the rebuilt Mackintosh building. Now it might seem that the question should be revised to what *did* it mean, since the physical structure as we knew it is lost. But there is a substantial portion of building sitting precariously on Garnethill that will not be ignored (fig. 5.1). The Mack lives on in our memories, in its design, in its ruin. So, what did and what *does* the Mack mean?

For the history of architecture and design, the Mack is a total work of art and a bewitching icon of fin de siècle architecture, be it Art Nouveau, Symbolist, Modern or simply Glasgow Style. It had an impact on a generation of architects too; to quote Aldo van Eyck:

I remember climbing that steep slope and, turning into Renfrew, being 'Struck' by what I saw. Like Michelangelo he accomplished a reconciliation of emotional extremes in architectural terms, thus mitigating inner stress by bringing together formal qualities and aspects deemed incompatible. Struck also by the way CRM, on the threshold of the modern movement, yet still within the nineteenth century, had, taking the past with him into the present without doing it again ... pointed to the future.[2]

Certainly this accolade would have pleased Mackintosh, giving him the recognition he always desired. In his lifetime though, the Mack's completion signalled the end of an era. Another commission of this calibre never came again, and difficulties arose at Honeyman, Keppie & Mackintosh that caused him to leave the partnership. He and Margaret left Glasgow for Walberswick in 1914 and, though it was not their intention, they never returned to live in the city, eventually settling in London. To our knowledge, he never returned to visit the school. Later, in France, when painting the

FIG. 5.1 View of the Mack from the south, June 2018.

watercolour *Collioure* (*c.* 1926–7, fig. 5.2), did he look at that building poised over the town and see in it his own bold masterpiece, high on its hill – did he wonder how it fared? What did the Mack mean to Mackintosh? His greatest achievement? His biggest disappointment? Mackintosh conceived the design ideas for the Glasgow School of Art within the most fruitful decade of his life, professionally and personally. It is curious to think now that there were both two phases of its creation and two phases of its destruction.

Mackintosh probably never imagined just how much his building would mean to his home city. The Mack represents civic pride for Glasgow, even though most Glaswegians have never been inside. It brought admirers from all over the world and added a bit of magic to the townscape. David Buri recalls:

There were invariably a lot of tourist groups being shown around the building, whatever the time of year, and while these could sometimes be a little disruptive for anyone working in the Mack library, it was an opportunity to meet people from around the world. The distances that some of them had travelled to see Mackintosh's work was always a reminder of how privileged I was to be regularly working in the space. But it was a particular pleasure when local people, who had perhaps lived all their lives nearby, came to visit the building for the first time, and it was a good reminder of the affection held for the building by Glaswegians.[3]

But in the aftermath of its destruction, for Glasgow and Scotland, the Mack meant anger, disbelief and despair. And truthfully, for some, apathy. It is unsurprising that there was, and still is, so much anger in the wake of the 2018 fire. It is the 'castle on a hill' that represents the best of the city's creative ingenuity. Some are rightly fuming at the destruction of a monument dear to them for a lifetime, and others, mostly younger people and even some GSA students who, having only experienced the building as a gap site, see a ruin cluttering their already overstretched campus. Knock it down and give them studio space, they think. I taught some of these students, and in my time at GSA I had the joy

FIG. 5.2 Charles Rennie Mackintosh, *Collioure, Pyrénées-Orientales*, *c.* 1926–7. Watercolour, 37.9 × 46.5 cm. The Art Institute of Chicago.

of watching them shift from confusion and apathy to designing projects advocating the Mack's full reinstatement, simply through studying its history and hearing first hand from the former restoration team how they were remaking it.

In the middle are those who have experienced the magic of the building but understand the need to move on to the next chapter in its life, whatever that entails. Those torn between the feeling that it will never be what it was and the desire to see it again, and the possibility that it could be something wonderful still. As time passes, I find myself drifting in that direction.

The vehement reactions and opinions this event has generated are yet another signifier of the power of this building, even in its state of ruination. In the wake of the 2018 fire things got terribly ugly for the GSA. In truth, a fair assessment of this period will require more distance. It was a very difficult period for Garnethill, primarily for the people who lived there, who were barred from their homes for months.[4] This came on the back of almost a decade of construction, from the building of the Reid through to the restoration project. One long-time resident opined:

The only interaction with local residents has been [GSA-hired] surveyors checking for movement/ subsidence due to demolition/building works. We have never been included or invited to any of the degree shows or to see the buildings in the 28 years I've lived in Garnethill, though we've endured the disruption and noise every year.[5]

Much of the building control during this period was regulated by the city, and it remains unclear why the police or the council did not facilitate access for at least essential items for residents shut out of their homes for ten weeks.[6] It was also challenging for staff and students, who needed to rethink their whole approach to teaching and learning when the campus was still not accessible by September 2018. It was an emotionally and physically trying period for all involved.

With catastrophes such as this, consequences will take years to resolve. Three years on, misleading headlines suggested that GSA was suing the fire alarm company and Page\Park Architects, when in reality it was the school's insurers following standard legal procedure 'to recover documents before time bar'.[7] History will offer better perspective, hopefully after the Mackintosh building is reconstructed and inhabited again by the school. As one early reader of this text observed in an insightful, humorous and typically Scottish fashion:

> *Remember some of the controversies when the school was built, like how Mackintosh built the west entrance without approval? It's now explained easily, but at the time you know it was a stramash. That's how this period will be looked at in a hundred years.*[8]

If there are to be any positive outcomes of this terrible event, it can be hoped that change will be implemented at the highest levels regarding care for our important and extensive historic environment in towns and cities across Scotland. The Scottish Government parliamentary committee criticised the GSA for the delay between the 2008 recommendation of a fire suppression system and its 2014 implementation. No one realised that the original recommendation for a suppression system came in 1964, and at that time Barnes could not acquire public support for the project.[9]

The situation had not changed by 2008, and even in their 2019 report the parliamentary committee had to concede:

> *The Committee notes that the approach taken by the GSA to fundraise in order to instal a mist suppression system in the Mackintosh building was considered by some to be unusual. The Committee recommends that the Scottish Government undertakes an assessment of whether the current funding models available to HEIs* [Higher Education Institutions] *to protect historic assets, such as the Mackintosh building, are adequate … We recommend that the Scottish Government, through its agencies, reviews the adequacy of powers to compel owners to put in place enhanced fire safety measures; the public funding available; and the flexibility attached to that funding, to protect buildings of national significance.*[10]

It is hoped the Scottish Government – and the wider international community – takes these recommendations to heart and acts on them, so that for Scotland the tragedy of the Mack finds purpose as a cautionary tale for the care and preservation of our built environment.

As for its reconstruction, what *could* the Mack mean? Wary of the term 'future proof', we can yet do our best to create a building for the future. The simplicity of Mackintosh's design means that with some ingenuity it could be recreated in a way that would be sustainable. Other recent and ongoing Mackintosh restoration projects offer a range of inspiring possibilities. The Hill House in Helensburgh, under the care of the National Trust for Scotland (NTS), has been protected by a 'box' since 2019 (*see* p. 95), which serves a dual function of both sheltering its problematic render and providing a fascinating visitor experience. It has proved very popular for visitors, who can explore its bridges around the upper stories of the house, and even over its roof, to watch its conservation in action. In partnership with the scientific team at HES, NTS has documented the drying phase while working towards a plan to sustainably treat the structure, and in 2023 began the process of slowly removing the render to repair it (fig. 5.3).

FIG. 5.3 The Hill House, Helensburgh, 1902–3, now sheltering under a 'box' while its render is removed and repaired.

FIG. 5.4 The Salon de Luxe at Mackintosh at the Willow after the 2018 restoration project, with a replica of Margaret Macdonald Mackintosh's gesso panel *O Ye All Ye That Walk in Willowwood*, made by Dai and Jenny Vaughn.

Meanwhile, the reconstruction of the original Willow Tea Rooms (now called 'Mackintosh at the Willow') on Sauchiehall Street was completed in 2018, for Mackintosh's 150th birthday, and opened just before the second GSA fire (fig. 5.4). This project took early guidance and inspiration from the GSA's MRP1 – indeed there was much consultancy overlap and communication between the two. It similarly employed a research-driven approach to internal reconstruction and external renovation, utilising specialist craftspeople and heritage experts to recreate its intricate interiors. However, it also took necessary liberties to facilitate the fact that this was to be not a museum but a working restaurant, for example integrating a new service and bar area in the ground floor, and a new rooftop tea lounge for rare sunny days. The team was also fortunate enough to acquire the building next door, and integrated it to make a new shop, exhibition space, educational suite and, most importantly, a lift to make the Willow fully accessible for visitors. All this was done in record time, just four years, perhaps because it was a largely private project undertaken by the Willow Tea Rooms Trust, founded in 2014 by Celia Sinclair after she purchased the buildings. As a testament to the success of the project, it was announced in January 2024 that Mackintosh at the Willow would join the portfolio of NTS, ensuring its future for the nation.[11] Perhaps the next Mack restoration project will take guidance from these two successes and build on them, cleverly combining faithful recreation with a sustainable and innovative approach, one that is greener and offers more flexible working space and 'smart' features, such as beacons in the Mackintosh lighting that connect the physical to the digital. Above all, it should be as fireproof as possible.

Can the Mack be rebuilt? Of course it can, as other projects have shown. Its material and materiality have gone, and have been for some time. But the design exists and our memories survive, though fading fast. Buildings are monumental testaments to our culture and achievements. Perhaps that is why such loss hits us so deeply, when the building is as wonderful, and beloved, as our Mack was. That building resides on Renfrew Street but also lives within us, like our homes and other places that speak to us profoundly. It survives in our stories and the moments we shared within it. And those that love it have the fear that when we are gone, if not rebuilt the Mack may also be gone. Even now at GSA whole cohorts of graduating students have

FIG. 5.5 Western stair to the sub-basement, February 2020.

never known it; and many staff who have loved and experienced the Mack have left the school, Glasgow, some even this world. By the time we can make the building whole again, how many of us will remember our time in it before? These are upsetting thoughts – but they also drive the desire to see the building live again.

The Mackintosh building is a masterpiece of architecture, but it is also a masterpiece of design. The design exists and much research has been completed already, as sketched in this book. In 2014 the GSA community stood in front of the Mack wondering if it could possibly be rebuilt. Now, under worse circumstances, there is evidence that it can be. Taking liberties as an author, here is my own vision: a faithfully restored Mack, cleverly connected to a new build that encompasses the defunct property down the hill on Sauchiehall Street, which, if present conditions in Glasgow are any indicator, is at risk of becoming another student accommodation high-rise. Create flexible teaching spaces, possibly even more staff offices (which are cramped and shared by most), studio space for postgraduate programmes and a theatre space in homage to the lost ABC. Join ranks with the nearby Centre for Contemporary Art (CCA) and the Royal Conservatoire of Scotland to make a contemporary cultural centre. Get an innovative but sensitive design team to create a dynamic and accessible connection to the Mack from down the hill. And include the community in a real and meaningful way. I don't know if that is possible, but at the very least I fully agree with Elizabeth Davidson's concerns and vision for the Mack, which was born from the passion, dedication and energy of the previous restoration team:

For the future, my biggest fear is that it is not reconstructed with a conviction that must imbue and infuse every member of the team from designers to bricklayers, if that happens it will ring false and futile; but my greatest hope is that if [GSA] can achieve this wholehearted reconstruction, one which deals with both materiality and spirituality and understands that intangible 'symbolism', then this project could be one of the greatest conservation projects ever and one which embraces and changes the debate around the climate emergency, inclusion and equality so pertinent to the world over a century later.[12]

I was immeasurably proud to be a small part of the first Mackintosh restoration project and humbled by the incredible experts in the fields of conservation, heritage, engineering and architecture working alongside me. But make no mistake: something went terribly wrong. The 2019 Scottish parliamentary investigation into this disaster, which can be read in full online, was protracted and heated but offered no clear resolve. The only conclusion was, in short, that there was an egregious error made in the protection of this building. We will never know what exactly happened: how the fire started, why alarms were seemingly malfunctioning, whether better protection in the form of fire systems (including temporary suppression and better compartmentalisation) would have helped to reduce, if not prevent, this calamity. But it is hoped that this was an 'honest error' and that the GSA, and the city, will bring back the Mack in a manner that celebrates and restores Mackintosh's vision.

The Mack of most people's memory is the one that was damaged in 2014. In the period following the fire, although no longer serving its intended function, it was very much a 'living' building throughout its restoration. Its community of users shifted from students, staff and visitors to project managers, engineers, architects, heritage professionals, researchers and craftspeople. Yes, it was largely a building site; but it was also a research project, a workplace, a place of creative response and, at times, a classroom. Outwardly, it is little more than a wreckage, and there has been confusion among some locals who think the 'School of Art' is closed. For many, the Mack is gone – an ephemeral thing, existing somewhere between wreckage and memory. But in its present state of ruin, there is still a place where one can stand on the west stairwell leading down to the sub-basement; a moment where, if you pause just at the bottom of the first landing and look up the sooty stairs and through the arched opening, you are back in the Mack (fig. 5.5). You can stop on that step and imagine – almost believe – the rest is soaring there above you.

The Glasgow School of Art is *not* the Mack. But the Mack is the Glasgow School of Art.

The Glasgow School of Art Club "At Home" in the Institute Galleries Sauchiehall St. on Saturday Nov. 25 from 3 to 5 P.M.

Margt. Menzies Macdonald inv & del.

NOTES

INTRODUCTION
A PLACE OF DREAMS

1   Alison Watt, 'Why I Wept for the Glasgow School of Art When I Heard of the Fire', *Guardian*, 24 May 2014, https://www.theguardian.com/commentisfree/2014/may/24/glasgow-school-of-art-fire-artist-alison-watts-reaction, accessed 3 July 2023.

2   Brian Ferguson, 'Glasgow School of Art Restoration "to Cost £35m"', *Scotsman*, 18 November 2015, https://www.scotsman.com/regions/glasgow-school-art-restoration-cost-ps35m-1489378, accessed 3 July 2023. No clear figure has ever been confirmed by the school as the project was unfinished, but it is thought the final cost would have been more than the £35 million cited in the press.

3   Christopher Platt, interview with the author, 2019.

4   'Notre-Dame Fire: International Call for Architects to Design New Spire', BBC News, 17 April 2019, https://www.bbc.com/news/world-europe-47959313, accessed 3 July 2023.

5   Gareth Harris, 'French Senate Says Notre Dame Must Be Restored "in the Same Way as Before"', *Art Newspaper* (blog), 29 May 2019, https://www.theartnewspaper.com/news/wim-delvoye-dismisses-french-senate-s-proposals-for-rebuilding-notre-dame, accessed 3 July 2023.

6   'Notre Dame Restoration Ready to Start as Safety Work Completed', *Guardian*, 18 September 2021, https://www.theguardian.com/world/2021/sep/18/notre-dame-restoration-ready-to-start-as-safety-work-completed, accessed 3 July 2023.

7   William Morris, Philip Webb and others, 'The SPAB Manifesto (1877)', Society for the Protection of Ancient Buildings, https://www.spab.org.uk/about-us/spab-manifesto, accessed 3 July 2023.

8   'The SPAB Approach', Society for the Protection of Ancient Buildings, 6 July 2017, https://www.spab.org.uk/campaigning/spab-approach, accessed 3 July 2023.

9   'The Burra Charter: The Australia ICOMOS Charter for Places of Cultural Significance 2013', Australia ICOMOS (International Council on Monuments and Sites), http://australia.icomos.org/wp-content/uploads/The-Burra-Charter-2013-Adopted-31.10.2013.pdf, accessed 3 July 2023.

10   'What is Intangible Cultural Heritage?', UNESCO, https://ich.unesco.org/en/what-is-intangible-heritage-00003, accessed 3 July 2023.

11   Burra Charter.

12   See, for example, Sally M. Foster and Neil G.W. Curtis, 'The Thing about Replicas – Why Historic Replicas Matter', *European Journal of Archaeology* 19:1 (2016), 122–48, and Sian Jones and Thomas Yarrow, 'Crafting Authenticity: An Ethnography of Conservation Practice', *Journal of Material Culture* 18:1 (2013), 3–26.

13   Stephen Mullen and Simon Newman, 'Slavery, Abolition and the University of Glasgow: Report and Recommendations of the University of Glasgow History of Slavery Steering Committee', September 2018, 21, https://www.gla.ac.uk/media/Media_607547_smxx.pdf, accessed 3 July 2023.

14   See Howarth 1977; Crawford 1995; Macaulay 2010; Billcliffe 2017.

15   Billcliffe 2017, 9.

16   Billcliffe 2017, 9.

17   Charles Rennie Mackintosh to Margaret Macdonald Macintosh, 16 May 1927, in Robertson 2001, 56.

18   See Nikolaus Pevsner, *Pioneers of Modern Design: From William Morris to Walter Gropius*, New Haven and London: Yale University Press, 4th edn 2005, 142.

19   Charles Jencks, *Towards a Symbolic Architecture: The Thematic House*, New York: Rizzoli, 1985.

20   See, for example, Brett 1992; Egger et al. 2000; Calvert 2012.

21   For example, two gesso panels were designed on the play *The Seven Princesses* for Fritz Waerndorfer. Macdonald's is in the collection of the MAK in Vienna; Mackintosh's was drawn but never realised as far as we know: the sketch is in the Hunterian collection at the University of Glasgow (GLAHA 41960).

22   Howarth 1977, 19–22.

23   '*Nommer un objet, c'est supprimer les trois quarts de la jouissance du poème ... le suggérer, voilà le rêve.*' Stéphane Mallarmé, interview in Jules Huret, *Enquête sur l'évolution littéraire* [A Survey of Literary Development], 1891.

CHAPTER 1
BEFORE THE MACK

1   Allan D. Mainds and Alexander Proudfoot, 'Dumble-Dum-Dearie, or How Fra Newbery Got his Cloak and Hat. The Glasgow School of Art Song' (*c.* 1916), repr. in full in McKenzie et al. 2009, 149.

2 Glasgow Centre for Population Health, 'Historic Population Trend: The Glasgow Indicators Project', 2019.

3 See Mullen 2009.

4 For a detailed discussion of design reform, see Kriegel 2008.

5 The South Kensington School became known as the National Art Training College in 1853 and finally became the Royal College of Art in 1896. For further reading, see Lawrence 2020.

6 Sonia Ashmore, 'Owen Jones and the V&A Collections', *V&A Online Journal*, no. 1 (Autumn 2008), http://www.vam.ac.uk/content/journals/research-journal/issue-01/owen-jones-and-the-v-and-a-collections/, accessed 4 July 2023.

7 This teaching collection became part of the South Kensington Museum, now the Victoria & Albert Museum.

8 Owen Jones, 'Lectures on Articles in the Museum of the Department of Science and Art', London, 1852, 4.

9 George Rawson, '"The Renfrew Street Panopticon": Francis Newbery and the Reinvention of Glasgow School of Art', in McKenzie et al. 2009, 18.

10 'Report of Lecture Entitled "Art Instincts" Delivered on 23 December, 1911, at Glasgow School of Art', *Glasgow Herald*, 25 December 1911.

11 'Glasgow School of Art', *Glasgow Herald*, 2 February 1897.

12 Charles Rennie Mackintosh, 'Architecture' (1893), in Robertson 1990, 208.

13 For further discussion of Artistic Dress and interiors, see Robyne Erica Calvert, 'Fashioning the Artist: Artistic Dress in Victorian Britain 1848–1900', PhD thesis, University of Glasgow, 2012.

14 Jackson 2013, 197–8.

15 See, for example, the work of Glasgow Boys painters E.A. Hornel and George Henry, who travelled to Japan and painted there together; both were good friends of Mackintosh's future employer John Keppie.

16 Jackson 2013, 199; Kimura 1982.

17 Kikuo Tanaka, *Iroha Biki Monchō: Illustrated Index of Japanese Coats of Arms*, Tokyo: H. Matsuzaki, 1881. The GSA copy is stamped 'The Glasgow School of Art and Haldane Academy', which indicates roughly when it entered the collection, as Haldane Academy was dropped from the school's name in 1891.

18 *Mackintosh Architecture*, M179 (Miss Cranston's Lunch and Tea Rooms, Ingram Street).

19 See Maryhill Burgh Halls Trust, https://www.maryhillburghhalls.org.uk/panels, accessed 19 February 2024.

20 Glasgow School of Art Archives & Collections (hereafter GSAA), GOV/1/53, Annual Report 1897–8, 16.

21 Crawford 1995, 9.

22 This has not been clearly documented and is repeated as part of Mackintosh folklore. However, errors in some of his extant manuscripts indicate irregularities beyond mere spelling mistakes, which might indicate dyslexia. See Robertson 1990, 26.

23 Charles Rennie Mackintosh, *House at Corner of McLeod Street*, 1889. Pencil on paper. Glasgow Museums (PR.1969.12.a).

24 Allan Glen's School Club, http://www.allanglens.com/index.php/allan-glen-s-school, accessed 4 July 2023.

25 For more on Glasgow's architecture, see Gomme and Walker 1987, still the best source on the subject.

26 See Chapter 4 for discussion.

27 Joseph Sharples, 'The Architectural Career of C.R. Mackintosh', *Mackintosh Architecture*.

28 Sharples, 'Architectural Career', *Mackintosh Architecture*.

29 This commission included the gesso panel *The Heart of the Rose* by Margaret Macdonald Mackintosh, which is now in the collection of the GSA. The project was a fully designed fire surround, with the gesso panel inset about the hearth. See Calvert 2018.

30 Charles Rennie Mackintosh, 'Diary of an Italian Tour' (1891), in Robertson 1990, 102.

31 Mackintosh's Northern Italian Sketchbook (1891), GSAA, https://gsaarchives.net/explore/mackintoshs-northern-italian-sketchbook/, accessed 4 July 2023.

32 Charles Rennie Mackintosh, *The Lido, Venice*, 1891. Watercolour drawing on paper. The Hunterian, University of Glasgow, GLAHA 41955.

33 See Robertson 1990; Rawson 2020. Mackintosh also undertook travels in Scotland and England that would have offered their own atmospheric experiences, and he took more direct influence from them – especially from his 1895 tour of Dorset. See Rawson 2020, 84.

34 Charles Rennie Mackintosh, 'A Tour in Italy' (1892), in Robertson 1990, 120.

35 Buchanan 2004, 22.

36 Mackintosh, 'Architecture', in Robertson 1990, 206.

37 For example the Willowwood theme, based on Rossetti's sonnets of the same name, at the Willow Tea Rooms. Such spaces can be looked at

in a cursory way as decoration, but also have narrative keys – Margaret Macdonald's gesso panels in many cases – that allow a story to unfold. See Calvert 2012.

38 Sharples, 'Architectural Career', *Mackintosh Architecture*.

39 See *Mackintosh Architecture*, M057 (Glasgow Art Galleries), M068 (Cheapside Street grain stores) and M069 (Craigie Hall), for example.

40 Sharples, 'Architectural Career', *Mackintosh Architecture*.

41 Andrew Graham Henderson, 'Obituary: John Keppie, RSA', *Journal of the Royal Institute of British Architects* (September 1945), 340.

42 *Mackintosh Architecture*, M072 (Glasgow Herald buildings).

43 Letter from Charles Rennie Mackintosh to Hermann Muthesius, 11 May 1898. Hermann Muthesius Estate, Werkbundarchiv, Museum der Dinge, Berlin.

44 *Mackintosh Architecture* has a complete list of known works by John Honeyman & Keppie in this period.

45 *Mackintosh Architecture*, M105 (Martyrs' Public School).

46 'Glasgow Municipal Meetings. Glasgow School of Art and Haldane Academy', *Glasgow Herald*, 16 October 1885.

47 For a detailed account of Newbery and his educational philosophy, see Rawson 1996.

48 Howarth 1977, 25. Howarth reports that this was related to him by Francis Newbery, who could not recall an exact date.

49 Jessie R. Newbery, 'Foreword: A Memory of Mackintosh', in *Charles Rennie Mackintosh, Margaret Macdonald Mackintosh: Memorial Exhibition*, Glasgow: McLennan Galleries, 1933, 1–2.

50 J.R. Newbery, 'Foreword: A Memory'.

51 The works Newbery references were in the April and September 1893 issues of *The Studio*. So 'the following autumn' may have been following the September 1893 issue, but it was more likely 1894.

52 Gleeson White, 'Some Glasgow Designers and Their Work': Part I, *The Studio* 11, no. 52 (1897), 86–99; Part II: *The Studio* 11, no. 54 (1897), 227–35; Part III: *The Studio* 12, no. 55, 47–50; Part IV: *The Studio* 13, no. 59 (1898), 12–24.

53 Burkhauser 1990, 49–50.

54 William Buchanan read the look between Margaret Macdonald and Jessie Keppie as a 'frisson', based on a rumoured broken engagement between Mackintosh and Keppie (Buchanan 2004, 8). However, any viewer who doesn't want to detect a 'catfight' in the image sees a look of warmth between friends. For detailed discussion, see Robyne Calvert, 'Immortals, Beloved?', https://robynecalvert.com/2018/02/20/immortals-beloved/, accessed 20 February 2024.

55 GSAA, MC/A/15/1–4.

56 Rather than Cabanel, I suggest that the vertical orientation, and long wavy strands of hair that merge with her dress, are also suggestive of Botticelli's famous *Birth of Venus* (1480), one of the 'old friends' Mackintosh will have visited at the Uffizi during his Italy trip. She is likewise suggestive of the female figures in the Pre-Raphaelite and Aesthetic paintings of Edward Burne-Jones, whose work – also informed by Botticelli – was influential for the young Glasgow artists.

57 Both George Rawson and Roger Billcliffe have noted the composition of these circular figures flanking a central tree to reference a wallpaper design by Voysey, which was reproduced in the September 1893 issue of *The Studio* that Jessie Newbery referenced. See Rawson 1996, 161; Billcliffe 2017, 37.

CHAPTER 2
DESIGNING THE MACK

1 GSAA, GOV/5/4/1, Conditions of Competition, 1896, 5.

2 Rawson 1996, 91–2.

3 GSAA, GOV/2/3, Governors' minutes, 22 February 1895.

4 Rawson 1996, 128–9.

5 Rawson 1996, 173.

6 Rawson 1996, 173.

7 Rawson 1996, 129–30.

8 GSAA, GOV/2/3, Governors' minutes, 28 January 1895.

9 The building committee included other notable governors, such as Leonard Gow, a philanthropist and businessman with interests in shipping, oil, explosives, gold mining and insurance, who was also a director of the Glasgow Institute of Fine Arts. Also included were the artist and shipping agent Patrick Smith Dunn and Baillie William Bilsland, a leading figure in local government and industry. With his brothers, Bilsland ran a bakery that employed 200 people and produced over ten million loaves a year. Like Newbery and so many others associated with the school

he had clear socialist values: in addition to free loaves of bread, his workers were well paid, and worked a maximum 40-hour week. A town councillor from 1886, Baillie Bilsland served as Lord Provost of Glasgow from 1905 to 1908. See *Mackintosh Architecture*, M134 (The Glasgow School of Art).

10 This included, for example, helping to organise Glasgow's International Exhibitions, notably as convenor for the applied and industrial art section in 1901. A political liberal, his services to art earned him a knighthood in 1906.

11 GSAA, GOV/2/4, Governors' minutes, 16 March 1896.

12 See *Mackintosh Architecture*, M134.

13 GSAA, GOV/5/1/1, Building Committee minutes, 15 July 1896, 12. Howarth reports that Burnet and Salmon had resigned as governors when they took part in the competition (Howarth 1977, 71) but their names appear in meeting minutes throughout this period (though Salmon may have taken a brief hiatus if absences are noted). Both had been part of the deputation to South Kensington three years earlier, which would have given them an advantage in understanding the school's needs. Salmon had also assisted in preparing the site for building, working on the project for a retaining wall; GSAA, GOV/2/4, Governors' minutes, 16 March 1896, 77–8. Given Leiper's ethical stance, one wonders whether the governors' participation in the competition caused any tension.

14 GSAA, GOV/2/4, Governors' minutes, 16 March 1896.

15 See *Mackintosh Architecture*, M105 (Martyrs' Public School) and M125 (Queen's Cross Church).

16 See *Mackintosh Architecture*, M233 (Scotland Street Public School).

17 GSAA, GOV/2/4, Governors' minutes, 12 August 1896, 92.

18 GSAA, GOV/2/4, Governors' minutes, 12 August 1896, 93.

19 GSAA, GOV/2/4, Governors' minutes, 27 August 1896, 95.

20 GSAA, GOV/2/4, Governors' minutes, 27 August 1896, 97.

21 GSAA, GOV/5/4/1, Conditions of Competition, 1896, 5.

22 Howarth 1977, 71.

23 GSAA, GOV/5/4/1, Letter to Directors from James King and Renny Watson, 7 December 1896.

24 GSAA, GOV/5/1/1, Building Committee minutes, 13 January 1897, 24.

25 See *Mackintosh Architecture*, M134.

26 GSAA, GOV/5/4/10, Keppie and Mackintosh, designs for the Glasgow School of Art, 1896.

27 GSAA, GOV/5/4/10, Keppie and Mackintosh, designs for the Glasgow School of Art, 1896, 2.

28 GSAA, GOV/5/4/10, Keppie and Mackintosh, designs for the Glasgow School of Art, 1896, 2.

29 Rawson 1996, 181.

30 GSAA, GOV/2/4, Governors' minutes, 11 October 1897, 159.

31 GSAA, GOV/2/4, Governors' minutes, 11 October 1897, 159–60.

32 *Mackintosh Architecture*, M134.

33 GSAA, GOV/2/4, Governors' minutes, 5 November 1897, 167.

34 GSAA, GOV/2/4, Governors' minutes, 20 April 1898, 199.

35 'Glasgow School of Art', *Glasgow Herald*, 26 May 1898, 8.

36 *Glasgow Herald*, 26 May 1898, 8.

37 *Glasgow Herald*, 26 May 1898, 8.

38 GSAA, GOV/1/53, Annual Report 1897–8, 4.

39 See GSAA, NMC/0447.

40 According to William Buchanan, 'the stone was lowered between two large windows on the first floor. It was said to be in full view of Renfrew Street although it can now neither be seen nor located.' He does not offer a source for this report. Buchanan 2004, 34.

41 For an account of the building construction process, see Sharples's research for *Mackintosh Architecture*, M134.

42 'Opening of the Art School', *Evening Times*, 21 December 1899, 2.

43 This remarkable key was only recently rediscovered by a descendant of James King and made a brief visit back to the GSA in April 2018, before being auctioned – a portion of the funds being donated in support of the restoration effort.

44 'Scottish Society Notes', *Madame*, 6 January 1900, 15.

45 GSAA, GOV/1/53, Annual Report 1897–8, 9.

46 Lewis F. Day, 'Decorative and Industrial Art at the Glasgow Exhibition (third notice)', *Art Journal*, (1901), 277.

47 Calvert 2018.

48 For a detailed discussion see George Rawson, '"The Renfrew Street Panopticon": Francis Newbery and the Reinvention of Glasgow School of Art', in McKenzie et al. 2009, 17–27.

49 GSAA, GOV/5/13, Fundraising pamphlet for the completion of the School building, n.d. [*c.* 1907].

50 William Burrell was a philanthropist whose extensive wealth came from the shipping industry. He was an avid collector of art and especially antiquities – he entered several notorious bidding wars for such items with other 'Gilded Age' millionaires like William Randolph Hearst. His vast collection was left to the city of Glasgow and is now housed in the Burrell Collection Art Museum.

51 GSAA, GOV/5/5/3, Appointment of the Architects, 1 February 1907.

52 *Mackintosh Architecture*, M233.

53 GSAA, GOV/5/1/3, Building Committee minutes, 10 September 1907.

54 *Mackintosh Architecture*, M134.

55 GSAA, DIR/5/2, letter sent by Director Francis H. Newbery to Professor G. Baldwin Brown, 19 February 1907. Inspired by discovering this note in the archives, former student Rosie O'Grady re-enacted the event by bringing a camel into the Mack as part of her 2013 degree show work entitled *Camellemac*. In a short video, she offers an uncanny vision of a live camel swaying its way about the basement corridor, wonderfully juxtaposed against a plaster cast of a lion, bringing to life Newbery's correspondence. Poignantly, this was the last degree show to be held in the Mack, and now that the space is lost, O'Grady's film has also become an important document of the building. At the event itself, just a video was played, but there were some live sheep, much to everyone's delight. The video can be viewed at the artist's website: https://rosieogrady.co.uk/Camellemac.

56 The School of Architecture was formed in collaboration with the Glasgow and West of Scotland Technical College to solve programmatic deficiencies faced by both in the face of stringent RIBA examinations. Eugène Bourdon, who was headhunted by Salmon and Burnet on a trip to the École des Beaux-Arts in France, was appointed the first head of the school. For a complete history of this era, see Robert Proctor, 'Tradition and Evolution: Glasgow School of Architecture under Eugène Bourdon', in McKenzie et al. 2009, 80–94.

57 Ranald MacInnes, interview with the author, 2020.

58 *Mackintosh Architecture*, M134, description, note 35.

59 Page\Park Architects, 'Glasgow School of Art: Applied Finishes Appraisal Report DRAFT', 2017.

60 Cairns 1992. Drawings made by Cairns can be found at https://gsaarchives.net/catalogue/index.php/cairns-george, accessed 5 July 2023.

61 *Mackintosh Architecture*, M134, description.

62 *Mackintosh Architecture*, 'McCulloch & Co'.

63 Now in the Victoria & Albert Museum, London; see https://collections.vam.ac.uk/item/O62460/casket-mackintosh-charles-rennie/, accessed 20 February 2024.

CHAPTER 3
A PLAIN BUILDING

1 *The Vista: The Quarterly Magazine of the Glasgow School of Architecture Club*, Autumn 1909.

2 Quoted in Grigor and Murphy 1993, 40. In 1990 the exhibition *Contemporary Visions*, celebrating Glasgow's year as European City of Culture, invited internationally renowned architects to make interventions in the Mack. One of these, a shower inspired by one at The Hill House and designed by British architect Edward Cullinan, remained in the director's toilet and was lost in the 2018 fire. The 1993 catalogue of the show included responses from the architects involved: Filippo Alison, Edward Cullinan, Aldo van Eyck, Hans Hollein, Arata Isozaki, Léon Krier and Stanley Tigerman.

3 Sarah MacKinnon, interview with the author, 25 June 2020.

4 This theory was put forward by Thom Simmons, the traditional skills officer for the project, who supported the salvage operations. Ranald MacInnes expressed uncertainty about Giffnock stone being used for carved detail.

5 Ranald MacInnes, 'Mackintosh and Materials', *Mackintosh Architecture*.

6 Charles Rennie Mackintosh, 'Scotch Baronial Architecture' (1891), in Robertson 1990, 61.

7 Charles Rennie Mackintosh, 'Architecture' (1893), in Robertson 1990, 206.

8 Elizabeth Davidson, interview with the author, 2021. At the time of publication, Davidson is project-managing the conservation of The Hill House, National Trust for Scotland.

9 Mackintosh, 'Scotch Baronial Architecture', in Robertson 1990, 63.

10 Frank Arneil Walker, 'Scottish Baronial Architecture', in Robertson 1990, 44.

11 Mackintosh, 'Scotch Baronial Architecture', in Robertson 1990, 52.

12 Louis H. Sullivan, 'Ornament in Architecture', *Engineering Magazine* 3, no. 5 (August 1892), 641.

13 Howarth 1977, 75.

14 GSAA, GOV/5/1/3, Building Committee minutes, 7 February 1908.

15 See, for example, Howarth 1977; Kimura 1982. Mackmurdo was a follower of Ruskin and a founder of the Century Guild of Artists with Selwyn Image; he helped to establish the Society for the Protection of Ancient Buildings (SPAB).

16 The 'Hennebique System' of reinforced concrete used on the Lion Chambers building on Hope Street offered an alternative to steel frames by casting concrete in situ, making the building more fireproof. The complexities of the material had an unfavourable result, however, and time has shown it to have the same weathering troubles as later Brutalist structures. The now A-listed Lion Chambers is currently mostly derelict and has been on the Buildings at Risk Register since 1997. It yet stands, covered in protective scaffold with authorities still determined to save it, but flummoxed as to how. It is a symbol of Victorian/Edwardian innovation gone awry.

17 Each floor has nine-square glazing for each window, with three windows per bay and three bays across, for a total of 81 panes of glass per floor. Some might suggest a nod to Freemasonry in the mathematical configuration.

18 GSAA, GOV/5/1/4, Building Committee minutes, 2 December 1908.

19 *Mackintosh Architecture*, 'George Adam & Son'. These were altered at a later date, according to Ranald MacInnes.

20 Neat 1994, 161–4.

21 Buchanan 2004, 22.

22 Buchanan 2004, 20–1.

23 Charles Rennie Mackintosh, 'Seemliness' (1902), in Robertson 1990, 225.

24 Quoted in Grigor and Murphy 1993, 52.

25 As described by Sharples in *Mackintosh Architecture*.

26 Jenny Brownrigg, interview with the author, 2021.

27 Alastair Macdonald, interview with the author, February 2019.

28 Bruce Peter, interview with the author, February 2019.

29 Grigor and Murphy 1993, 54.

30 Grigor and Murphy 1993, 72.

31 Grigor and Murphy 1993, 72.

32 Christopher Platt, 'The Experience of Place', in Roderick Kemsley and Christopher Platt, *Dwelling with Architecture*, Routledge, 2012, 13–46.

33 Bruce Peter, in conversation with the author, 2020.

34 Buchanan 2004, 122.

35 John Brown, interview with the author, 2020.

36 These doors have been relocated throughout the history of the school, notably when Keppie Henderson worked on improvements and fire prevention strategies *c.* 1966. Thus it is difficult to pin down a specific east versus west analysis, since some doors may have moved from their original positions.

37 Macdonald interview, February 2019.

38 Frances Robertson, interview with the author, February 2019.

39 Frightened Rabbit was one of several successful rock bands to have ties to the school over the last few decades, including The Soup Dragons, Travis and Franz Ferdinand. Hutchison founded Frightened Rabbit while still a student in 2003; he sadly passed away in 2018 and his family established the youth mental health charity Tiny Changes in his name, https://tinychanges.com.

40 Scott Hutchison, interviewed in *Mackintosh's Masterpiece*, BBC Films, 2009, dir. Louise Chapman.

41 Rawson 1996, 188. Groundwater was subsequently also Treasurer, following the death of Edward Catterns in 1909. Catterns was rather a fixture, having been with the school for decades and through the appointment of Newbery as well as through most of the building of the Mack. A painter and sculptor, he is worth further research in terms of his importance in the history of the school.

42 For more on gender coding in nineteenth-century interiors, see Kinchin 1996, 12–29.

43 Sarah Smith, interview with the author, February 2019.

44 William Buchanan, James Macaulay and Andrew MacMillan, 'A Tour of the School', in Buchanan 2004, 108.

45 Brownrigg interview, 2021.

46 Mackintosh notably designed a large, heavy desk that provided study space for staff. It was very plain, designed for three users (so may have been placed under the window) with the slightest sloping top at either end for reading material. This piece

found little use in its later life, and was lost in 2014 along with other furniture stored in the west end of the building (GSA MC/F/72).

47 Macdonald interview, 2019.

48 Alison Watt, interview with the author, February 2019.

49 Gregory Rankine, interview with the author, March 2019. This is part of the oral history of the school which has been told to me by many, though few wished to go on record after the controversy of the second fire. Many current staff are former students and have a wide variety of interesting experiences to recollect from the past forty or so years. There is certainly a 'secret history' of the Mack to be written in terms of the intangible heritage of this building.

50 The conversations with Anne Ferguson and Barbara Dryburgh occurred during a 2017 'Mack Memories' event inside the building, in which former students over the age of about seventy-five were invited to talk to members of the restoration team and GSA archives about their experiences in the building. Their memories were noted and given to GSA archives to be catalogued.

51 David Buri, interview with the author, February 2019.

52 Duncan Chappell, interview with Dawn Worsley, 25 May 2017, in Worsley 2019.

53 Buchanan, Macaulay and MacMillan, 'A Tour of the School', in Buchanan 2004, 120.

54 Calvert 2012.

55 Buchanan, Macaulay and MacMillan, 'A Tour of the School', in Buchanan 2004, 120.

56 Davidson interview, 2021.

CHAPTER 4
ASHES TO ASHES

1 Elizabeth Davidson, interview with the author, September 2021.

2 Nicky Imrie, 'Building Process and Records', note 15, *Mackintosh Architecture*.

3 *Mackintosh Architecture*, M072 (Glasgow Herald buildings).

4 For a detailed discussion of fireproofing history and Mackintosh-designed buildings, see Purse 2021.

5 GSAA, GOV/2/4, Governors' minutes, 11 October 1897, 161.

6 Purse 2021, 48.

7 Brown 2018. The quote is from V&A Archives, MA/1/9793; RP/1914/196 CIRC, V&A Museum Minute Paper, Glasgow School of Art, 23 September 1913.

8 Black and Swanson 1964, 1.

9 The building was listed in 1966 (and A-listed in 1983), which was good for its stature, but may have added a layer of complication in terms of any structural changes.

10 Buro Happold FEDRA, 'Fire Protection Strategy Options Study', July 2006, 3.

11 From personal experience, while I had to submit risk assessment forms for events, no such training was provided to me prior to 2014, beyond the Design History department head Nicholas Oddy vehemently reminding us to unlock both doors to the lecture theatre in case of fire.

12 Elizabeth Davidson, 'GSA Report on Compartmentation' (2019), Glasgow School of Art, https://themackintoshbuilding.co.uk/wp-content/uploads/2023/01/GSA-Report-on-Compartmentation.pdf, accessed 9 July 2023.

13 Glasgow School of Art, written submission of evidence to the Scottish Parliament Culture, Tourism, Europe and External Affairs Committee, 15 November 2018, 9, https://archive2021.parliament.scot/S5_European/General%20Documents/CTEEA_2018.11.15_GSAEvidence.pdf, accessed 9 July 2023.

14 Glasgow School of Art in association with Page\Park Architects, 'The Mackintosh Conservation & Access Project: The Importance of Fire Suppression' (2009), Glasgow School of Art, https://themackintoshbuilding.co.uk/wp-content/uploads/2023/01/PP-paper-about-non-funding-of-mist-suppression-July-2009-.pdf, accessed 22 February 2024. For a detailed discussion of HES grant funding policies and their relationship to EU regulations, see Purse 2021.

15 It should be noted that risk assessments were required by all students or staff who wanted to hold any event or exhibit in the school, including assessing fire risk; I have experience of completing these for several events myself.

16 For the complete list, see Purse 2021, 67.

17 Purse 2021, 68.

18 Scottish Fire and Rescue Service (SFRS), 'Fire Investigation Report for the May 2014 Fire at The Glasgow School of Art', 2014, 10.

19 SFRS, 'Fire Investigation Report' 2014, 10–11.

20 Davidson, 'GSA Report on Compartmentation'.

21 Despite enquiries to current and former staff, no clear answer has

been given as to this decision outside the fact that the school was pressed for space for collection storage. One imagines it was thought this would be a safer space than rooms in newer, less secure buildings on campus.

22 The paintings had all been photographed by the Art UK project and appear in their digital collection. All items lost in the fire were recorded as such in the school's catalogue at the earliest possibility – a process that took some time in the wake of recovery efforts. The school has since been criticised for not making a published list of items more easily available.

23 See Roger Billcliffe, written submission of evidence to the Scottish Parliament Culture, Tourism, Europe and External Affairs Committee, 20 September 2018, https://archive2021. parliament.scot/S5_European/ General%20Documents/CTEEA_ GSoA_WritEv_Roger_Billcliffe.pdf, accessed 9 July 2023.

24 Phil Miller, 'The Mack Can Be Rebuilt, Says Muriel Gray', *Herald Scotland*, 20 June 2018, https://www. heraldscotland.com/news/16301644. mack-can-rebuilt-says-muriel-gray/, accessed 9 July 2023.

25 'Phoenix Bursaries', Glasgow School of Art, 2015, http://gsaphoenix. blogspot.com, accessed 9 July 2023.

26 'GSA Mack Building – Glasgow School of Art Degree Show', *The Skinny*, 4 June 2015, https://www. theskinny.co.uk/art/emerging-artists/mack-building-glasgow-school-of-art, accessed 9 July 2023.

27 Inns's departure was the subject of much speculation and sensation in the press, with the official statement stating that he resigned. See Mike Wade, 'Glasgow School of Art Principal Tom Inns Resigns amid Turmoil Following Mackintosh Fire', *The Times*, 3 November 2018, and John Jeffay, 'Emails Reveal Rift at Heart of Glasgow School of Art', *The Times*, 2 September 2019.

28 Clarke 2015, 48.

29 'The Glasgow School of Art Mackintosh Library: Data Structures Report by Kirkdale Archaeology', Mackintosh Restoration Project, 2015, 3.

30 This process has been completed at The Hill House through a HES/National Trust for Scotland partnership.

31 'Public Get First Opportunity to See Stunning 3D Visualisations of the Mackintosh Building Post Fire', Glasgow School of Art, 6 October 2016, http://gsapress.blogspot. com/2016/10/public-get-first-opportunity-to-see.html, accessed 9 July 2023.

32 Almost immediately after the fire, GSA alumna Lizzie Malcolm created the Mac Photographic Archive, a crowdsourced project to collect images, which could be mapped to an interactive plan of the building. It is full of wonderful personal memories, some of which have been used in this book.

33 Jo Crotch sadly passed away in 2021 after a long and difficult illness. These 'Mack Memories' remain unpublished; they were given to me as custodian and to use in my own work when Jo became too unwell to complete her project. Rather than include them here, I feel that they should be published elsewhere, in Jo's memory.

34 Contributors included non-GSA artists such as Grayson Perry, Anish Kapoor, Antony Gormley, Rachel Whiteread and Tacita Dean, as well as notable GSA alumni like Alison Watt, Douglas Gordon, Jenny Saville, Simon Starling, Martin Boyce and Chantal Joffe. All works can be viewed at http://ashtoart.org/ artwork, accessed 9 July 2023.

35 The work was exhibited at Christie's, London, before the auction on 8 March 2017, and the gallery also smelled of burnt wood on entering. The project raised nearly £570,000 for the restoration effort. The rest of the funds came from the insurance payout, Scottish and UK Government promises, and private donations, which, in the end, became part of a wider 'Campus Appeal' managed by the GSA Development Trust, a £32 million campaign to rebuild the Mack and expand the already overstretched campus by purchasing and refurbishing the nearby Stow Building for the School of Fine Art. This campaign had not yet reached its goal when the 2018 fire struck.

36 Alexander 2021; Worsley 2019; Purse 2020. Alexander and Purse's projects were co-supervised by HES.

37 All these activities were of course made with full Health & Safety compliance; site visits and community engagement activities are normal in a project like this. It was very strange that during the parliamentary enquiry this was translated into the GSA allowing 'illegal acts' to take place in the building.

38 Alongside Davidson and MacKinnon, a Collections Recovery Project Manager, Polly Christie, was also appointed to work with former GSA Archives & Collections Manager Susannah Waters to oversee the vast project associated with moving and safeguarding the archives and collections (including furnishings and fixtures recovered from the Mack); my own former role of Mackintosh Research Fellow was created to foster and support these, alongside offering research support for the project itself. This internal group of GSA staff became, informally, the 'three Rs': Restoration, Recovery and Research. More formally, the entire project was originally overseen by a subcommittee of the governors and the Mackintosh Restoration Committee, which additionally included the presidents of the GSA Students' Association, various board members, Inns and, from HES, Ranald MacInnes. The committee increasingly focused on 'big picture' items such as contractual arrangements and financial concerns, which left an advisory gap for some of the more day-to-day decisions about the building and its needs. There were several staff consultations throughout the project, but ultimately a new subcommittee was formed in 2017 that was to advise the Mackintosh Building Committee through project completion, the Mackintosh Operations Group. This comprised the design team members, various heads of departments such as Finance, IT, Learning Services (Archives, Collections & Library), Inns, Davidson and myself representing Mackintosh research and teaching. After the second fire, and Inns's departure, senior management never convened this group again.

39 Elizabeth Davidson, 'The Mackintosh Building: Brief to Design Team', 2015, 2–3. GSAA.

40 Page\Park 2016, 56.

41 Page\Park 2016, 56.

42 Page\Park 2016, 68.

43 Duncan Chappell, interview with Dawn Worsley, 25 May 2017, in Worsley 2019.

44 GSAA, GOV/2/7, Governors' minutes, 1909, 58.

45 GSAA, GOV/5/1/4, Building Committee minutes, 18 February 1910, 129.

46 Natalia Burakowska, interview with the author, 2020.

47 Formerly the Royal Commission on the Ancient and Historical Monuments of Scotland (RCAHMS), it merged with HES in 2015.

48 Burakowska interview, 2020.

49 While the school was 'opened' in December 1909, the job books and invoices revealed many sundry works still going on inside the building into the new year, for example the removal and refitting of sinks in the architecture studios in February 1910.

50 Clarke 2015.

51 Clarke 2015.

52 Burakowska interview, 2020.

53 Alongside Paul Clarke, the expert panel comprised conservation architect Andrew Wright, who has worked closely on other Mackintosh properties like The Hill House, and Alan Hooper, Programme Leader in the Mackintosh School of Architecture at GSA.

54 The invoices also prove that these well-known photos, previously dated to 1910, must have been taken some time between 7 August 1909, when the main library table was delivered, and 22 October 1909, when the nine cypress library tables were delivered, as they are also absent from the photos.

55 GSAA, GOV/5/1/4, Building Committee minutes, 26 January 1909, 65.

56 GSAA, GOV/5/1/4, Building Committee minutes, 8 February 1909, 72.

57 Natalia Burakowska, 'Atlas', unpublished draft report, Page\Park Architects, 2018.

58 See, for example, Macaulay 2010, 147.

59 Nick Clifford, 'In-Situ Strength Assessment and Species Identification at the Mackintosh Building, Glasgow School of Arts', Page\Park Architects, 2016. Tulipwood was facing material; the interior of posts was spruce.

60 George Lister Sutcliffe, *The Modern Carpenter and Joiner and Cabinet-Maker: A Complete Guide to Current Practice*, vol. 1, London: Gresham Publishing, 1903, 74. Thanks to Rachael Purse for this discovery.

61 Charles Rennie Mackintosh, 'Untitled Paper on Architecture' (c. 1892), in Robertson 1990, 193–4.

62 'Sales Ledger, 1907–1909, Letters A–K', Robinson Dunn & Co Ltd Timber Importers and Sawmillers, 1909. University of Glasgow Business Archives, UGD 203/1/26.

63 Clifford, 'In-Situ Strength Assessment'.

64 Page\Park Architects, 'Glasgow School of Art: Applied Finishes Appraisal Report DRAFT', 2017.

65 This was useful very briefly, as shortly thereafter a full set of detailed photos were discovered uncatalogued in the GSA archives. We also learned they were roughly sketched in a 1973 article, 'Casabella' by Alison Filippo.

66 This was notably commented on by Roger Billcliffe at various workshops and public talks. In an article in *The Times* (14 August 2018) he was also quoted as saying to an audience at the Edinburgh International Book Festival that the school 'should not be rebuilt by pedantic architects ... the computer will make the drawings of the building ... it won't be tempted to put in the twiddly bits that architects might add'.

67 According to Burakowska, these casts were made by Robert Pollock, who worked on House for an Art Lover, and were gifted to the project design team for research.

68 This group included Mackintosh furniture scholar Roger Billcliffe, University of Glasgow Mackintosh Professor Emerita Pamela Robertson, Glasgow Museums' curator Alison Brown and Charles Rennie Mackintosh Society Chair Stuart Robertson.

69 Glasgow Museums Curator of European and Decorative Arts Alison Brown, who has worked closely on the Oak Room conservation for well over a decade and oversaw its installation at the V&A Dundee (without furniture), shared with us her theory that these chairs were not actually designed by Mackintosh. On close inspection, she has a point: the chamfering, she noted, was not like that any seen in any other Mackintosh chairs, and the overall look was closer to the kinds produced in the 1920s and 1930s by firms like Heal's, or more locally, Wylie & Lochhead. Further research needs to be undertaken, but in terms of 'Mackintosh authenticity', it complicates any replication decisions in future.

70 This micro-project was led collaboratively by the Restoration Project Manager Sarah MacKinnon and the Recovery Project Manager Polly Christie.

71 'Data Structures Report by Kirkdale Archaeology', 2015.

72 Purse's project, co-funded by GSA and HES, was originally centred on documenting the restoration. But in the wake of the second fire it was revised to focus on how to protect our heritage. See Purse 2021.

73 Scottish Fire and Rescue Service (SFRS), 'Fire Investigation Report: The Glasgow School of Art, 15 June 2018', January 2022.

74 SFRS, 'Fire Investigation Report', 18.

75 The exclusion zone was one of the true disasters of the fire. Residents were unable to access their homes and local businesses had to close indefinitely. This was not the school's decision, nor was it in their power to allow access; however, all parties agree that there should have been better communication throughout this period. The anger of the community was understandable.

76 SFRS, 'Fire Investigation Report', 43.

77 SFRS, 'Fire Investigation Report', 37–8.

78 Glasgow School of Art and Avison Young (preparer), 'Strategic Outline Business Case', 22 October 2021, https://themackintoshbuilding.co.uk/wp-content/uploads/2023/03/211020_GSA_business_case_PRECIS-375-FINAL-FOR-HOARDING93.pdf, accessed 22 February 2024. Options explored included: 'Option 1 – Do Minimum, comprising the stabilisation of the existing structure and façade. This is included for comparison purposes only rather than a realistic option to pursue. Option 2 – Faithful Reinstatement, comprising a reinstatement of the original building yet in a manner that is compliant with all relevant legislation and digitally enabled. Option 3 – Hybrid, comprising a reinstatement of the original design ethos and the recreation of certain iconic rooms and finishes, digitally enabled with flexible space. Option 4 – Modern equivalent, comprising the demolition of the fire-damaged building and the construction of an entirely new facility on site', 29.

79 'Strategic Outline Business Case', 34.

80 Glasgow School of Art, 'Media Release: Mackintosh Building Update', 24 January 2023, https://gsapress.blogspot.com/2023/01/media-releasemackintosh-building-update.html, accessed 9 July 2023.

81 The external steering group members are listed on the recently established project website, but only some bios were available there at the time of going to press. Of those listed, several included are practising architects, property developers or risk managers. Heritage authorities, including the Charles Rennie Mackintosh Society, are listed among external stakeholders in the Business Case document, but it is unclear from the website how they are engaging with the steering group. As of February 2024 the website lists steering group membership as: Professor John French (Convenor), James Sanderson (Vice-Convenor), Ann Faulds, Michael McAuley, Ken Ross, Lesley Thomson, Paul Brewer, Professor Hanif Kara, Kim Hitch, Stephen Hodder, Professor Neal Juster, Iain Marley, Jill Miller, Lucy Musgrave, Stuart Patrick and Dale Sinclair. See: https://themackintoshbuilding.co.uk/project-governance/steering-group/, accessed 16 February 2024.

82 'Statement: The Mackintosh Building Procurement Exercise', GSA, 1 March 2023, https://gsapress.blogspot.com/2023/03/statement-mackintosh-building.html, accessed 9 July 2023.

83 Merlin Fulcher, 'The Mac scraps search for restoration architect after procurement error', *Architects' Journal*, 2 March 2023, https://www.architectsjournal.co.uk/news/the-mac-scraps-search-for-restoration-architect-after-procurement-error, accessed 9 July 2023.

84 Fulcher, 'The Mac scraps search'.

85 Sir David Chipperfield, 'The Responsibilities of Practice', NORR ed., 31 January 2024. https://www.youtube.com/watch?v=4C1_mHZlgxo, accessed 22 February 2024. Another eloquent case for

rebuilding has been made by Frank Arneil Walker in his essay 'Glasgow School of Art: The Building and its Future', *Journal of the Charles Rennie Mackintosh Society*, 105/106 (2023), 17–23.

EPILOGUE
THE EPHEMERAL
SCHOOL OF ART

1 Neil Bickerton, 'Mackintosh Didn't Build an Art School', Facebook post, 23 June 2018.

2 Quoted in Grigor and Murphy 1993, 47.

3 David Buri, interview with the author, February 2019.

4 Phil Miller, 'Residents Lambast Glasgow School of Art in Submission to MSPs', *Herald Scotland*, 5 October 2018, https://www.heraldscotland.com/news/16961757.residents-lambast-glasgow-school-art-submission-msps/, accessed 10 July 2023.

5 Written submission on behalf of the Sauchiehall Street Inner Cordon Businesses and Garnethill Displaced Residents Group re the Mackintosh Building to the Scottish Parliament Culture, Tourism, Europe and External Affairs Committee, October 2018, 1, https://archive2021.parliament.scot/S5_European/General%20Documents/CTEEA_WriteEv_GSOA_Sauchiehall.pdf, accessed 10 July 2023.

6 'Garnethill residents consider legal action in wake of Art School fire', *Glasgow Live*, 21 August 2018, https://www.glasgowlive.co.uk/news/glasgow-news/garnethill-residents-consider-legal-action-15056146, accessed 10 July 2023.

7 Mark Aitken, 'Glasgow School of Art Sues Fire Alarm Firm after Catastrophic Blaze'. *Sunday Post*, 23 August 2020, https://www.sundaypost.com/fp/art-school-sues-fire-alarm-firm-after-catastrophic-blaze/, accessed 10 July 2023.

8 Many thanks to this reader, who wishes to remain anonymous.

9 See Chapter 4; for a detailed discussion of this history, see Purse 2021.

10 Scottish Parliament Culture, Tourism, Europe and External Affairs Committee, 2nd Report, 2019, 4, https://www.gsa.ac.uk/media/1691659/CTEEAC-Response-March-2019.pdf, accessed 10 July 2023.

11 'Mackintosh at the Willow Joins the Trust', National Trust for Scotland, 11 January 2024, https://www.nts.org.uk/stories/mackintosh-at-the-willow-joins-trust, accessed 5 February 2024.

12 Elizabeth Davidson, interview with the author, September 2021.

SELECTED BIBLIOGRAPHY

Alexander, Carolyn, 'The Materiality, Authenticity and Aura of the Creative Replica: Can the use of visual art and socially engaged practice facilitate deeper engagement with lost or vulnerable heritage?', PhD thesis, Glasgow School of Art, 2022

Baines, Mark, John Barr and Christopher Platt (eds), *The Library: Glasgow School of Art*, Glasgow: MSA Publications, 2015

Billcliffe, Roger, *Charles Rennie Mackintosh and the Art of The Four*, London: Frances Lincoln, 2017

Billcliffe, Roger, *Charles Rennie Mackintosh: The Complete Furniture, Furniture Drawings & Interior Designs*, Dumfries & Galloway: Cameron & Hollis, 2010

Brett, David, *C.R. Mackintosh: The Poetics of Workmanship*, Cambridge MA: Harvard University Press, 1992

Brown, Alison, '"Remarks on Fire Danger" – Inspectors' Reports on the Glasgow School of Art in 1913 and 1914', *Journal of the Charles Rennie Mackintosh Society* 103/104 (2018), 30–1

Buchanan, William, ed., *Mackintosh's Masterwork: The Glasgow School of Art*, 2nd edn, London: A&C Black, 2004

Burkhauser, Jude, *Glasgow Girls: Women in Art and Design 1880–1920*, Edinburgh: Canongate Publishing, 1990

Cairns, George, 'The Glasgow School of Art: An Architectural Totality', PhD thesis, University of Glasgow, 1992

Calvert, Robyne Erica, 'A Walk in Willowwood: Decoding the "Willowwoods" of Dante Gabriel Rossetti and Margaret Macdonald Mackintosh', *Journal of the Scottish Society for Art History* 17 (2012), 24–31

Calvert, Robyne Erica, 'The Künstlerpaar: Mackintosh, Macdonald & The Rose Boudoir', *Journal of the Charles Rennie Mackintosh Society – Celebratory Issue for Mackintosh 150*, no. 102 (2018), 32–5

Cameron, Dugald, *A Home for Lost Dogs: Glasgow School of Art and Parallel Passions*, Irvine: Kestrel Press, 2018

Carruthers, Annette, *The Arts and Crafts Movement in Scotland: A History*, London: Paul Mellon Centre for Studies in British Art, 2013

Chu, Petra ten-Doesschate and Max Donnelly, *Daniel Cottier: Designer, Decorator, Dealer*, New Haven and London: Yale University Press, 2021

Clarke, Paul, 'Glasgow School of Art: The Measure of Things', in Mark Baines, John Barr and Christopher Platt (eds), *The Library: Glasgow School of Art*, Glasgow: MSA Publications, 2015, 48–66

Crawford, Alan, *Charles Rennie Mackintosh*, London and New York: Thames & Hudson, 1995

Cumming, Elizabeth, *Phoebe Anna Traquair: 1852–1936*, Edinburgh: National Galleries of Scotland, 2005

Cumming, Elizabeth, *Hand, Heart and Soul: The Arts and Crafts Movement in Scotland*, Edinburgh: Birlinn, 2006

Dianat, Alborz, 'The Re-Making of Charles Rennie Mackintosh: A Study of the 1933 Memorial Exhibition', *Architectural History* 62 (2019), 145–69

Egger, Hanna, Pamela Robertson, Peter Vergo and Manfred Trummer, *A Thoroughly Modern Afternoon: Margaret Macdonald Mackintosh and the Salon Waerndorfer in Vienna*, Vienna: Bohlau, 2000

Gomme, Andor and David Walker, *Architecture of Glasgow*, rev. edn, London: Lund Humphries, 1987

Grigor, Murray and Richard Murphy, eds, *The Architects' Architect: Charles Rennie Mackintosh*, London: Bellew, 1993

Helland, Janice, 'Frances Macdonald: The Self as Fin-de-Siècle Woman'. *Woman's Art Journal* 14, no. 1 (1993), 15–22

Howarth, Thomas, *Charles Rennie Mackintosh and the Modern Movement*, rev. edn, London and New York: Routledge, 1977

Jackson, Neil, 'Found in Translation: Mackintosh, Muthesius and Japan', *Journal of Architecture* 18, no. 2 (2013), 196–224

Kelley, Stephen J., Donald Friedman, Kyle Normandin and Pamela Jerome, 'The Paradox and Dilemma of Reconstruction', *APT Bulletin: The Journal of Preservation Technology* 51, no. 1 (2020), 49–55

Kimura, Hiroaki, 'Charles Rennie Mackintosh: Architectural Drawings', PhD thesis, University of Glasgow, 1982

Kinchin, Juliet, 'Interiors: Nineteenth-Century Essays on the "Masculine" and the "Feminine" Room', in Pat Kirkham, ed., *The Gendered Object*, Manchester: Manchester University Press, 1996, 12–29

Kriegel, Lara, *Grand Designs: Labor, Empire, and the Museum in Victorian Culture*, Durham, NC: Duke University Press, 2008

Lawrence, Ranald, 'The Internal Environment of the Glasgow School of Art by Charles Rennie Mackintosh', *Construction History* 29, no. 1 (2014), 99–127

Lawrence, Ranald, *The Victorian Art School: Architecture, History, Environment*, Abingdon and New York: Routledge, 2020

Lethaby, W.R., *Architecture, Mysticism and Myth*, London: Percival & Co., 1892

Macaulay, James, *Charles Rennie Mackintosh*, New York: W.W. Norton, 2010

McKenzie, Ray, Alison Brown and Robert Proctor, *The Flower and the Green Leaf: Glasgow School of Art in the Time of Charles Rennie Mackintosh*, Edinburgh: Luath Press, 2009

Monie, Ian C., 'The Survival of the Works of Charles Rennie Mackintosh', *Art Libraries Journal* 2, no. 3 (Autumn 1977), 33–43

Mullen, Stephen, *It Wisnae Us: The Truth About Glasgow and Slavery*, Edinburgh: The Royal Incorporation of Architects in Scotland, 2009

Neat, Timothy, *Part Seen, Imagined Part: Meaning and Symbolism in the Work of Charles Rennie Mackintosh and Margaret Macdonald*, Edinburgh: Canongate Publishing, 1994

Owen, Alex, *The Place of Enchantment: British Occultism and the Culture of the Modern*, Chicago: University of Chicago Press, new edn 2007

Page\Park, 'Conservation Atlas, The Glasgow School of Art, Mackintosh Building', Glasgow: Page\Park Architects, 2016

Purse, Rachael, 'In Case of Emergency: What Do the 2014 and 2018 Fires in the Mackintosh Building Tell Us about How We Manage Our Built Heritage?', PhD thesis, Glasgow School of Art, 2021

Rawson, George, 'Francis Henry Newbery and the Glasgow School of Art', PhD thesis, University of Glasgow, 1996

Rawson, George, *Charles Rennie Mackintosh's Italy*, Catrine: Stenlake Publishing, 2020

Robertson, Pamela, ed., *Charles Rennie Mackintosh: The Architectural Papers*, Wendlebury: White Cockade Publishing in association with the Hunterian Art Gallery, 1990

Robertson, Pamela, ed., *The Chronycle: The Letters of Charles Rennie Mackintosh to Margaret Macdonald Mackintosh, 1927*, Glasgow: Hunterian Art Gallery, 2001

Robertson, Pamela, ed., *Doves and Dreams: The Art of Frances Macdonald and J. Herbert McNair*, London: Lund Humphries, 2006

Rodger, Johnny, 'Putting Holl and Mackintosh in Multi-Perspective: The New Building at the Glasgow School of Art', *Arq: Architectural Research Quarterly*, 17:1 (2013), 2–14

Rodger, Johnny, 'The Vanishing Library', *New Left Review*, 119 (September/October 2019), 94–103

The Scottish Parliament Culture, Tourism, Europe and External Affairs Committee, session 5, The Glasgow School of Art, https://archive2021.parliament. scot/parliamentarybusiness/ currentcommittees/109732.aspx

Shaw, Michael, *The Fin-de-Siècle Scottish Revival: Romance, Decadence and Celtic Identity*, Edinburgh: Edinburgh University Press, 2020

Trowles, Peter, 'The Glasgow School of Art Mackintosh Conservation and Access Project', *Journal of the Charles Rennie Mackintosh Society* 94 (2008)

Walker, Frank Arneil, *Mousa to Mackintosh: The Scottishness of Scottish Architecture*, Edinburgh: Historic Environment Scotland, 2023

Welter, Volker M., 'Arcades for Lucknow: Patrick Geddes, Charles Rennie Mackintosh and the Reconstruction of the City', *Architectural History* 42 (1999), 316–32

Worsley, Dawn, 'Three Burnt Books: An Unconventional Conservation Narrative', PhD thesis, Glasgow School of Art, 2019

ONLINE ARCHIVES AND RESOURCES

Space constraints have not allowed me to include all the many wonderful images I would have liked in this book. I recommend further browsing at these rich online resources:

The Glasgow School of Art's Archives & Collections (GSAA): gsaarchives.net

Mackintosh Architecture: Context, Making and Meaning (2014): http://www.mackintosh-architecture.gla.ac.uk/
A digital catalogue raisonné edited by Pamela Robertson, Joseph Sharples and Nicky Imrie, this is a definitive resource on the architectural projects of John Honeyman & Keppie/Honeyman, Keppie & Mackintosh 1889–1913, providing drawings, images, archives, chronologies and critical essays of the highest calibre.

Historic Environment Scotland's CANMORE website: http://canmore.org.uk
This contains many images of the Mack throughout its history, including the complete set of Harry Bedford Lemere's photos, which were taken over three visits in 1909–10.

The Mac Photographic Archive: http://the-mac-photo-archive.net
A wonderful crowdsourcing project organised by Lizzie Malcolm and Daniel Powers to collect images of the building after the first fire.

ACKNOWLEDGEMENTS

Thank you to the Scottish Fire and Rescue Service for doing everything possible to save this beloved building, twice.

This book was originally meant to be published in 2019 as a celebration of a completed restoration project. The team at Yale University Press have been unflagging in their support from the start, not just professionally but also emotionally as the events of 2018 unfolded and through the state of the world since. Mark Eastment has been a joy to work with, offering guidance with humour, practicality and sympathy. Equally, Felicity Maunder has been brilliant in turning the chaos I offered into a beautiful book, and I can't begin to thank her for all she has taught me about this process. A very special thanks to Kathrin Jacobsen for designing the book with such thought and care, as appropriate to the subject, with nary a 'Mackintosh' font in sight. I would also like to thank Stuart Weir for overseeing the production of the book, Clare Double for proofreading, and Amanda Speake for compiling the index. The Yale marketing team have been superb; many thanks to Lizzie Curtin, Charlotte Stafford and Emily Richardson. I am also grateful for the advice of my anonymous readers.

The production of this book has been assisted with generous funding support from the Paul Mellon Centre and the Royal Society of Edinburgh's Small Grant Scheme and I am enormously grateful for the generosity of both organisations.

I must also acknowledge The Glasgow School of Art for making this book possible by choosing me to be the Mackintosh Research Fellow for six unforgettable years, and supporting my academic freedom in writing this story throughout.

The assistance of archives and libraries was essential to this project. The Glasgow School of Art Archives have been stellar, particularly in providing me with access to previously uncatalogued material when I was a staff member. I am very grateful to Cat Doyle and Jennifer Lightbody for image research assistance, as well as to Stella Hook, Michelle Kaye, Helen Victoria Murray and Susannah Waters. I also wish to thank two former GSA Librarians, David Buri and the late George Rawson (d. 2022) – perhaps the single best source on the history of the Glasgow School of Art and Francis Newbery, to which this text owes a very deep debt. The research here also owes much to the brilliant *Mackintosh Architecture: Context, Meaning and Making* project at the University of Glasgow/Hunterian Art Gallery, and I must thank Pamela Robertson, Joseph Sharples and Nicky Imrie for many years of guidance and assistance. Also at The Hunterian, thanks to Steph Scholten and Graham Nisbet. At Historic Environment Scotland, Ewan Hyslop, Al Rawlinson and Lyn Wilson are always a joy to work with; and I must also thank Joseph Waterfield in their archives for image support. At Glasgow Life I wish to thank Nerys Tunnicliffe and Barbara McLean at Glasgow City Archives, and Alison Brown at Glasgow Museums. At the Charles Rennie Mackintosh Society thanks to Stuart Robertson, and a special shout to Dylan Paterson, Sven Burghardt and Ewan Mill Keith for letting me in the 'stage door' to take pictures in perfect light. For help and kindness with images I must also thank: Scott Abercrombie and Matt Bridgestock at John Gilbert Architects; Douglas Annan; Gordon Barr at the Architectural Heritage Fund; Ben Blossom; Wattie Cheung; GSA's School of Innovation and Technology (formerly Sim+Vis); John Mackie at Lyon & Turnbull; Niall Murphy at Glasgow City Heritage Trust; Isabella Scott at NTS Mackintosh at the Willow; David Walsh of Duille; and Norry Wilson of Lost Glasgow. Last, but most definitely not least, my deepest thanks to Alan McAteer, who has been photographing the Mack for many years (often gratis) and who provided many gorgeous and heartbreaking images for this book.

There is a substantial list of people who have inspired this book, and I must start by acknowledging all my previous students who studied the Mackintosh building with me with, inside and out, before fires and after. Chief among these are my former PhD students, Dr Rachael Purse and Dr Carolyn Alexander. Cohort: you are ever my muses.

At the heart of this story are the amazing women and men who comprised the team rebuilding the Mack. My deepest gratitude goes to my former 'Three R's' team at GSA: Liz Davidson, Sarah MacKinnon and Polly Christie, along with Hannah Patching and Thomas Simmons. I am also incredibly grateful to David Page, who very early on welcomed me to the design team table by saying 'what we need is a fashion historian' to help date some research images. From that moment, I no longer felt an imposter. Even in the wake of all that has happened I am grateful to have had the privilege of working with Page\Park Architects and the extended design team from Gardiner & Theobald Management Services, Harley Haddow, David Narro Associates and Kier Construction (Scotland). From that group I am particularly indebted to Page\Park's Brian Park, John Brown and Natalia Buraskowa; Dominic Echlin of David Narro; Graciela Ainsworth Conservation; and project advisers Paul Clarke of the University of Ulster, Ranald MacInnes of Historic Environment Scotland, and Kevan Shaw of KSLD – all of whom provided invaluable research insight for this book.

Memories and personal accounts underpin this text, and these have been derived from both casual conversations and formal interviews with former and present staff and students of the Glasgow School of Art who loved the Mack. For their time and generosity in support of this research I particularly wish to thank: Sam Ainsley, Mark Baines (1952–2020), Neil Bickerton, Claire Biddles, Ross Birrell, Helena Britt, Jenny Brownrigg, Paul Chapman, Joanna Crotch (1963–2021), Barbara Dryburgh, Anne Ferguson, Tom Gardner (1923–2019) and Audrey Gardner (1924–2020), Laura Glennie, Giovanna Guidicini, Tom Inns, Stuart Jeffrey, Will Judge, Helen Kendrick, Colin Kirkpatrick, Alastair Macdonald, Mairi Mackenzie, Patrick Macklin, Alan Miller, Ken Neal, Nicholas Oddy, Bruce Peter, Christopher Platt, Bob Proctor, Frances Robertson, Nicola Simonson, Ross Sinclair, Sarah Smith, Thea Stevens, Susannah Thompson, Peter Trowles, Nick Walker and Alison Watt.

I also owe a massive debt to my mentors, colleagues and friends, old and new, some of whom were also generous readers. These are the people who got me here; many are an ocean away and had no idea how much they helped, even across the miles: River Aaland, Duncan Chappell, Annie Chase, Mina Coleman, Stephanie Fratino Conte, Abby Cox, Colin Cruise, Hilary Davidson, Kristin Dean, Rachael Drummond, Winsome Duncan, Ashley Good, Jacquelin Erwin, Donato Esposito, Gayle Goudy, Laura Hamilton, Emma Hanley, James Harper, Jane Herring, (Princess) Dave Horalek, Lynn Hulse, Sally-Anne Huxtable, Veronica Isaac, Juliet Kinchin, Margaret MacDonald, Karen Mailley, Stewart McKnight, Joanna Meacock, Synthia Molina, Robin Rayn, Kristi Robinson, Suzanne Rowland, Hannah Rumball, Sally Rush, Samantha Sherry, Sandy Sessler, Evelyn Silber, Monica Smith, Rhoda Stefanatos, Paul Stirton, Fergus Sutherland, Alice Strang, Kate Strasdin, Emily Taylor, Sally Tuckett, Anna Vaughn-Kett, Elisa Velasquez, Lisa Wages, Kim Wahl, Kirsty Walker, Sabine Wieber, Lucy Weir, Clare Willsdon and Alison Yarrington.

Finally, with all my heart, I fervently thank my dearest friends and family (they are all both), who supported me through this whole debacle, and not without the shedding of tears, particularly after the 2018 fire and ultimately the personal fallout I experienced as a consequence. My gratefulness is beyond words, but perhaps ink will suffice: Ailsa Boyd and Gregory Rankine; John and Cindy Findley; Robin and David Governale; Nelson Fraga; Jade Halbert; Bill, Jackie and Lesley Muir; Amy Walker; and Peter Wilson. *Endlich*: John Muir, thank you for your red pen, your rambling japes, all the tunes, keeping me sane, *und alles*.

IMAGE CREDITS

Every effort has been made to contact the copyright holders of the illustrations, but should there be any errors or omissions, Yale University Press would be pleased to insert the appropriate acknowledgement in any subsequent printing of this publication.

0.1 Photo Jeff J. Mitchell/Getty Images; **0.2** McAteer Photo; **0.3** Robyne Calvert; **0.4** The Hunterian, University of Glasgow; **0.5** Glasgow School of Art Archives & Collections; **0.6, 0.7, 0.8** McAteer Photo; **0.9** Wandrille de Préville, CC BY-SA 4.0; **0.11** © The Trustees of the British Museum, CC BY-NC-SA 4.0; **0.12** McAteer Photo; **0.13, 0.14** Glasgow School of Art Archives & Collections.

1.1 Glasgow School of Art Archives & Collections; **1.2** photo courtesy Douglas Annan; **1.3** National Galleries of Scotland, D3757, purchased 1930; **1.4** photo courtesy Douglas Annan; **1.6** McAteer Photo; **1.7** Tom Parnell, CC BY-SA 2.0; **1.8** The Hunterian, University of Glasgow; **1.9** Scott Abercrombie/John Gilbert Architects; **1.10** The Hunterian, University of Glasgow; **1.11** Robyne Calvert; **1.12** Ben Blossom Photography; **1.13** Robyne Calvert; **1.14** Library of Congress; **1.15** Robyne Calvert; **1.18** RIBA; **1.17, 1.18** Robyne Calvert; **1.19** Glasgow Art Club; **1.20** Robyne Calvert; **1.21** Glasgow School of Art Archives & Collections; **1.22, 1.23, 1.24, 1.25** Robyne Calvert; **1.26, 1.28, 1.29, 1.30, 1.31, 1.32, 1.33, 1.34** Glasgow School of Art Archives & Collections; **1.35** National Museums Scotland; **1.36** Lyon & Turnbull; **1.37, 1.38** The Hunterian, University of Glasgow; **1.39** *Dekorative Kunst*, 5 (1902), p. 216.

2.1 The Hunterian, University of Glasgow; **2.2, 2.3** Glasgow School of Art Archives & Collections; **2.4** Glasgow City Archives Collection; **2.5** Robyne Calvert; **2.6, 2.7** National Archives of Scotland; **2.8** HES (Bedford Lemere Company Collection); **2.9** Glasgow School of Art Archives & Collections, T. & R. Annan and Sons; **2.10** Glasgow City Archives Collection; **2.11** Glasgow School of Art Archives & Collections; **2.12** Glasgow School of Art Archives & Collections, © estate of Edith Lovell Andrews; **2.13** The Metropolitan Museum of Art, Edward Pearce Casey Fund, 1981. Image copyright The Metropolitan Museum of Art/Art Resource/Scala, Florence; **2.14** Lyon & Turnbull; **2.15** Glasgow School of Art Archives & Collections; **2.16, 2.17, 2.18, 2.19** HES (Bedford Lemere Company Collection); **2.20** McAteer Photo; **2.21** The Hunterian, University of Glasgow; **2.22** Robyne Calvert.

3.1 Glasgow School of Art Archives & Collections; **3.2** Glasgow School of Art Archives & Collections, © Brian & Shear Industrial Photographers, Glasgow; **3.3** McAteer Photo; **3.4, 3.5** Glasgow School of Art Archives & Collections; **3.6** Michael McCarthy; **3.7** Cafferty; **3.8** Glasgow School of Art Archives & Collections, T. & R. Annan and Sons; **3.9** Bruce Peter; **3.10** Glasgow School of Art Archives & Collections; **3.11** Bruce Peter; **3.12** Robyne Calvert; **3.13** Glasgow School of Art Archives & Collections; **3.14** The Hunterian, University of Glasgow; **3.15** Stuart Robertson; **3.16** Glasgow School of Art Archives & Collections, © Keith Gibson; **3.17** Glasgow School of Art Archives & Collections; **3.18** Glasgow City Archives Collection; **3.19, 3.20, 3.21** Glasgow School of Art Archives & Collections; **3.22** McAteer Photo; **3.23** HES; **3.24** Glasgow School of Art Archives & Collections, © Keith Gibson; **3.25** HES (Bedford Lemere Company Collection); **3.26** Glasgow School of Art Archives & Collections, T. & R. Annan and Sons; **3.27** HES; **3.28** Glasgow School of Art Archives & Collections, T. & R. Annan and Sons; **3.29** Glasgow School of Art Archives & Collections, © Brian & Shear Industrial Photographers, Glasgow; **3.30, 3.31** McAteer Photo; **3.32** Glasgow School of Art Archives & Collections; **3.33** HES (Bedford Lemere Company Collection); **3.34, 3.35, 3.36** HES; **3.37** Glasgow School of Art Archives & Collections; **3.38** Glasgow School of Art Archives & Collections, © Keith Gibson; **3.39** HES; **3.40, 3.41** Glasgow School of Art Archives & Collections; **3.42, 3.43** HES; **3.44** HES (Bedford Lemere Company Collection); **3.45** Glasgow School of Art Archives & Collections, T. & R. Annan and Sons; **3.46** McAteer Photo; **3.47** HES (Bedford Lemere Company Collection); **3.48** McAteer Photo; **3.49** Glasgow School of Art Archives & Collections; **3.50** Robyne Calvert; **3.51, 3.52** Glasgow School of Art Archives & Collections; **3.53** McAteer Photo; **3.54** © The Glasgow School of Art. 3D assets created jointly by Historic Environment Scotland and The Glasgow School of Art; **3.55** HES; **3.56, 3.57** Robyne Calvert; **3.58** Glasgow School of Art Archives & Collections; **3.59** Glasgow School of Art Archives & Collections, T. & R. Annan and Sons; **3.60** Glasgow School of Art Archives & Collections, Studio Swain; **3.61** HES (Bedford Lemere Company Collection);

INDEX

Illustrations are shown by a page reference in italics and caption information not in the main body of the text is shown in bold.